CYPRUS 1974-1975: SCENARIO FOR TRAGEDY

* An independent island republic in eastern Mediterranean half the size of New Jersey

* Per capita income in 1973: $1,313

* Population 650,000: 80% Greek Orthodox Christians; 18% Turkish Muslim; remainder Armenians and Maronites

* Invaded July 20, 1974, by Turkish land, sea and air forces termed "Operation Attila" by Turks

* Murdered by Turkish aggressor: 5,000 Cypriots

* Weapons of murder: napalm, bombs, machine guns, armored vehicles

* Supplier of all Turkish military equipment: United States of America

* Destroyed:
  41% of all schools
  45% of all hospitals
  70% of economy's productive capacity

* 200,000 refugees bereft of homes and farmlands seized by Turks

* U.S. Congress votes December 17, 1974, to uphold U.S. laws and agreements under the Foreign Assistance and Military Sales Acts by cutting off military aid to Turkey

* Turks continue to occupy 40% of northern part of country with 40,000 soldiers

* De facto Turkish-Cypriot puppet state in Turkish held area announced February 13, 1975

* Greek Cypriots continue to appeal to Security Council for help

CRISIS
ON
CYPRUS

*A Report Prepared
for the
Subcommittee to Investigate
Problems Connected with
Refugees and Escapees
for the
Committee on the Judiciary
of the
United States Senate*

American Hellenic Institute
Washington, D.C.

Published 1975 by
The American Hellenic Institute, Inc.
1730 K Street, N.W.
Washington, D.C. 20006

TABLE OF CONTENTS

PART I

N 106

Page
Preface, by Senator Edward M. Kennedy, Chairman_____ v
Introduction _____ 1
  Seeds of Conflict_____ 9
    1. Independence _____ 9
    2. Communal Conflict of 1963–64 and 1967_____ 11
    3. Role of the United Nations_____ 12
    4. Communal Tensions_____ 12
  Cyprus, 1974: Scenario for Tragedy_____ 14
    1. Coup Against Makarios_____ 14
    2. Turkish Invasion_____ 15
  Consequences of the Invasion_____ 18
    1. Humanitarian Consequences_____ 18
    2. Economic Consequences_____ 30
    3. Political Consequences_____ 31
    4. Impact of Partition_____ 32
    5. Hazards of Economic Partition_____ 37
    6. Costs of the Invasion to Turkey_____ 38
  Humanitarian Needs and International Assistance_____ 39
    1. International Relief Assistance_____ 40
    2. Role of the United Nations Force in Cyprus_____ 40
    3. Role of the International Committee of the Red Cross_____ 42
    4. Role of the U.N. High Commissioner for Refugees_____ 42
  Notes on United States Policy_____ 44
Summary of Findings_____ 53
Recommendations _____ 59

APPENDIX

  I. Address by Senator Kennedy on the Cyprus Crisis, Testimonial
     Dinner Honoring Archbishop Iakovos, New York, Oct. 20, 1974___ 65
  II. Text of Senator Kennedy's Statement and Senate Concurrent Reso-
     lution 110, relating to Cyprus_____ 69
  III. Text of Senator Kennedy's Amendment for Relief and Rehabilita-
     tion Assistance to Cyprus (Africa and Bangladesh)_____ 71
  IV. Text of Secretary of State Kissinger's News Conference of August
     19, 1974, and Official Statements on Cyprus before the United
     Nations Security Council_____ 77
  V. United Nations Security Council Resolutions on Cyprus, 1974_____ 91
  VI. Reports of the Secretary-General on Developments in Cyprus, and
     first report of the U.N. High Commissioner for Refugees_____ 95
  VII. Documents Relating to the Founding of Cyprus, including the Treaty
     of Guarantee, 1959_____ 105
  VIII. Memorandum prepared for the Study Mission by the Ministry of
     Foreign Affairs, Republic of Cyprus on Conditions in Cyprus____ 113

PART II

Statements of:
  His Eminence, Archbishop Iakovos, Primate of the Greek Orthodox
    Church in the Americas 4
  William G. Chirgotis, Supreme President, Order of AHEPA, and
    William P. Tsaffaras, cochairman, AHEPA Justice for Cyprus
    Committee 13

APPENDIX

  I. AHEPA Report: Humanitarian Mission to Cyprus, November 1974 23
  II. Text of subcommittee's correspondence with Secretary of State Henry
    Kissinger on U.S. policy toward Cyprus 37
  III. Selected press reports and commentaries on the Cyprus situation 45

PREFACE

By Senator Edward M. Kennedy, Chairman

This is a perilous time for the people of Cyprus—as it also is for the renewal of democracy and freedom in Greece, and for the future of NATO and of progress and peaceful relations in the Eastern Mediterranean. The repercussions of recent events in this part of the world have been widespread, and will continue to aggravate international relations and bedevil United States foreign policy for many months to come. This report examines some of these events, but concentrates on the Turkish invasion of Cyprus.

The Turkish invasion turned the island into shambles. In political terms, it violated the integrity of an independent state. In economic terms, it shattered the island's flourishing economy. And in human terms, it brought personal tragedy to thousands of families—and turned half the population into refugees, detainees, or beleaguered people caught behind ceasefire lines.

In too many quarters—including our own government—the human dimensions of the Cyprus crisis, and the plight of Cypriot civilians, has taken second place to the political and military issues at stake—and to the special interests of those who have much to lose or to gain by the outcome of the conflict. But the civilians of Cyprus—both Greeks and Turks—also have interests. And for hundreds of thousands, recent weeks have been a nightmare of death and tragedy and grief.

This report reviews the human and political tragedy of Cyprus. It is based on the findings of a recent Study Mission to the area, public hearings before the Subcommittee, and additional inquiry. As the report indicates, a drive along the roads of Cyprus quickly tells the tragic tale of the Cypriot people—of the human consequences of an armed invasion and deadlocked diplomacy, of bombing and napalm, of ceasefire violations, of military occupation, and man's inhumanity to man.

In the Turkish occupied northern areas only a small percentage of the population remains—including an estimated 8,000 Turkish refugees bombed or shelled out of their homes. Desolation and destruction mark many areas. Whole villages and towns and cities are empty of people, who fled their homes in fear of advancing Turkish forces. The 15,000 to 20,000 Greeks who remain are being held as virtual hostages—confined to their villages or elsewhere, and usually separated from family members and without adequate food and water and medical care. Some 500 of these people, for example, are being cruelly detained by Turkish forces in Kyrenia's Dome Hotel.

Government controlled areas of the island have been inundated with refugees from the north. Since the invasion on July 20, over 200,000 men, women and children—at least a third of the population—have sought shelter wherever they could find it—in open fields, under trees, along the roadsides, and in schools, monasteries and public buildings. Only in the last few weeks have relief supplies begun to arrive in meaningful quantities; but food, blankets, medicines, other relief goods, and shelter are still in short supply. And, with the onslaught of the rainy season and the winter cold, the condition of the people will inevitably deteriorate—unless adequate relief measures are taken now, or a political settlement is accomplished, which will permit refugees to return to their homes. The overwhelming majority of needy people in government controlled areas are Greek Cypriots. But significant numbers of Turks—including some 10,000 Turkish Cypriot refugees—also command our help and concern.

A great deal has been said over America's role in the Cyprus crisis—and over the apparent complicity of our government in the human and political tragedy of the Cypriot people.

Our government suggests, for example, that Americans should recognize and appreciate legitimate Turkish grievances over developments on Cyprus, since independence more than a decade ago. Americans are told by their government that "the position of the Turkish community on Cyprus requires considerable improvement and protection. We [the U.S. Government] have supported a greater degree of autonomy for them." And, given this, we Americans must be practical in our approach to the Cyprus crisis. What has happened is understandable, and we must accept, therefore, the "new realities" on the island.

But what are these "new realities"? And what are we being asked to understand and accept?

Are we to condone the invasion and occupation of Cyprus? Are we to condone ceasefire violations? Are we to condone the nibbling away of an independent state, and a continuing threat of a new offensive in the so-called Turkish "peace operation"? Are we to condone the human tragedy brought about with the illegal use of American supplied weapons? Are we to condone the failure of our government to condemn the Turkish invasion? Are we to condone the omissions in our diplomacy, and the efforts by our Government to cover up these omissions and the tilt toward Turkey? Are we to stand silent in the face of *these* realities.

I believe the American people expect more of their government, and this is clearly reflected in the views and recent actions of Congress. The time is long overdue for the President and members of the Administration to give some greater evidence of concern and action over the human and political tragedy of Cyprus—and over the needed diplomacy by our government to help restore the island's territorial integrity and the right of the Cypriot people, working together, to determine their own destiny. We must do all in our power to accomplish this end. Important first steps should include a strengthened United Nations presence on the island, the orderly and phased withdrawal of Turkish troops, and the return of refugees to their families and homes.

With such goals in mind, the United States should also strengthen its support of relief and rehabilitation efforts by the Cyprus Government, the Turkish Cypriot Administration, the United Nations High

Commissioner for Refugees, (UNHCR) the International Committee of the Red Cross (ICRC) and others.

The United States can assist in a number of ways. For example, we should be doing more to encourage greater international support of UNHCR and ICRC relief efforts on Cyprus. We should lend our diplomacy to help guarantee the free access of these international relief agencies to the Turkish occupied areas of the island. And we should also be doing more to encourage the reopening of the Nicosia airport, which would, among other things, greatly facilitate the work of the relief agencies.

Of immediate importance is a more substantial American contribution to the UNHCR relief program of some $22,000,000 through the end of this year. So far, we have committed only $3,000,000—a paltry sum which falls far below our normal share of support for UNHCR programs. This token contribution for humanitarian programs is distressing, particularly in light of the millions of dollars in military hardware we are continuing to ship to Turkey.

If Cyprus today is on the brink of new conflict and even greater tragedy, our government's policy bears a special responsibility. For the omissions in our diplomacy over Cyprus, our support of the Turkish position, and the President's insistence on maintaining a business-as-usual attitude toward military shipments to Turkey, only encourages Ankara's intransigency and feeds frustrations on Cyprus and among our friends in neighboring Greece. It is long overdue for us to rescue our foreign policy from a course that is disastrous both to our best traditions and interests in the Eastern Mediterranean.

INTRODUCTION

The Subcommittee has closely followed humanitarian problems on Cyprus since the outbreak of violence and the Turkish invasion of the island in mid-July 1974. As the situation deteriorated, and following consultations with officials in the United Nations and the Department of State, on August 8, the Chairman expressed in the Senate the Subcommittee's public concern over the plight of the Cypriot people. Among other things, the Chairman stated:

> Reports from the area—including official reports to our own Government and elsewhere—fully confirm the human tragedy of Cyprus. Tens of thousands of women and children have been forcibly expelled from their villages—especially in Turkish occupied areas—or have fled their homes as refugees. Thousands of able-bodied men have disappeared—and some apparently have been deported to camps or prisons in southern Turkey. Refugees tell of 'much suffering' and 'systematic' arson, looting, murder, and rape. And civilian casualties—both wounded and dead—number in the hundreds, if not the thousands.
>
> I do not rise to offer any magic solution for meeting the immediate political and humanitarian problems of Cyprus. But I do rise to express a deep personal concern over the plight of Cypriot civilians—especially over the continuing violations of human rights and the rules of common human decency which are evidenced in Turkish occupied areas. A spokesman for our own Government suggests that 'some very rough stuff' continues. This is a deplorable situation, and I appeal to the Turkish Government and all parties involved to make every effort in behalf of bringing peace and relief to Cyprus.
>
> Apart from securing a meaningful separation of forces and a political settlement at the conference table in Geneva, there are three items of immediate concern to me as chairman of the Subcommittee on Refugees:
>
> First, the emergency relief needs of refugees and others in distress—including food, water, shelter, medicine, and protection;
>
> Second, the condition, treatment, and release of civilian detainees—including those who may have been deported to Turkey or other areas; and
>
> Third, the free movement of international relief convoys and humanitarian personnel from the United Nations or the International Committee for the Red Cross—ICRC—including the free access of Red Cross personnel to detention centers on both sides.

Nearly a week later, on August 14, and following important "land grabs" by Turkish forces in violation of the United Nations sponsored ceasefire, Ankara ordered phase two of the invasion. Sensing the growing humanitarian needs on Cyprus, and particularly in light of new appeals for relief assistance by the Cypriot government, on August 16 the Chairman made a personal appeal to the United Nations High Commissioner for Refugees (UNHCR), Prince Sadruddin Aga Khan, for his "favorable consideration of good offices for meeting humanitarian needs and for providing care and protection to the refugees." The United Nations responded to the Cypriot Government's appeal for help. On August 20, United Nations Secretary General Kurt Waldheim designated the High Commissioner as "coordinator of United Nations humanitarian assistance for Cyprus." Shortly thereafter, during a visit to the island in late August, the High Commissioner established a field office in Nicosia to help meet humanitarian needs among both Greek and Turkish Cypriots.

Also on August 20, during the sweep of Turkish forces over more than forty percent of Cyprus, the Subcommittee held a public hearing on the escalating humanitarian problems with Assistant Secretary of State for European Affairs, the Honorable Arthur A. Hartman, and others from the Executive Branch. And shortly thereafter, the Chairman dispatched a Study Mission to the Eastern Mediterranean.

The field study was conducted by Mr. Dale S. deHaan, Staff Director to the Subcommittee; Mr. Jerry M. Tinker, Staff Consultant; and Dr. Dennis Skiotis, Assistant Professor of Greek and Turkish History at Harvard University and a Special Consultant to the Subcommittee. The Study Mission's departure for the field was delayed for several days. Citing the violent and senseless death of U.S. Ambassador Roger P. Davies on August 19, and very strong anti-American feelings among Greek Cypriots, the Department of State, at the highest levels, expressed concern over the physical safety of the Study Mission and over other factors relating to the national interest. Finally, with the approval of the Department, the Study Mission left Washington on the evening of August 27. It returned on September 12.

The Study Mission spent a week on Cyprus, and traveled extensively in both government controlled and Turkish occupied areas. On the government side, the team visited Greek refugee concentrations in greater Nicosia, the Larnaca area where the bulk of the refugees are located, the Limassol area on the southern coast, and the British Sovereign Base areas at Akrotiri and Dhekelia. The Study Mission also visited Turkish Cypriot detainees and other Turks in government controlled areas. The Cypriot Government was fully cooperative, and readily accommodated the Study Mission's interests and concerns.

In the Turkish occupied areas, the Study Mission visited Turkish Cypriot refugees in the Turkish quarter of Nicosia, and traveled north to Kyrenia and east to the port of Famagusta. In addition to visiting some 450 Greek civilians detained in Kyrenia's Dome Hotel, the team also visited the Greek population remaining in Bellapais, a village near Kyrenia. Although the Study Mission was received cordially by the Turkish Cypriot Administration in the occupied areas, its movement in the northern part of the island was restricted. Permission to travel west of Kyrenia was not granted, and requests to visit the

Karpasian peninsula in the northeast, where several thousand Greeks remain as virtual hostages, were never cleared by "the authorities".

In addition to talking with hundreds of refugees and others in distress in all parts of the island, the Study Mission met twice with the Acting President of Cyprus, Glafcos Clerides, and with members of his Government and representatives of the Cyprus Red Cross. Talks were also held with Rauf Denktash, the constitutional Vice President of Cyprus and head of the Turkish Cypriot community, and with members of his administration and representatives of the Turkish Cypriot Red Crescent Society. Representatives of the International Committee of the Red Cross (ICRC), the UNHCR, the United Nations Forces in Cyprus (UNFICYP), and others were readily available for consultations, and in London the Study Mission met with the President of Cyprus, Archbishop Makarios. The American Embassy in Nicosia extended every courtesy to the Study Mission, and useful conversations were held with Ambassador William Crawford and members of his staff.

After leaving Cyprus, the Study Mission traveled to Ankara, Athens, Geneva and London. In Ankara, the team met with Turkish Foreign Ministry officials, and with representatives of the Turkish Red Crescent Society and the ICRC. Extensive conversations were also held with U.S. Ambassador William B. Macomber, Jr., and members of his staff.

In Athens, the Study Mission met with Acting Foreign Minister Dimitrios Bitsios and other Greek officials, as well as with members of the U.S. Embassy staff. In Geneva, additional meetings were held with the ICRC and the UNHCR, and in London talks were held with appropriate officials in the British Foreign Ministry and others.

As suggested in the Chairman's preface, this report—based mainly on the recent field study—is part of the Subcommittee's continuing effort to underscore the distressing human consequences of the Turkish invasion of Cyprus, and to make the case again that normalizing the life of the Cypriot people and restoring the territorial integrity and full independence of Cyprus must be a matter of vital concern to the American people and their government. A preliminary report of the Study Mission's findings and recommendations was presented by Dr. Skiotis at a Subcommittee hearing on September 26. Secretary Hartman also testified at this hearing.

Copies of the Subcommittee's hearings on Cyprus are available by writing the Subcommittee office.

CRISIS ON CYPRUS

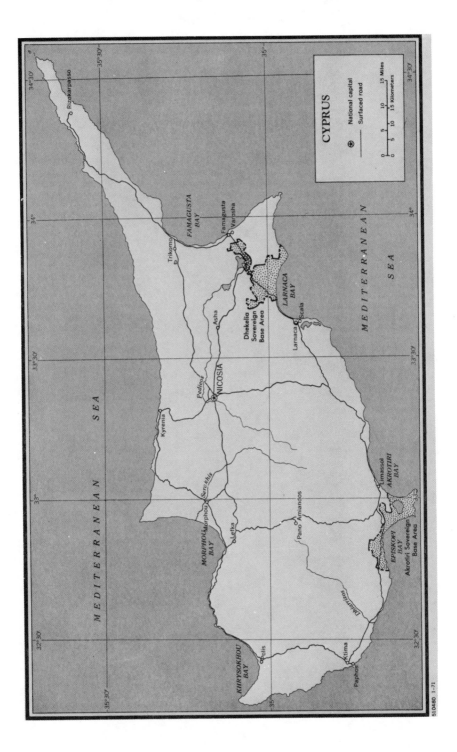

CYPRUS

⊕ National capital
— Surfaced road

0 5 10 15 Miles
0 5 10 15 Kilometers

MEDITERRANEAN SEA

MEDITERRANEAN SEA

Rizokarpasso

FAMAGUSTA BAY

Trikomo

Famagusta
Varosha

LARNACA BAY

Asha

Dhekelia Sovereign Base Area

Scala
Larnaca

NICOSIA

Pedieos

Kyrenia

Serakhis

MORPHOU BAY

Morphou

Lefka

Pano Amiandos

Limassol

AKROTIRI BAY

Dhiarizos

EPISKOPI BAY

Akrotiri Sovereign Base Area

KHRYSOKHOU BAY

Polis

Ktima

Paphos

510480 1-71

SEEDS OF CONFLICT

Cyprus is situated in the eastern Mediterranean, 40 miles south of Turkey, 60 miles west of Syria and 500 miles east of mainland Greece. It is the third largest island in the Mediterranean (after Sicily and Sardinia) with a maximum length of 138 miles and a maximum breadth of 59 miles. Its total area—some 3572 square miles—is only about half the size of the state of New Jersey.

Two thirds of Cyprus is mountainous. Two mountain ranges stretch from east to west. One, the Kyrenia range, is in the north. The other, the Troodos range, rises in the southwest. Between these two ranges lies the chief agricultural area, the Mesaoria plain, where the capital Nicosia is situated.

In recent years, Cyprus had attained a considerable degree of prosperity. The economy was doing well and living standards were increasing year after year. In 1973 the per capita income was $1,313. While not as wealthy and advanced as western nations, Cyprus was much better off than most countries in Asia, Africa and Latin America. Its economy is usually compared with that of Israel.

Of Cyprus' estimated population of 650,000, some 80% speak Greek and are Greek Orthodox Christian by religion. Some 18% are Turkish speaking Muslims. Armenians and Maronites are prominent among the remainder.

I. INDEPENDENCE

The presence of Greeks on Cyprus can be dated to the end of the thirteenth century B.C. But down through the ages to 1960, the island was conquered and ruled sucessively by Phoenicians, Egyptians, Assyrians, Persians, Macedonians, Romans, Byzantines, Lusignans, Venetians, Ottomans, and the British. It was in 1571 that Cyprus was conquered by the Ottoman Turks, and it is from this time that the emergence of a Turkish speaking Muslim community on the island can be traced. Ottoman rule in Cyprus lasted until 1878 when Cyprus was leased to the British. The British annexed it in 1914 when Turkey became Germany's ally in World War I. Cyprus was made a Crown Colony in 1925.

During the late Ottoman and British periods, the political movement among the Greek Cypriot majority for union with Greece—enosis—became the most powerful force in Cypriot politics. By and large, agitation for enosis was successfully contained—sometimes even suppressed by the force of arms (1931)—until the 1950's, when matters came to a head and the Greek Cypriots launched a guerrilla campaign against the British. The Greek Cypriot revolt, led by Archbishop Makarios and Colonel Grivas, proved impossible for the British to crush.

In reaction to the greatly increased threat of enosis, the Turkish Cypriots sided with the British and supported the maintenance of

British rule. They argued, however, that, if British rule were to end, Cyprus should revert to Turkish sovereignty. In the late 1950's, the idea of partitioning the island into separate Greek and Turkish areas was advanced by Ankara and endorsed by the Turkish Cypriot leadership.

The Greek Cypriot campaign was terminated by the conclusion of the Zurich and London agreements of February 1959.* These agreements, aimed at solving the Cyprus problem, were worked out among the governments of Greece, Turkey and Britain, and members of the western alliance (NATO). Archbishop Makarios, the leader of the Greek Cypriots, had serious reservations about the arrangements, particularly regarding the constitutional structure of the new state that was to be founded. But, in the end, he acccepted. Dr. Kutchuk, the leader of the Turkish Cypriots, also initialed the agreements on February 19, 1959.

According to the terms of these agreements, Cyprus was to become an independent republic. Britain, however, would have two military bases over which she would maintain sovereign rights. Greece and Turkey were also to maintain small military contingents on the island. The three powers would jointly guarantee the independence of, and respect for, the constitution of the new republic. Both union with any other state, and partition, were expressly forbidden. Although the three powers pledged joint consultations with each other in the event of a breach of the treaty, each also reserved the right to act unilaterally to defend the treaty provisions.

The agreements provided for a presidential form of government, with the President a Greek, elected by the Greek community, and the Vice President a Turk, elected by the Turkish community. The President and the Vice President were both granted a veto right over foreign affairs, defense and internal security. In the Council of Ministers and the House of Representatives, the Turks were granted 30% of the seats, again elected on separate rolls. They were also given 30% of the posts in the civil service and security forces, and 40% in the Army. The Turks were also granted complete legislative and administrative autonomy in educational, religious, and cultural affairs, and in matters of personal status and taxation. Moreover, any modification of the constitution's articles, which were open for amendment, required the consent of a separate two-thirds majority from representatives of each community. In sum, the recognition of specifically designated and separate rights for the Turkish community form the distinguishing feature of the Cyprus constitution. But the effort to minimize misunderstandings between the two communities, with detailed provisions in all areas of government and administration, had the opposite result—the institutionalisation of governmental dualism and ethnic separatism between Greek and Turkish Cypriots.

From the very establishment of Cyprus as an independent state on August 16, 1960, the constitutional machinery failed the new republic. The Greek majority saw the aspects of the constitution described above as hindrances to their becoming masters in their own house, and as legislating the maintenance of a state within a state. The Turks, on the other hand, feared that any erosion of their constitutional guarantees

---

*For the complete text of these agreements, see Appendix VII.

would leave them with no rights at all. Given the peculiarities of the constitution, political conflict was probably inevitable. And such conflict intensified as the Greeks tried to show that only a unitary system of government would work on Cyprus, and as the Turks took every opportunity to block government business whenever they felt that their rights were infringed upon or their needs unmet. The two communities were soon deadlocked on a host of issues: civil service staffing, the Army, separation of municipalities, and the use of the Turkish veto on central government taxation, among other things.

2. COMMUNAL CONFLICT OF 1963-64 AND 1967

All this forms the background to the ethnic conflict that erupted in 1963. Makarios, the Republic's first President, suggested a number of constitutional amendments whose primary purpose was to reduce separatism and bring about a greater measure of majority rule. Ankara, followed by the Turkish Cypriots, rejected his proposals. Intercommunal fighting broke out five days later, in December 1963, with each side accusing the other of having planned war beforehand.

The pattern of events which occurred during the first Cyprus crisis (1963-64) was closely paralleled during the 1967 flare-up. On both occasions, the Greek Cypriots, being far more numerous than the Turkish Cypriots, seemed about to overwhelm them in the early stages of the conflict. Turkey would then threaten to interevene militarily—and in August 1964 Turkish fighter bombers did indeed strike Greek Cypriot positions—and this, in turn, would lead to real dangers of war with Greece. Since both Turkey and Greece were NATO allies, the U.S. would become immediately involved, as would Britain, a guarantor of Cyprus independence. The Soviet Union would then react quickly to NATO military and diplomatic activity in the eastern Mediterranean. And finally, as a non-aligned nation, Cyprus would count on the concern of a great many states, which together with the great powers, would call for the United Nations to undertake the thankless task of peace-keeping and even mediation on the island.

It should be stressed, however, that in both the 1963-64 and 1967 confrontations over Cyprus the U.S. played the active and crucial role, as the leader of the western alliance, in defusing the crises. High level American diplomats, George Ball and Cyprus Vance, worked diligently to avoid war. In 1964, for example, Turkey was warned in the strongest terms that the U.S. would not tolerate precipitate action or invasion. And in 1967, the Greek colonels were forced to suffer a humiliating diplomatic defeat requiring the recall of Grivas from Cyprus and the withdrawal of 9,000 Greek soldiers from the island.

However, American efforts to arrange for NATO peace-keeping forces on Cyprus (advanced by George Ball in 1964), as well as the "Acheson plan" (union of Cyprus with Greece, one or two Turkish cantons and a Turkish military base on the island, and the cession of the remote Greek island of Castellorizon to Turkey), were not acceptable to President Makarios, who was abandoning Enosis and becoming increasingly identified with a policy favoring independence and neutrality. Makarios' own view was that greater reliance should be placed on the U.N., regarding both peace-keeping functions and guaranteeing the independence and territorial integrity of Cyprus.

3. ROLE OF THE UNITED NATIONS

Thus, since March 4, 1964, a U.N. peace-keeping force (UNFICYP) has been present on Cyprus. The Security Council mandated UNFICYP "to use its best efforts to prevent a recurrence of fighting and, as necessary, to contribute to the maintenance and restoration of law and order and a return to normal conditions." Until the most recent crisis. UNFICYP has played a very important role in the stabilisation and maintenance of peace on Cyprus, and there was general agreement that it has been one of the more successful operations of the international organization.

The U.N. also appointed a mediator whose report (Galo-Plaza Report), published in 1965, was intended to serve as the basis for a new solution. The main points of the Report were:

1. Cyprus should remain an independent state renouncing its right to unite with Greece.

2. The island should be demilitarised. The question of the British bases was set aside for later consideration.

3. There should be no partition or physical separation of the Greek and Turkish communities. However, Turkish Cypriot rights should be guaranteed by the U.N. and supervised by a U.N. commissioner on Cyprus.

4. A settlement should depend in the first place on agreement between the people of Cyprus themselves and talks should take place between Greek and Turkish Cypriots.

This plan was rejected summarily by Turkey. It was, however, "noted" by the Political Committee of the General Assembly and so it can be said to have been approved to that extent by the U.N. Moreover, in December 1965, the General Assembly adopted a resolution which took "cognizance of the fact that Cyprus should enjoy full sovereignty and complete independence without any foreign intervention or interference," and which called on "all states to respect the sovereignty, unity, independence and territorial integrity of Cyprus."

4. COMMUNAL TENSIONS

As a result of the upheavals of 1963–64, the Turkish Cypriots abandoned many of their villages and gathered for self-protection and the facilitation of partition in the more defensible areas. According to the U.N., there were some 25,000 Turkish Cypriot refugees who were forced to relocate in this manner. Greek Cypriots were not permitted to enter these areas, nor were Turks permitted to leave their enclaves without permission from their leaders. Confined in these enclaves, without sufficient resources, it was only direct economic aid from Turkey (an estimated $25 million annually) that enabled the Turks to survive as a separate entity.

Although intercommunal tensions eased after 1967, the situation on Cyprus remained at an impasse. The most promising signs of progress were the discussions that began in early 1968 between Glafcos Clerides and Rauf Denktash (representing the Greek and Turkish Cypriot communities) aimed at resolving the differences between them. In 1972, these inter-communal talks were expanded to include, in advisory capacities, a U.N. Special Representative and constitutional experts from Greece and Turkey.

At about the same time, however, the Greek Cypriots found themselves plunged into a domestic political crisis of their own. President Makarios' policy of abandoning enosis for the "unfettered independence of a unitary state" was opposed both by the extreme right wing in Cyprus (EOKA–B) and by the military junta that had seized power in Athens in April 1967. In contrast to the dictatorship in Greece, Makarios was democratically elected, enjoyed the support of the left wing AKEL party in Cyprus, and pursued a policy of non-alignment.

Former EOKA leader Grivas returned to Cyprus clandestinely in 1971, and plots and attempts to assassinate Makarios became frequent. In late 1973, there were several armed clashes between the rebels and security forces. And Christos Vakis the Cypriot Minister of Justice, was kidnapped by EOKA–B terrorists.

CYPRUS, 1974: SCENARIO FOR TRAGEDY

In the summer of 1974, the terrorists intensified their activities on Cyprus. On July 2, Makarios complained to the Greek Government that the 650 Greek officers commanding the Greek Cypriot National Guard were planning to overthrow him, and he demanded their immediate recall. By this time the plot was something of an open secret. The Greek Foreign Minister, Tetenes, his aides, and over 20 Greek officers resigned in disgust. And on July 5, the Nicosia newspaper *Apoyevmatini* printed an account of the plot against Makarios, adding that the Greek officers and their EOKA–B henchmen planned to kill the President and put a "puppet" in his place.

1. COUP AGAINST MAKARIOS

This is almost exactly what happened 10 days later. On July 15, Greek officers, on instructions from the military junta ruling in Athens, overthrew the legitimate government of Cyprus in a coup d'etat. Nikos Sampson was appointed President. But Makarios escaped death and was flown to London by the British. In London, as well as at the U.N., Makarios called for the restoration of Cyprus' independence and sovereignty.

In spite of later statements by Secretary of State Henry A. Kissinger, that information about the coup "was not exactly lying in the street," there is abundant evidence suggesting that the U.S. knew of the impending coup well in advance. But there are doubts that Washington was fully successful in conveying a warning signal to the Greek junta to refrain from action on Cyprus. Trying to establish what happened at this period is complicated by the fact that the U.S. apparently was in the habit of communicating with the junta via the C.I.A. station chief, while the regular Embassy channels in Athens were rarely used. In any case, much more forceful and forthright measures should and could have been employed at this early, critical stage of the Cyprus crisis; for the half-hearted, complacent tactics of the U.S. failed to deter the junta.

After the coup on Cyprus, Britain—a guarantor power—and other NATO countries condemned Sampson and came out strongly for the restoration of Makarios. Once again the U.S. dragged its feet and carefully refrained from putting the responsibility for the coup on the junta. The State Department spokesman called for "moderation" and a return to "constitutional arrangements", and Makarios' status was left deliberately ambiguous.

And in the United Nations, Ambassador John Scali was putting the best possible face on the Greek Cypriot junta. On July 19, he told the Security Council—which had just heard a plea from Makarios—that "my government has always opposed intervention in the internal affairs of one country by another, and to the extent that *this may be the case in Cyprus*, I repeat we deplore it." (italics added) Thus, Scali and the United States Government, far from labeling the Athens inspired Sampson coup as "intervention," was saying "it may be" and that "it would be a serious error to rush to judgment on an issue of this gravity."

These "even-handed" statements emanating from the State Department were interpreted by Ankara as tacit U.S. acceptance of the new state of affairs on Cyprus. To Turkey, Sampson's elevation to power signalled the strong possibility of enosis, and Ankara therefore immediately prepared for a military solution to the problem. Prime Minister Bulent Ecevit first flew to London to consult with the British. In London he demanded the recall of the Greek officers and the establishment of a federal system of government on Cyprus to be worked out immediately in talks between Clerides and Denktash. Here again clear-cut U.S. support of the Turkish *diplomatic* position would probably have significantly reduced the chances of Turkey opting for military action. Instead, Under Secretary of State Joseph J. Sisco was dispatched to shuttle between Athens and Ankara in a futile effort to effect, apparently, a compromise on Cyprus that would save face for the Greek military junta. And, it now appears, that he did not seriously warn the Turks that, if they were determined to seek a military solution, the U.S. would find itself obliged to at least consider cutting off military assistance to Ankara.

2. TURKISH INVASION

On July 20, Turkish forces began landing on Cyprus. They were resisted stubbornly by the Greek Cypriots who managed, surprisingly in view of their military inferiority, to limit initial Turkish gains to a slim corridor from Kyrenia to Nicosia. On that same day, the U.N. Security Council adopted the first of a series of strongly-worded resolutions calling for an immediate ceasefire; urging an end to foreign intervention and the withdrawal of all foreign troops; and requesting the guarantor powers of Cyprus—Greece, Turkey and Britain—to start negotiations for a settlement.

The first of a series of ceasefires was effected on Cyprus on July 22; but, from the outset, the Turkish military kept reinforcing its forces and steadily expanding the width of its Kyrenia-Nicosia salient. During this time, the U.S., in public statements, professed to be unconcerned about what it called minor military actions.

The Turkish invasion of Cyprus and the ensuing possibility of war with Greece so concerned the Greek junta that it recalled Constantine Karamanlis to Greece to form a civilian government of national unity. On the same day, July 23, Clerides replaced Sampson as Acting President of Cyprus.

The renewal of democracy and constitutional government in Greece (after 7 years of military rule), as well as on Cyprus, raised hopes throughout the world for a negotiated settlement. Indeed, under British leadership, the three guarantor powers met in Geneva on July 26, and on the 30th signed a declaration in which they agreed to implement the U.N. sponsored cease-fire on Cyprus. The second phase of the Geneva Talks, to consider political issues, opened on schedule on August 8. The following day, Greek, Turkish, British and U.N. military observers agreed on a cease-fire line separating opposing forces on Cyprus.

But the negotiations reached an impasse when Turkish proposals—first, for a federal system under which Turkish Cypriots would have a separate administration in a zone covering 38% of Cyprus, and secondly, for a cantonal system under which the Turkish Cypriots would administer several smaller areas—were received cooly by the Greek negotiators and Clerides, who requested 36 hours to discuss the Turkish proposals with their governments. Turkey, probably intent upon winning on the battlefield what it had demanded at the conference table, rejected the Greek request for an adjournment. The British describe the Turkish position as "arbitrary and unreasonable". But once again the U.S. did very little, and failed to prevail upon the Turks to remain at the negotiating table.

In an incredible move of bad timing, if not bad policy, the Department of State at this crucial juncture of the talks issued a statement, which stressed the equity of the Turkish position. The following is the text of the statement issued by Department spokesman Robert Anderson at a news briefing on August 13th:

"The U.S. position is as follows:

"We recognize the position of the Turkish community on Cyprus requires considerable improvement and protection. We have supported a greater degree of autonomy for them.

"The parties are negotiating on one or more Turkish autonomous areas. The avenues of diplomacy have not been exhausted. And therefore the United States would consider a resort to military action unjustified.

"We have made this clear to all parties."

Regrettably, the statement was not clear to Turkey. Moreover, it appeared—from the timing of the statement and the stress made on Turkish grievances—that Washington was supporting Ankara's position in Geneva.

Thus, one day later, on August 14, before dawn, the Turkish Army, heavily reinforced with armor and wielding the advantage of complete air superiority, slashed across Cyprus towards both east and west. In three days, this overwhelming military thrust sliced off at least 40% of Cyprus which was slightly more than what the Turks had been demanding in the Geneva talks. The rapid and effortless Turkish advance on Cyprus had both a profound repercussion at the international level and a devastating effect on the population of the island.

At the international level, the Karamanlis government in Greece considered war with Turkey, then rejected that option, but withdrew militarily from NATO. Both widespread public disillusionment and the military's bitterness dictated this course of action regarding the U.S. and NATO. This is a development of profound significance in Greek history—at a critical juncture in the fresh democratisation process—which has already fostered a radical move towards the left in the country's political profile.

U.S. policy, which at every crucial stage of the Cyprus crisis seems to have been one of hasty improvisation and coldly calculated to mini-

17

mise disturbances within NATO, failed in the end. Not only did it achieve the opposite result, but more importantly in human terms, it failed the defenseless people of Cyprus.

APPROXIMATE AREAS OF TURKISH OCCUPATION AFTER 1ST PHASE OF INVASION

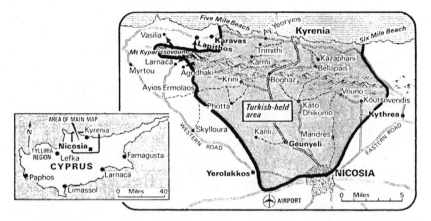

—from The Economist, Aug. 10, 1974

APPROXIMATE AREAS OF TURKISH OCCUPATION AS OF OCTOBER 1974

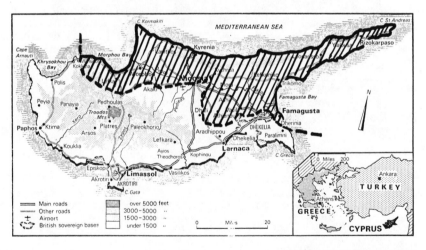

— — — — — Approximate Demarcation
—from The Economist

CONSEQUENCES OF THE INVASION

There are today two stark realities on Cyprus. The first is the presence of an army of occupation—approximately 40,000 heavily armed Turkish troops. The second is the humanitarian crisis confronting over 282,000 Cypriots—nearly half the population of the island—who are now refugees, civilian detainees, prisoners of war, or others in need of humanitarian assistance, on both sides of the uncertain ceasefire line.

Regrettably, there is too little understanding outside of Cyprus as to the consequences of the invasion and conditions in the field. To comprehend what has happened to Cyprus—and especially to appreciate how central the resolution of humanitarian issues is to a settlement of the Cyprus problem—it is important at the outset to review current refugee and related humanitarian problems on the island.

1. HUMANITARIAN CONSEQUENCES OF THE INVASION

As Table 1 outlines, there are several categories of displaced persons and other people in need of help. The first, and by far the largest category, are the Greek Cypriot refugees in the Government controlled area of the south. Official statistics in the field estimate that at least 200,000 Greek Cypriots have been displaced from Turkish occupied areas. Some 30,000 of these people have found shelter with relatives or friends, and need a minimum of relief assistance. The remainder, however, have needed shelter as well as general relief. In addition to these "semi-permanent" refugees, thousands of other Greek Cypriots, living in areas bordering the ceasefire line, have been temporarily displaced, because of actual Turkish troop movements in their area or the fear and threat of new military operations by Turkish forces.

TABLE 1.—*Humanitarian Problems in Cyprus* [1]

I. Refugees:	
1. In Government controlled areas:	
Greek Cypriot refugees	194, 400
Post-ceasefire refugees (from Athna and other areas along cease-fire line)	20, 000
Turkish Cypriots displaced or cut-off	34, 000
2. In Turkish occupied areas:	
Greek Cypriots displaced or cut-off	20, 000
Turkish Cypriot refugees	8, 000
II. Prisoners of war and detainees, both sides	6, 000
Total	[2] 282, 000

[1] Based upon statistics of the UN High Commissioner for Refugees and International Committee of the Red Cross, as of September 15, 1974.

[2] Subsequently, revised statistics on displaced persons in Cyprus, compiled as of Nov. 1, 1974 by the Government of Cyprus, UNFICYP, the UNHCR and ICRC, indicate the total has been reduced slightly. According to sources in the field, this is accountable to the subsequent release and repatriation of over 6,000 detainees and prisoners of war on both sides, a more accurate census of Greek Cypriot refugees by the Government of Cyprus, and revised U.N. estimates of Turkish Cypriot refugees.

[Footnote 2 Continued on Following Page]

(18)

To drive along the roads of southern Cyprus, is to drive through an endless refugee camp. In early September, refugees were encamped under trees, along the roadside, in cars, in open fields, under small lean-to huts made of pine branches and sticks, and in tents provided by International Relief agencies. Every available public building and accommodation was filled with refugees—schools, churches, monastaries, and civic buildings. District towns had been flooded with refugees, and with idle men swelling the unemployment rolls. Small towns and villages along the way had doubled or tripled in size.

Athna Forest.—Following the second phase of the Turkish invasion, some one hundred thousand Greek Cypriot refugees fled south for safety. They brought whatever they could cart along with them, as this old woman from the Famagusta area, standing beneath the trees of Athna Forest with her family's meager household goods.

Footnote 2—Continued

The following table presents the revised estimate of displaced persons and others in need on Cyprus, as of Nov. 1, 1974:

I. Refugees:
    1. Greek Cypriots in Government-controlled areas:

Satisfactorily sheltered with friends/relatives or in second homes rented	57,600
Living in public buildings, schools, etc.	5,800
Housed in permanent structures, but overcrowded conditions and will have to move	89,700
Living in shacks, garages, unfinished structures	11,000
Living in tents	9,000
Living in the open, under trees, in makeshift, open shelters	7,700
Total	**180,800**

    2. Turkish Cypriots in Government-controlled areas:

Living in tents on British Sovereign Base areas	8,500
In isolated villages, cut off, or in controlled villages/enclaves	22,000
Total	**30,500**

    3. Greek Cypriots in Turkish-occupied area:

Living in cut off villages, or displaced	9,000

    4. Turkish Cypriot refugees in Turkish-occupied area:

Moved from the south to the north, and includes some refugees from 1963–64	8,500

II. Prisoners of war and detainees, both sides:

All have been released under U.N. auspices	6,000
Total	**234,800**

The Larnaca district, around the British Sovereign Base Area of Dhekelia, was overwhelmed by refugees, mostly from Famagusta. A typical situation was that of Ormidhia town, whose population had jumped by some 300%. Refugee families were scattered everywhere, and relief supplies were just beginning to arrive—over two weeks after many of the refugees first moved. An empty soccer field was being turned into a refugee city of tents—camping tents for six people, now holding one or two families with as many as 14 men, women and children huddled together.

Xylophaghou village.—On the outskirts of a small town, an old man sits idly beneath the trees of the roadside. To drive through the southern portions of Cyprus is to drive through an endless refugee area, where this old man and his grand-daughters, await the prospect of returning to their home, but with little to do, and with even less hope, in the meantime.

Athna Forest.—The fear of the Turkish army is widespread after the reports of brutality at the end of the first phase of the invasion. As a result of this fear—real or imagined—people fled at the instant they saw or thought Turkish forces were on their way—dropping everything, and taking very little with them. Here two women sit in their "home" of straw, blankets, and a small canvas overhead.

Athna Forest.—A former high school teacher from Famagusta, whose only shelter is a lean-to canvas and straw bed among the bushes of Athna Forest, talks to the leader of the Study Mission, Dale S. deHaan, about his narrow escape from the Turkish sweep into Famagusta and the dispersal of his family—many of whom are still missing.

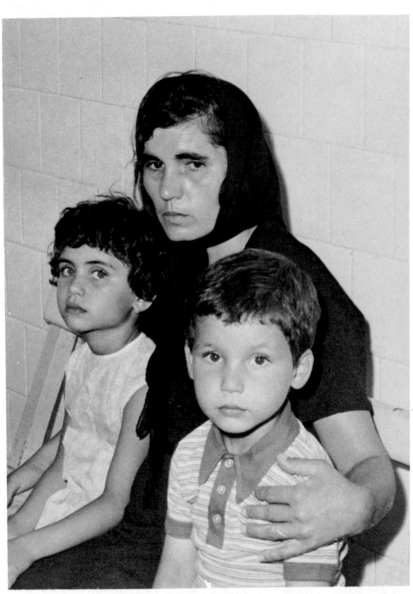

Nicosia.—A mother huddles two of her children, anxiously awaiting news of their missing father—caught on the Turkish side of the ceasefire line. Thousands of men are still missing on both sides; a constant theme heard by the Study Mission was the systematic rounding-up of village men between the ages of 16 to 65— many of whom are still unaccounted for or are still held hostage.

Ormidhia town.—The population of the small town of Ormidhia has jumped by over 300% after the influx of refugees. Here Study Mission member Dennis Skiotis speaks to a refugee family eating its lunch beneath the trees on the outskirts of the town. They hope soon to receive tents, but even more, they hope to be able to return to their homes only a few miles away.

Nicosia school.—Refugees are everywhere and every available public building and accommodation is filled with refugees—schools, churches, monasteries, and civic buildings. Here Study Mission members, Jerry Tinker (left) and Dale S. deHaan, meet with children in a school in Nicosia—living as refugees in the schools they should be attending.

Ormidhia town.—Shelter has now begun to arrive for the refugees. Here an empty soccer field has been transformed into a small refugee city of tents—camping tents for six people, now holding one or two families with as many as 14 men, women and children huddled together until more tents arrive.

Ormidhia town.—Sanitation and other facilities for refugee camps are only now being established. Here a mother bathes a child in the only place she can—outdoors. As winter approaches, and refugee camps become more crowded, serious sanitation and other health problems must be anticipated.

Nicosia, Turkish Quarter.—Although there are approximately 8,000 Turkish Cypriot refugees from the current crisis, whose needs are the same as those on the Greek Cypriot side, the refugees most mentioned, by Turkish Cypriot officials, are the refugees displaced from the 1963–64 communal violence. Vice-President Denktash emphasizes their long neglect, and provided the above photographs showing the crowded and unsanitary conditions in which these Turkish Cypriot refugees of 1963–64 still live.

Reflecting the fluidity of the refugee movement, and the serious lack of shelter and relief supplies in many areas of Larnaca district, a substantial number of the refugees were moving westward to the Limassol district. In early September, the Limassol District Officer estimated that some 1,200 refugees were arriving daily in and around Limassol city. And, because of a lack of adequate shelter and the approaching winter cold, thousands of refugees who had fled to the Troodos mountains from Northwest Cyprus, were heading for greater Nicosia and other populated areas.

The critical problems of the Greek Cypriot refugees are all the classic problems which confront refugees everywhere—the need for shelter, blankets, food, medicine, and other necessities of life. In Cyprus, all are still in short supply, and in some areas many are unavailable. In particular, there was, and remains, a desperate need for blankets. Despite the arrival of thousands of blankets in September, there was clear evidence of the need for more. In the town of Xylophaghou, for example, the school was crowded with refugee families who were forced to sleep on cold, concrete floors. Food supplies were rapidly dwindling, but a Government sponsored food distribution and rationing program was getting underway. Starting with a daily distribution of bread, relief officials were hoping to expand the ration program to include protein foods, milk, and other supplies, *if*—and it was a big "if"—relief supplies from abroad arrived on schedule before government stocks were depleted.

During the Study Mission's visit to the Dhekelia area, the Turkish army undertook what United Nations officials later described as "armed reconnaisance in force" along the ceasefire line above Athna. This type of military action or its threat, which occurred regularly in August and September—and variously described as Turkish "land grabs" or "salami tactics"—produced thousands of new refugees or temporarily displaced persons. Like the thousands before them, they fled for safety out of fear of the Turkish army.

Whether real or imagined—and it is probably real—the fear of what the Turkish military might do is widespread. Whenever and wherever the Study Mission talked with Greek Cypriot refugees, the story was basically the same: People moved the instant they saw or thought the Turkish army was advancing towards their town or village. And they moved *instantly*—dropping everything, taking very little with them, and by foot, car, tractor, truck, bus, or wagon, moved to safety in Government controlled areas. The stories of rough and sometimes brutal treatment of civilians by Turkish forces in Kyrenia, after the first phase of the invasion, had spread over the island like wildfire. Thus, during the second phase of the invasion, Greek Cypriots fled the moment there was rumor or sight of military forces—creating a virtual vacuum into which the Turkish army could and did move without resistance and without the presence of people.

The Study Mission saw direct evidence of this the day it visited the Athna forest, bordering the British Base Area at Dhekelia. Cars and trucks were moving down the road from Athna town, loaded with people and with whatever they could carry— clothes, baskets, mattresses, a few pots and pans—and heading for the safety of the British Base and the shelter of the trees. But conditions were miserable—hot, dusty, no tents, few blankets, no water, little sanitation, and a meager amount of food distributed by the British. Yet the refugees continued to come that day—by the hundreds.

The night before the fall of Famagusta, some 8,000 refugees came into the forest area, and in the days that followed some 7,000 more arrived. It was, for many, a first stop before moving onward, but over 9,000 refugees were still encamped last month under the trees. Before long, the winter cold and rains will come, and a major question for the refugees is whether tents will arrive in time, or other shelter will be found.

Another category of refugees and persons in duress are the Turkish Cypriots in Government controlled areas—a total of some 34,000. Approximately 10,000 are refugees at Episkopi (on the Akrotiri British Base), where camps have been established under the auspices of the ICRC and the UNHCR. In almost every way, the plight and the needs of these refugees are identical to that of their Greek Cypriot counterparts. In addition, about 24,000 Turkish Cypriots are cut-off or isolated—either by choice or by circumstance—in Turkish villages or in the Turkish quarter of larger towns in the south. These beleaguered villages are under the observation and protection of United Nations Forces in Cyprus, and are also receiving relief assistance under international auspices.

The Study Mission visited one mixed village, Kalokhorio, where the Turkish quarter has not been disturbed—having hoisted a white flag above the mosque as a signal of the lack of hostile intentions. There was no indication of any harm being done to these Turkish Cypriots. However, there can be no question that other Turkish villages are, and do, feel beleaguered and isolated. International observers indicated that physical conditions in these cut-off villages and towns are not as bad as suggested by the Turkish Cypriot administration in Nicosia. As one United Nations official, who has been on the island for many months, stated: "Objectively nothing has changed in these Turkish villages, except the fear that something has changed." But in the context of the violence and random mass killings that have occurred on the island since the fighting broke out, the apprehension that conditions may change for the worse does not reassure Cypriots huddled in enclaves, on whatever side of the ceasefire line they find themselves at the moment.

The last categories of refugees and persons in need are those in the Turkish occupied areas. These people include some 8,000 Turkish Cypriot refugees, and an estimated 20,000 Greek Cypriots displaced or cutoff. The Turkish Cypriot refugees are those reportedly displaced during the fighting, such as around the old city of Famagusta, and those who have fled from the south to the north. In September, some of these refugees were in schools in the Turkish sector of Nicosia. They appeared to be in good condition, with no overcrowding, and adequate relief assistance from the Turkish Cypriot Red Crescent Society.

However, the refugees the Turks most often mention are not those from the current conflict, but rather those from the 1963 intercommunal violence, when some 25,000 Turkish Cypriots were displaced. One deserted and run down area bordering Nicosia, called Omorphita, remains a symbol of the neglect the Turks feel the Greek Cypriots and others paid to their needs 11 years ago.

The sense of Turkish Cypriot grievance is real and runs deep. As Vice President Denktash told the Study Mission, "the many drops of

Greek injustice to the Turkish minority has, over the years, filled the ocean in which we are all now drowning." And to many officials of the Turkish Cypriot community, the current suffering of the Greek Cypriots, although quantitatively far greater, is in principle the same as that suffered in the past by the Turkish Cypriots. As one official phrased it "the refugee problem is not the numbers involved, it's the principle." And, given what they feel has been world indifference to suffering among Turkish Cypriots, they only grudgingly recognize the current plight of Greek Cypriots and say they do not understand the current international concern over these victims of the Turkish "peace operation" in Cyprus.

The second type of refugee problem in the Turkish occupied areas is that of some 20,000 Greek Cypriots isolated in such places as Kyrenia and Bellapais, and in several villages cutoff in the so-called panhandle area of Karpasia.

In Kyrenia, about 450 Greeks are still being cruelly detained by Turkish authorities in the waterfront Dome Hotel. They had been rounded up from their nearby homes by the Turkish military during the early stages of the invasion, or had fled on their own to the hotel in search of safety.

Bellapais, a small village of some 400 Greek Cypriots and in normal times a favorite tourist spot, has now become a virtual prison for the local population as well as some 450 Greek Cypriot refugees who are also held within the confines of the village. At the peak of the fighting during the first phase of the Turkish invasion, well over 2,000 refugees fled to the sanctuary of this small village. But after the Turkish military occupied the village, cordoning it off, most were forcibly moved across the Green Line in Nicosia. The Turkish army also rounded-up the male population, taking some 150 men to destinations unknown. At the time of the Study Mission's visit, the families of these men still had no word as to their fate—whether they were in prisons or dead.

The situation in Bellapais had improved from the worst days of over-crowding and panic. But although the number of refugees in the village had decreased, the conditions had become more desperate physically as well as psychologically, as the days of uncertainty and confinement press on. Only minimal food was being provided through the Red Cross. And, contrary to the official Turkish line that there are only local people in Bellapais staying in their homes, there were at least 450 refugees cut-off and separated from their families, and told by Turkish authorities that "reunification of families is not sufficient grounds for permission to move."

In the abandoned city of Famagusta, with the old Turkish quarter of the city sealed off by the Turkish army, no life stirs on the empty streets, which were once home for over 40,000 people. The only population left behind are an undetermined number of old people—old men and women, hiding in their homes, some too feeble or ill to move, others afraid to come out in sight of the Turkish army. The Swedish contingent of UNFICYP located in the new city area, has reported sighting a number of old people scavenging for food and supplies in the darkness of night.

In Famagusta, as elsewhere, Turkish authorities said they have attempted to search abandoned areas in order to find elderly Greek Cypriots who have stayed behind. They indicated that whenever these old people were found and were unable to care or provide for themselves—as was generally the case—they were then handed over to representatives of the International Committtee of the Red Cross to be reunited with their families in refugee areas in the Government-controlled zone. While visiting Famagusta, the Study Mission witnessed such a round-up of old people, observing six or seven old men and women, huddled together in the back of a guarded Turkish army truck, with troops at fixed bayonet, hauling a group of old people from their homes—a scene tragically reminiscent of pictures from Germany in 1939.

As noted earlier, the Study Mission was not able to arrange a visit to Karpasia, and United Nations officials have had only very limited access to the area. Reports suggest, however, that the Greeks remaining in Karpasia are in increasingly desperate straits. They are, in fact, prisoners of the Turkish Army. They are confined to their villages or are being detained in churches and other civic buildings. The younger men have been taken away. Food, medicine and other materials are in short supply. And international relief is generally denied by the Turkish authorities.

Until outside observers and relief officials are able to freely deliver relief supplies and to have unrestricted access to refugees in the Turkish occupied areas, the world will not know the full tragedy of Cyprus, nor will international relief agencies be able to provide all the help they can. And until the Turkish policy of isolating inhabitants of Karpasia ends, the world must assume the Turkish authorities have something to hide. This policy contrasts sharply with the free access enjoyed by the United Nations and the Red Cross throughout the Government controlled area in the south.

Finally, there is the humanitarian problem of releasing prisoners of war and civilian detainees—some 6,000 on both sides. Considerable and very encouraging progress has been made in this area, resulting from the recent talks, under U.N. auspices, between President Clerides and Vice-President Denktash. Two prisoner exchanges have been made, and more are promised in the coming weeks.[1]

2. ECONOMIC CONSEQUENCES OF THE INVASION

It is exceptionally difficult to quantify the full extent of the damage and destruction caused by the conflict, nor all the ramifications the invasion has had, and will have, on the economy. But, for a state as small as Cyprus, there can be no doubt that it has been catastrophic.

Regarding the extent of physical destruction, the evidence suggests that minimal bomb or structural damage occurred—with the exception of areas in and around the Kyrenia-Nicosia enclave, which was the site of the original Turkish landing and the staging ground for phase two of the invasion. Considerable looting has occurred in many areas. Kyrenia city, for example, has been looted beyond description, and in driving across the island to Famagusta, there is wide-spread evidence of looting of Greek Cypriot villages along the road. In fact, the Study Mission observed two military trucks and a lorry loaded with miscellaneous pieces of furniture heading for some unknown desination down the road from Famagusta.

The new city of Famagusta—the "Miami Beach" area known as Varosha—is the major exception to the problem of looting. As of early

---

[1] By the end of October, 1974, nearly all of the prisoners of war and detainees on both sides had been released under a series of exchanges at the Ledra Palace Hotel, arranged under the auspices of the United Nations and the ICRC.

September, evident care had been taken by Turkish military commanders to seal this area off from all potential looters. It was relatively untouched. However, it symbolizes what has happened to the economy of Cyprus. This once bustling city, a key element in the island's tourist industry, is now a ghost town. Standing on the empty main street—"John F. Kennedy Blvd.,"—amid high-rise hotels and apartments and expensive shops, one can see only a few stray dogs and cats, and a lonely contingent of Swedish U.N. troops. The Greek population had fled.

Since the Turkish invasion, the Government of Cyprus estimates that the country is losing some $4.5 million in economic production every day. The vast citrus industry in the Morphou area rots on the trees. The wheat fields, which should have been planted, lie fallow. Unknown numbers of livestock and cattle are dead because of the lack of food and water. The mines and light industry lie idle. And not a single tourist remains on the island. It will not be too many months before the foreign exchange crisis becomes critical—a fact that has only been delayed temporarily by the action of Greece in providing some direct financial support to the Government of Cyprus.

There can be little doubt today that the damage to the economy of Cyprus will only serve to heighten the plight of the people, and make the life of the refugees all the more precarious. With each passing day the economic situation worsens, as will the condition of the refugees, if something more is not done soon.

3. POLITICAL CONSEQUENCES OF THE INVASION

There can be little doubt today that the Turkish invasion succeeded in altering the political situation on Cyprus. Indeed, it is generally accepted that the invasion has destroyed the constitutional framework and political structure of the Government of Cyprus, as it was established in 1960, and there can be no turning back the clock. The future of Cyprus will be a future governed by a new and different governmental and political structure. The precise form of this new structure will be a primary focus of negotiations in the days and weeks ahead. There are currently a number of options and arrangements being discussed in Nicosia, Athens, Ankara, and other capitals.

Most frequently mentioned, particularly in Ankara and Washington, is some form of Federal system involving territorial separation of the two communities on the island—of geographic separation between Turkish and Greek Cypriots, in order to create a Turkish majority area on Cyprus. By whatever name it is called, this is tantamount to partition, and it will mean traumatic shifts in the current economic and population patterns of the island.

To an outside observer, it may seem possible, even easy, to work out some new "bi-regional", "zonal", or "federal" arrangement on Cyprus. It may seem today only a question of where the line should be drawn. But the central question is whether any Greek Cypriot government can be found that would accept a settlement imposed by the force of arms, and predicated on the non-return of two out of five of the Greek Cypriot refugees. If that kind of "solution" is forced upon the Greek Cypriots, there can be little question that they will resist it, perhaps with violence and guerrilla war—with all that that implies for the future peace and stability of the Eastern Mediterranean. The very likely outcome, then, would probably be *de facto* partition in its extreme form—in effect, double enosis. With a political, or at the very minimum, administrative and economic union of the two separate parts of Cyprus with Greece and Turkey, Cyprus would cease to exist.

Turkey insists that this is not the outcome it seeks, even as the Greek Cypriots insist that it is an outcome they cannot accept. In the middle lies a solution. Where that is today, much less tomorrow, is for all parties to negotiate.

The Greek Cypriot position, supported by Greece, is that before negotiations can resume, there must be some gesture, on Turkey's part, to accommodate Greek Cypriot demands to have a substantial number of refugees return home. Greek Cypriot spokesmen have indicated privately and publicly that the Government of Cyprus will be flexible in negotiations—that it is prepared to accept new constitutional arrangements, including perhaps some form of "cantonal" system granting Turkish Cypriots full communal security and autonomy. But Greek Cypriots insist that progress must be made at the very outset on the return of refugees to their homes.

The Turkish Cypriot position, as well as Ankara's, emphasizes that speedy progress on a political solution involving biregionalism would enable both sides to address the refugee problem on a permanent basis. Their spokesmen emphasize the past failures and long-standing grievances of the Turkish Cypriots, and speak of new realities on Cyprus. They stress that Turkey does not seek partition, either political or economic, and that they wish to preserve the independence of the island. Precisely how these contrary objectives can be accommodated is the large unanswered question.

4. IMPACT OF PARTITION

Whatever name or label is used to describe partition in Cyprus—whether it is called "bi-regionalism," "geographic federalism," "consolidated cantonments," or "double enosis"—the reality of any partition on an island the size of Cyprus is that there will inevitably be serious human and economic consequences.

The partition line most frequently envisaged in discussions on Cyprus, particularly within the Turkish community, relates to the so-called "Attila line." This line was first proposed by the Turkish Cypriot Communal Chamber in 1964, and was raised again this past July by Turkey during the Geneva talks. As the accompanying map indicates, the Attila line runs from Kokkino in the northwest, via Xerarkaka, south of Lefka, Akaki, through Nicosia, east through Angastina and Prestio, to Famagusta. The area north of this line is approximately 1,170 square miles, comprising roughly one-third of the territory of Cyprus. Currently, the Turkish Army occupies land considerably beyond the Attila line.

But no matter where a line is finally drawn, any artificial division of the island will bring immense economic problems as well as massive population dislocation—the general character of which can only be imagined after an analysis of important economic and population factors. The following information was obtained from official sources in the field, and serves to document some of the population and economic factors related to partition in Cyprus.

THE ATTILA LINE PROPOSED BY TURKEY

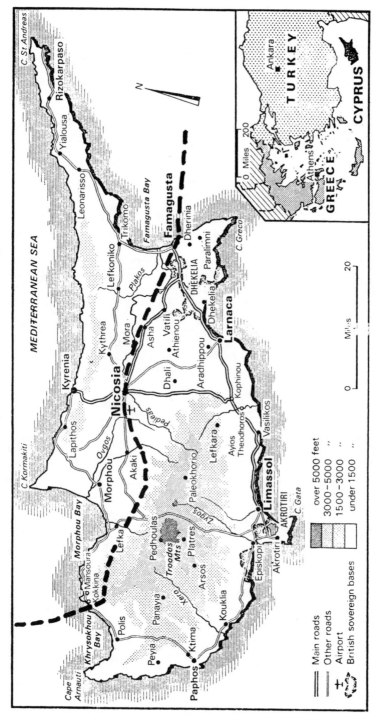

Map legend:

Main roads
Other roads
Airport
British sovereign bases

over 5000 feet
3000–5000 ,,
1500–3000 ,,
under 1500 ,,

0   Miles   20

■ ■ ■ ■ Approximate Demarcation

a. *Impact of Partition on Population Patterns*

Drastic changes in the population patterns of Cyprus would come with partition—changes every bit as serious and disruptive as those which have already come with the Turkish military invasion, which has, in effect, turned the island upside down. Most severely affected, of course, is the Greek Cypriot community, which comprises some 78% of the population.

A partition along the Attila line, which would require a significant segregation of Greek Cypriots and Turkish Cypriots into separate areas—and which seeks to assure a Turkish majority in their area—would mean moving nearly half the total population and resettling them elsewhere on a permanent basis. Based on 1972 population estimates, this would amount to moving some 51,800 Turks (44.6% of the total Turkish Cypriot population) from scattered areas around the island into the northern zone. In turn, this would require moving out of that northern area at least 147,500 Greek Cypriots (or some 29.3% of the total Greek Cypriot population), who, until the invasion, lived there.

Official estimates indicate that such a shift could involve as many as 40,000 families, and it would significantly alter the population density in each of the two ethnic areas.

According to Cyprus Government estimates, this would reduce the density of population in Turkish areas by half—from 185 to only 76.9 persons per square mile. Yet, at the same time, it would force the population density in the Greek area to jump from 181 to 202.6 persons per square mile. The following table, based on official estimates from the last detailed census in 1960, provides a population profile of Cyprus.

Table 2.—Population profile of Cyprus

Total population:

		1972
Greek (78%)		503, 100
Turkish (18%)		116, 100
Armenians, Maronites, others (4%)		25, 800
Total (100%)		**645, 000**
Average population density per sq. mile		181

Population of area north of the Attila lines:

Greek (67.7%)		147, 500
Turkish (29.5%)		64, 300
Others (2.8%)		6, 000
Total (100%)		**217, 800**

Population of important urban centers in the northern area

Morphou (120 Turks, 7,360 Greeks)	7, 480
Kyrenia (1,383 Turks, 2,800 Greeks)	4, 183
Lefka (Turks, no Greeks)	5, 400
Famagusta (6,900 Turks, 27,700 Greeks, 4,800 others)	39, 400
Nicosia:	
Turkish sector	27, 400
Greek sector (Greeks)	72, 600
Others	10, 500
Total	**110, 500**

In short, if partition in Cyprus is to mean significant segregation between Greek and Turkish Cypriots, and if it also means the Turks are to have a majority in their area, as Turkey now seems to demand, it would require a drastic rearrangement of existing population patterns—rearrangement that cannot help but be painful, and probably inequitable, to the Greek Cypriots. An example is the city of Morphou, which falls above the Attila line, and which seems clearly within the Turkish area from the Turkish point of view. If Morphou were made to become a Turkish majority area, well over half of 95% of the city's current population would have to leave their homes. In Kyrenia, 30% to 60% of the population would have to leave and be replaced by Turks.

The impact upon land ownership would be no less severe, and would obviously be a major stumbling block in any partition plan. It would require compensation for Greek privately owned land in the northern areas of Cyprus, as well as extensive land exchange programs between Turkish and Greek Cypriots. Because the Greeks own more land in the north than the Turkish Cypriots do in the south, land exchange would obviously be complicated no matter whose statistics one uses on current land ownership. The Government of Cyprus claims the 1960 Census shows some 20.4% of the total agricultural land in Turkish hands, while the Turkish Communal Chamber says arable Turkish land is 30%.

The discrepancy may not seem great in terms of total land tenure, but when the critical differences of land location, its level of development, and its crop, are added to land distribution patterns, exchanging land on an equitable basis would be difficult, if not impossible—regardless of what the actual total of land may be respective to the two communities.

b. Impact of Partition on the Economy

Being a relatively small island, the economy of Cyprus is necessarily homogeneous and, even as it has prospered and grown remarkably over the past decade, it remains a fragile and developing economic system. Partition of this totally integrated economy would have disastrous consequences, and to partition it in an equitable fashion would try the wisdom of Solomon—because it works, prospers, and grows only as a whole.

If the Attila line forms the basis of partition, it would include many of the principal foreign exchange earning portions of the economy on the Turkish side. It would include the copper mining region in the Morphou Bay area, the whole of the highly-developed agricultural Morphou plain (including the mostly Greek citrus industry), all of the perennial springs in the Kyrenia mountain range, most of the irrigated plain of the eastern Mesaoria, large areas of citrus groves in the Serrakhis river valley, large forest areas in the Kyrenia region (although two thirds were burned during the invasion), many of the best tourist resorts, and portions of Famagusta, including the largest port facilities on the island.

In comparison, the Greek controlled area, although retaining a sizeable portion of the fertile Mesaorian plain, would contain a high proportion of uncultivable mountainous and forested terrain (the Troodos Mountain area), and undeveloped land.

Agriculture.—Because Cyprus is basically an agricultural country, with approximately 47% of the land cultivated and well over half of the population engaged in some form of agriculture, partition would inevitably have a severe impact upon its agricultural sector.

For example, the fertile Mesaorian plain, the breadbasket of Cyprus, contains the bulk of the island's cultivable lands. Its principal crops are wheat, barley, vegetables, and citrus fruits. Extensive irrigation in the area is required during the summer dry season, and this has been developed over the past decade. If this plain is partitioned along the Attila line, it would place within Turkish control some 37% of all croplands, and provide the Turkish Cypriot community with more than half of the valuable irrigated crop land, and over half of the wheat cultivated areas—to feed less than a quarter of the island's population.

The Morphou plain would also fall in the Turkish area, and as a result Turkish Cypriots would control two thirds of the best citrus growing region of Cyprus. These include the orange and grapefruit groves in the Famagusta and Morphou areas, and the lemon orchards near Karavas and Lapithos in Kyrenia. Citrus fruits represent the most important export of the island, valued at some $17.3 million in 1970 according to Cyprus Government statistics.

Turkish controlled areas would also have the second best potato growing region of Cyprus, along the Nicosia-Morphou road, as well as approximately half of the carob and olive producing areas. The value of potato exports, mostly to England, was almost $16 million in 1970.

A breakdown of what partition of the Mesaoria plain would do to cultivation of cropland, is outlined in Table 3, based upon data from a 1956 British land utilization map and from a 1967 Government of Cyprus directory on Commerce.

TABLE 3.—PARTITION OF MESAORIA

Overall crop lands	Irrigated crop lands	Area under barley cultivation	Area under wheat cultivation
Area of 456 square miles (37.7 percent) Turkish control.	184 square miles (50.3 percent).	57,812 acres (45 percent)___	43,045 acres (62 percent).
Area of 692 square miles (57.5 percent) Greek control.	168 square miles (46 percent).	56,527 acres (44 percent)_____	23,049 acres (33.2 percent).
United Kingdom sovereign base of 56 square miles (4.8 percent) territory Dhekelia.	14 square miles (3.7 percent).	14,131 acres (11 percent)_____	3,332 acres (4.8 percent).
Total 1,204 square miles (100 percent).	366 square miles (100 percent).	128,470 acres (100 percent)_	69,426 acres (100 percent).

Tourism.—In recent years, tourism has grown as a significant foreign exchange earner for Cyprus, and it has almost been exclusively Greek Cypriot investments and management that have made it possible. Partition of the island, especially if Famagusta is divided differently than it is now, would also cut the tourism business in half.

The Greek controlled areas would retain many of the tourist and ski attractions in the western part of the island and in the Troodos mountains. But the tourist trade concentrated in the Kyrenia and northern coastal resorts would fall into Turkish hands. Loss of

Kyrenia would be especially hard for Greek Cypriots, largely because of its flourishing, Greek-owned hotel business. In 1970, Kyrenia and Famagusta (now both in the Turkish occupied area), and Nicosia, together accounted for 82% of the tourist accommodations and are clearly the most significant aspects of the foreign exchange earnings of tourism.

Forestry.—Although the timber resources of Cyprus provide less than 30% of its timber requirements, the forests represent a key resource in the island's economy. Partition would mean that the northern area, which contains some 197 square miles of timber, or about 29% of all state and privately owned forest land, would be in Turkish hands. Roughly one-third of the island's timber output would be reserved for less than a quarter of the population.

Mining.—The Turkish occupation of the Morphou Bay area brings within its control the U.S.-owned Cyprus Mines Corporation, the island's largest copper producing company and another significant foreign exchange earner. According to information in Nicosia, this copper mine's output in 1970 totalled some 18,000 metric tons, a substantial drop from the peak years of the 1960's, and it would, officials say, decline further unless there are new investments of capital equipment. All other mining areas would remain in Greek held territory.

Industry.—Officials indicate that this branch of the economy would be least affected by partition, largely because there is little heavy industry on the island aside from the mines. Light industry is largely concentrated around Nicosia, and the southern port cities, and remain in Greek controlled areas. The significant winery industry, almost wholly Greek-owned, is in the Limassol areas and would be in Greek areas under a partition plan.

5. THE HAZARDS OF ECONOMIC PARTITION

Over the past decade, the economy of Cyprus has grown at a remarkable rate, and it has become one of the most dependable members of the International Monetary Fund, and one of the highest rated recipients of United Nations Development Program funds. Indeed, Cyprus has prospered and has developed economically at a far better rate than its neighbors, including Turkey and even Greece. It has one of the highest per capita incomes in the Eastern Mediterranean—nearly three times that of Turkey.

However, this prosperity and economic performance has been based upon the integrated economy of the whole island. What political partition would mean in economic terms is anyone's guess—even if the intention is not, as Turkey says it is not, to divide the island's economy. But how a political partition line can be drawn without also dividing or disrupting the economy of the island, is clearly one of the most troubling questions confronting negotiations over the fate of Cyprus.

The results of the Turkish invasion have already, in less than three months, wrecked havoc with the economy of Cyprus. As already noted, the losses from physical damage and dislocation, caused by the military activity since July, have already run into the millions. But as serious as the economic effects of Turkish occupation have been to date, consequences of partition may be even more damaging. Every indicator suggests that Cyprus could not easily recover economically from a permanent political partition—certainly not in the near future, and perhaps not for many years to come.

6. COSTS OF THE INVASION TO TURKEY

Whatever sense of national fulfillment and political triumph Turkey may feel over its action on Cyprus, it clearly has come at considerable cost. According to the U.S. Embassy in Ankara, the invasion and occupation of Cyprus adds heavily to the already substantial problems of Turkey—of a 35% inflation rate, an unofficial unemployment rate of 20%, and a potential reduction of foreign exchange earnings from remittances of a declining number of Turkish migrant workers in Western Europe. Now the costs of the Cyprus occupation are added, which, according to official estimates in the field, will total some $1 billion by the end of this year.

Nearly 10% of Turkey's military force is now stationed on Cyprus, and there have been heavy logistical and support requirements. Civilian "technicians" and others have also gone to the island. Moreover, there were considerable losses during the invasion. According to responsible military sources in the field, the performance of Turkey's armed forces during the first phase of the invasion was very poor. Although Turkey apparently employed a basic plan its general staff had drafted and perfected over a period of several years, military observers say there was poor operational planning, inadequate communications, and a near total failure of joint operations among Turkish air, sea, and ground forces.

As a result, through tactical errors Turkey lost an estimated 15 aircraft during the invasion. It sank one of its own destroyers. Casualties were considered light, but included some 300 men killed and another 500 wounded. Had there been any substantial Greek Cypriot forces and tanks in the northern part of the island, casualties undoubtedly would have been considerably higher. One military observer suggested, for example, that because the Turkish airborne assault came at too high an altitude, a better organized and equipped Greek Cypriot army could have easily eliminated an entire Turkish airborne regiment swinging helplessly in the air.

Currently stationed on the island are some 40,000 mainforce Turkish troops, with more than 200 tanks. There are some naval vessels around the island, but the presence of aircraft is limited until airstrips can be improved and extended.

Recent field reports suggest that Turkey is digging in to stay on Cyprus. Unconfirmed reports indicate that the Turkish army has already erected barriers along the ceasefire line, and has established extensive fortifications across the island. And as a "Berlin wall" divides Cyprus, Turkish currency, laborers, equipment and goods pour in from the mainland to fill the vacuum created by the isolation of the north from the island's economy.

HUMANITARIAN NEEDS AND INTERNATIONAL ASSISTANCE

Within days after the first phase of the Turkish invasion, when some 40,000 Greek Cypriots had fled the Kyrenia area, it was apparent that a serious refugee problem was developing on Cyprus. Both the Government of Cyprus, the International Committee of the Red Cross, and UNFICYP responded in mid-July. Subsequently, in August, the UNHCR assumed principal responsibility for the international relief effort.

Massive humanitarian relief needs were created by the advance of the Turkish army, particularly after the second phase in August. Within a month, some 40% of the Greek Cypriot population was rendered homeless, fleeing into government controlled areas of the south. Their need for shelter, food, medicine, blankets, and other supplies, were immediate and serious. As refugees moved from one area to another in search of shelter, the Government of Cyprus attempted to marshall the stocks of food, tents and blankets on the island. But supplies were clearly inadequate.

The relief requirements for some 160,000 Greek Cypriot refugees who are unable to move-in with relatives or find accommodation with their own resources, have been listed down by the Cyprus Government in the following quantities: 30,000 tents to accommodate five persons each, also 100 large tents for camp sites; 320,000 blankets, counting two blankets for each refugee, particularly children; 156,000 camp-beds; 33,000 heating sets for winter; 320 mobile kitchens; and continuing outside food supplies.

The office of "Special Services for the Relief and Rehabilitation of Displaced Persons" in Nicosia has estimated that to establish refugee camp sites for all those who are now in need of shelter will cost over $22 million. The Government of Cyprus is currently planning for between 70 to 90 such camp sites, accommodating between 1,000 and 4,000 people each. The UNHCR has urged the government to avoid establishing large refugee camps, and to place all sites around existing communities.

The leveling of ground, provision of water, sanitary and medical facilities, and the erection of tents and support facilities, are now well underway. The Government of Cyprus has pledged to provide shelter for all refugees by the middle of October, and to have all schools reopened which have until now been occupied by refugees. The speed and thoroughness of the government's response to the refugee crisis is evidence of its capacity to undertake relief programs and to absorb outside relief assistance. The government has the talent, the energy, the infrastructure, and most of all, the concern, to carry forth a meaningful and significant relief effort—*if* they are given the tools and the resources to help them help themselves.

1. INTERNATIONAL RELIEF ASSISTANCE

Although there was a commendable and early response from many nations to the plight of Cyprus—particularly from Greece, the European Economic Community, and the United States—the appeals of both the ICRC and the UNHCR have not been fully met to date. In fact, the UNHCR's appeal for some $22,000,000 through the end of this year has only met with token response from the United States and the world community, and the initial enthusiasm and support for Cyprus relief now threatens to dry up.

Bi-lateral aid from Greece has been substantial, and by far the largest contribution to Cyprus. In addition to providing some $17.7 million per month in budget support to the Government of Cyprus, Greece has also contributed well over $5 million in relief supplies, principally tents, clothes, blankets and food.

Although the United States has so far pledged no budgetary support to the Cyprus Government, it has made some relief contributions. As of October 1st, the United States had allocated or pledged, in cash and kind, close to $6,000,000—mainly through the ICRC and UNHCR. U.S. assistance to date breaks down as follows:

TABLE 4.—U.S. Government assistance to date (as of Oct. 10, 1974)

Ambassador's fund	$25, 000
Grant to ICRC	725, 000
Grant to UNHCR	[1] 1, 000, 000
Blankets (64,570 wool and cotton)	264, 814
Tents, family—5,600 each	690, 890
Tents, general purpose large, 100 each	102, 300
Cots, folding—9,998 each	101, 625
Body bags—200 each	4, 120
Red Cross markers—79 each	4, 090
Water cans—10,000 each	10, 500
Tent repair kits	218
Water trailers—4 each	8, 000
Tent flies—5,600 each	[1] 400, 000
TDY expertise, FDR coordinator and staff	5, 515
Estimated air transport commodities	1, 282, 043
U.S. Government total	4, 624, 115

[1] Obligations of $1.4 million against $3 million UNHCR pledge.

2. ROLE OF THE UNITED NATIONS FORCE IN CYPRUS

For over ten years, the United Nations Peace-Keeping Force on Cyprus (UNFICYP) has helped to reduce communal tensions and prevent the spread of violence by interposing itself between the two Cypriot communities. The direct costs to the U.N. of keeping UNFICYP on the island have totaled some $350 million since 1964.

The effectiveness of UNFICYP's role on Cyprus was shattered with the invasion of the Turkish Army. The mandate of UNFICYP under these conditions made it a "peace-keeping force" in name only. As it watched the Turkish army move across Cyprus, UNFICYP became more of a "peace observing force," watching the breakdown of peace, with no power to maintain it, much less to enforce it. This is stated neither to denigrate the important role of the United Nations in the past, nor to underestimate its potential contribution in the future. Rather, it is to indicate the severe limitations under which UNFICYP now labors, and the critical need to revise and expand the scope of its mandate.

Today, as before the Turkish invasion, UNFICYP's operations are primarily based around a framework of static posts, which have been established wherever possible, but particularly in sensitive places. These static posts are supplemented by frequent mobile patrols, of regular military units or U.N. Civilian Police (UNCIVPOL). Since the invasion, UNFICYP has had relatively free and unrestricted access only to districts outside of the Turkish occupied areas.

According to UNFICYP officials, their main activity under current conditions is an effort to generate a feeling of confidence and to obtain information concerning the local situation—particularly in areas where humanitarian and relief measures, including the security of population, are required. A special problem exists in Nicosia, where military confrontation continues to exist along the so-called "Green Line" separating the Greek and Turkish quarters. UNFICYP is endeavoring to interpose itself along the line to prevent violence. There are several UNFICYP posts along the line and active patrolling between them. Still, violence has erupted, and numerous fires have been started in buildings along the line on the Greek side—fires reportedly set by the Turks.

Within the Turkish occupied area, UNFICYP activities are very limited. UNFICYP provides trucks for the delivery of food and other supplies to Kyrenia, Bellapais and some other areas. But, in the main, UNFICYP is restricted to the few static posts it was able to hold through the invasion—such as the Swedish post in the abandoned city of Famagusta. There is little, if any, freedom of movement.

As noted above, in the Government controlled areas, UNFICYP has relatively free access, and is making special efforts, in cooperation with the Government, to provide care and protection to the Turkish Cypriot population. The complete resources of UNFICYP, including logistic support, are made available to the ICRC and UNHCR through a special humanitarian/economics office established at UNFICYP headquarters on July 22.

The humanitarian efforts of UNFICYP cover the following items:

1. Information gathering to spot areas of humanitarian need;

2. The transport of supplies, principally to Turkish Cypriot villages cut-off in Government controlled areas;

3. The provision of warehouse and logistic assistance to the Red Cross, UNHCR, and the Government of Cyprus;

4. Medical care and medivac, particularly in Turkish Cypriot areas;

5. UNICIVPOL assistance to investigate alleged atrocities and to support ICRC efforts in tracing the missing;

6. Assisting in the restoration of water and electricity across communal zones; and,

7. Agricultural support efforts, including the provision of food and water to abandoned livestock and other animals.

The current strength and composition of UNFICYP, nearly doubled in response to an urgent request by Secretary-General Waldheim in August, stands as follows:

Austria	300
Canada	950
Denmark	432
Finland	626
Ireland	4
Sweden	575
United Kingdom	1,391
Hospital unit (Austria)	14
Total UNFICYP personnel	4,292

In addition, UNCIVPOL personnel is being increased from 153 to 200. The U.S. has also doubled its contributions to UNFICYP operations.

3. ROLE OF THE INTERNATIONAL COMMITTEE OF THE RED CROSS

On July 19, shortly after the coup against President Makarios, and before the Turkish invasion, the ICRC sent two delegates to Cyprus. Within three days, as conditions deteriorated, 14 additional ICRC delegates, including three doctors, arrived in Nicosia. Some 3.5 tons of medicaments, including blood plasma and other emergency supplies, were air lifted to the island. This early and swift response by the ICRC to the crisis developing in Cyprus was the first alert the international community had as to the scope and dimension of humanitarian needs.

Within a week, the ICRC, in close cooperation with the local Cypriot Red Cross, had established a full scale relief operation in addition to their normal responsibilities during conflict. Some forty ICRC delegates are now stationed on the island, and the ICRC role is in transition from general relief operations to its more traditional mandate under the Geneva Conventions. This mandate includes tracing missing persons, inspection of civilian detainee and prisoner of war facilities, and similar responsibilities. Relief operations are being absorbed by UNHCR.

Throughout the crisis on Cyprus, the leadership and activities of the of the ICRC have been crucial. The ICRC assumed, without hesitation, relief responsibilities when no other organizations were available to help, and their presence and contributions on Cyprus continue as important links in the international effort to help meet the humanitarian needs of Cyprus.

4. ROLE OF U.N. HIGH COMMISSIONER FOR REFUGEES

Since August 20th, and following an appeal by the Cyprus government, the UNHCR has been the focal point for international humanitarian assistance on Cyprus. The UNHCR, Prince Sadruddin Aga Khan visited Cyprus in late August, and has established a field office in Nicosia, headed by Mr. John Kelley.

Initially, the UNHCR concentrated on supplementing the emergency relief efforts already underway by the ICRC, in cooperation with the local authorities. Concurrently, however, the UNHCR also initiated, with the Cyprus government, the necessary planning for longer term relief and rehabilitation efforts. On August 30, the UNHCR issued an international appeal for contributions to an emergency relief fund of $9,000,000. Several days later the amount was increased to $22,000,000 to cover anticipated relief needs through the end of this year. As of October 3rd, the total amount received, in cash and kind, has only been $6,800,000—less than a third of the total need.

The UNHCR has representatives in both the Turkish occupied zone and the Government controlled areas. UNHCR has complete and free access in Government controlled areas, and effective mechanisms for coordination has been established in Nicosia with Government relief officials. However, in Turkish occupied areas, the UNHCR, like other international agencies, has been unable to travel freely. It was not until late September, for example, that the UNHCR representative was permitted to travel to Karpasia and other areas of serious need in the occupied territories. Moreover, relief convoys are severely limited in their efforts to reach people in need.

5. ROLE OF INTERGOVERNMENTAL COMMITTEE FOR EUROPEAN MIGRATION (ICEM)

The primary purpose of ICEM is the movement of refugees and migrants, mainly in Europe, to resettlement areas elsewhere. In recent years, however, ICEM has also assumed important responsibilities in arranging air charters and sea movements, of both people and materials, for the U.N. and its specialized agencies. In this connection, ICEM is currently supporting UNHCR efforts on Cyprus, by arranging for the transportation of thousands of tons of blankets, tents and relief supplies for the refugees and others in need on the island.

NOTES ON UNITED STATES POLICY

In his August 8th statement on the Senate floor, the Chairman made these comments:

"I fully appreciate the immense difficulties in the Cyprus issue. It is a complex matter for diplomats and humanitarians alike. But should not our Government give more evidence of concern? What are American policy objectives? What is the substance of our activities? What have we done to help meet humanitarian needs among the Cypriot civilians who are refugees or detainees on either side?

"The American people and their representatives in Congress deserve some answers, and should not be in the dark over United States policy toward Cyprus. I am extremely hopeful, that the administration will finally give some additional evidence of a very active concern over the needed efforts to bring peace and relief to the people of Cyprus."

These comments by the Chairman in the early stages of the Cyprus crisis were prompted by the virtual silence at the highest levels of our government over developments on the island. Apart from some rather routine statements at the United Nations, and some occasional comment by "sources" or spokesmen in the Department of State, American officials said very little about Cyprus—or at least about the substance of American policy.

Although flatly denied in all quarters of the Administration, to many observers there has been a perceptible "tilt" toward Turkey in the American approach to Cyprus—especially following the demise of the short lived Sampson regime in Nicosia. But, as suggested elsewhere in this report, given the variety and rapidity of developments in Cyprus and related events, United States policy in these early days seems to have been one of hasty improvisation, coldly calculated to minimize disturbances within NATO, more than anything else. This has not only achieved the opposite result in the end, but more importantly in human terms, it has failed the defenseless people of Cyprus—and, for many observers, has confirmed a Turkish "tilt" in United States policy toward Cyprus.

After a month of virtual silence at the highest levels of our government, on August 19, immediately following the senseless death of Ambassador Davies in Nicosia, Secretary of State Henry A. Kissinger held a news conference and finally made a public statement in behalf of the President over American policy toward Cyprus. The statement.[1] in part, reads as follows:

President Ford has asked me to make the following statement on behalf of the United States:
First, the United States shall insist on the strict maintenance of the cease-fire on Cyprus.

---

[1] For the complete text of this statement, as well as other official United States statements on Cyprus, see Appendix IV.

Second, the imperative and urgent need is to begin negotiations.

Third, we will continue to support efforts to bring the parties to the negotiating table.

Fourth, the United States will play any role requested by the parties. We are also prepared to support the able efforts of the British Foreign Secretary, (James) Callaghan, in this regard.

Fifth, in these negotiations, we believe it will be necessary for Turkey, as the stronger power on the ground, to display flexibility and a concern for Greek sensitivities, both in terms of territory and the size of military forces on the island. I have made this point directly this morning to the Prime Minister of Turkey. I have been assured that the Turkish Government considers the demarcation line negotiable and that it will carry out the provisions of the Geneva agreement calling for phased reductions of troops on Cyprus.

Sixth, the United States greatly values the traditional friendship of Greece. It has the highest regard for Prime Minister Karamanlis and wishes every success to his democratic government. We will use our influence in any negotiation to take into full account Greek honor and national dignity. At the same time, we assume that all of our allies, including Greece, join in collective defense in their own interests. We are willing to strengthen these common alliance ties and to help the Greek Government in any way possible. We will not be pressured by threat of withdrawal from the (NATO) alliance, or anti-American demonstrations, which in any event are totally unjustified by our record.

I repeat that this statement has been gone over by President Ford.

On its face, the Secretary's statement was well-rounded in generally defining the immediate issues and possible American contributions toward a resolution of the Cyprus crisis. Notably missing, however, was, among other things, any acknowledgement that the territorial integrity and independence of Cyprus had been violated, and any evidence of regret or concern over the Turkish invasion of the island, the continuing and blatant "salami tactics" of the Turkish occupation army, or the important fact that nearly half of the island's people were becoming refugees or virtual hostages as a result of advancing Turkish forces.

These are significant omissions in the Secretary's statement. And, when combined with other statements by Administration spokesmen—including those in hearings before the Refugee Subcommittee—the Study Mission's findings in the field and the Administration's general record on Cyprus, an American "tilt" toward Turkey seems to characterize American policy towards Cyprus.

Nothing dramatizes this more, perhaps, than the simple fact that the Study Mission was told again and again, by Turkish spokesmen in the field and in Washington, that they felt that United States policy toward Cyprus was "right", "equitable", "fair", and "good". Needless to say, the same kinds of feelings were not expressed in Athens or in the Government controlled areas of Cyprus.

What is some of the substance in the American "tilt" toward Turkey? It is readily seen in the omissions of our diplomacy, in our apparent acquiescence in the Turkish invasion, in our tacit recognition of a Turkish *fait accompli* through the force of arms, in our clear association with the fundamentals of the Turkish negotiating position, and in our cynical use of humanitarian aid for Greek Cypriot refugees to support our political and diplomatic ends.

Some omissions in our diplomacy have been referred to elsewhere in this report, and they have been widely discussed in the press and elsewhere. Suffice it to say that a listing of missed opportunities can be dismissed as hindsight, and it is conceivable that nothing beyond what we did would have worked. But, America's public silence, and private timidity and vacillation, in the early stages of the crisis—beginning with the overthrow of President Makarios—add up to a failure of diplomacy. If nothing else, a better record of our efforts to help maintain the peace, would at least counter the widespread feeling today that the United States was unconcerned over the issues of national independence and human suffering in a small, non-aligned country.

The United States has never fully acknowledged that the sovereignty and territorial integrity of an independent government and state has been violated through the invasion and occupation of the island by foreign troops. This seems to be of little concern to American policy makers. In the field, for example, the Study Mission was told by our diplomats that the United States was well aware of Turkish plans, but, in contrast to American actions in previous and similar crises on the island, we really did nothing effective to stop phase one of the invasion, and, very little, if anything, to discourage phase two.

Apart from the omissions in Secretary Kissinger's statement on August 19, other public indicators support this general conclusion. For example, as noted earlier in this report, on August 13, State Department spokesman Robert Anderson issued a statement which not only stressed equities in the Turkish position and American concurrence in some general Turkish objectives, but which also gave tacit approval to some of the reasoning given by Turkish authorities to justify their "peace operation" on Cyprus. And, during an August 18 interview over CBS, Secretary of Defense James R. Schlesinger expressed little concern over the reality of 40,000 Turkish occupation troops on Cyprus, but he did say that "we've understood the desire of the Turks to protect the minority Turkish problem, but the Turkish moves at this point have gone beyond what any of its friends or sympathizers would have accepted. . . ." Secretary Hartman, in commenting on the Cyprus issue and the Schlesinger statement, spoke in a somewhat similar vein before the Refugee Subcommittee.

In this regard also, the legitimate Government of Cyprus is given little standing in public statements by American officials—apparently because, as part of what some of our diplomats call the "new realities," we conveniently ignore the presence of an occupation army and for all intents and purposes accept a *de facto* form of partition on the island as a result of the Turkish invasion. And so, like the Turkish Cypriot and mainland leadership, American officials seem to all but accept the demise of a legitimate Cyprus government, and prefer to speak of separate and equal administrations on the island. A good example of this is Secretary Hartman's comment to the Subcommittee on August 20. In referring to "the two communities on Cyprus", he said: "It really is quite a divided country now. There is no single administration, and there really has not been for some time. Mr. Clerides heads up the Greek Cypriot administration and Mr. Denktash heads up the Turkish administration." The omission of references to the legitimate Government of Cyprus is a small item, perhaps, but one which carries some importance when put in the total context of American statements on developments in Cyprus, beginning with the Sampson coup, and in the overall perspective of recent American policy toward the island.

Given the omissions in our country's diplomacy, and our apparent acquiesence in the Turkish invasion, it is inevitable, perhaps, that the United States would give its tacit recognition to Turkey's *fait accompli* on Cyprus, and clearly associate itself with the fundamentals of the Turkish negotiating position—a bi-regional settlement, or geographical separation of the Greek and Turkish communities. This conclusion—based on what some American diplomats call the "new realities"—was fully confirmed in the Study Mission's conversations in the field, as well as in conversations in Washington and in Secretary Hartman's testimony before the Refugee Subcommittee on August 20 and September 26. Also, this is clearly implied in Secretary Kissinger's August 19 statement on American policy towards Cyprus. The Secretary states that, in negotiations, "we believe it will be necessary for Turkey . . . to display flexibility . . . both in terms of territory and the size of military forces on the island. . . . I have been assured that *the Turkish Government considers the demarcation line negotiable . . .* [italics added]." In short, the United States agrees that there should be some "demarcation line" across Cyprus—in effect some form of partition, which was a stated objective of the Turkish invasion—and we are publicly committed to this objective in our diplomacy over the future of the island.

In responding to a reporter's question over American initiatives toward Cyprus, the Secretary also said on August 19: "We have not yet made any specific proposal as to a particular solution, but you will see in the statement that I have just read our view as to *the direction in which the negotiations should go* [italics added]."

And this raises the issue of American policy towards the refugees and humanitarian needs on Cyprus. There can be no doubt that the 200,000 Greek Cypriot refugees—about a third of the island's population—want to return to homes they fled in the Turkish occupied areas. And the return of refugees is a key element in the negotiating position of the Cypriot and Greek governments—in terms of both a resumption of negotiations and a final settlement over the future of Cyprus. Regarding a resumption of negotiations, most Cypriot and Greek leaders are looking first for a "gesture of goodwill" from Turkey, which would involve the orderly withdrawal of Turkish troops from some areas and the return of refugees to their homes.

The record of American policy on the refugee issue is not only a said commentary on the callous nature of American policy towards the vast human tragedy in Cyprus, but it also helps to define our bias toward Turkey, and it confirms once again that the lives of people caught in the crunch of disaster and war are not very important in our efforts to build a structure of peace—even when people problems are immediately central to resolving the issue at stake. Secretary Kissinger's policy statement of August 19, for example, is silent on the refugee issue. So are the President's two messages to Congress vetoing legislation to bar further military assistance to Turkey. Secretary Kissinger's September 23 statement to the United Nations General Assembly does refer to "the conditions under which refugees can return to their homes and reside in safety"; but, in testimony before the Refugee Subcommittee on September 26, Secretary Hartman, in response to the Chairman's question, seems to define more fully the Administration's position and policy bias toward Turkey.

Although Secretary Hartman suggested that "the refugee question will be one of the most important issues [in negotiations over a settlement of the Cyprus dispute]", he did not tie the issue to the Administration's efforts to find "common ground" between Greece and Turkey for a resumption of negotiations or to any gesture of goodwill Turkey could make "as an aid to the negotiating process." In fact, Secretary Hartman, while conceding that "the refugee question will be one of the most important issues [in negotiations]", seems to follow the basic Turkish position, that any return of refugees would be an end result of negotiations and part of the final settlement over the future of Cyprus. The hearing record, in part, reads as follows:

Senator KENNEDY. Is it our position that there is going to have to be a withdrawal of all foreign troops?

Mr. HARTMAN. Well, let me state what the last agreed position of the parties was.

On July 30th they agreed to a declaration in Geneva calling for the phased withdrawal of forces. . . .

Senator KENNEDY. Well, should not—

Mr. HARTMAN. They both agree there should be a phased withdrawal of forces. Clearly, 40,000 Turkish troops on the island is not—

Senator KENNEDY. Should there not at least be some gesture on the part of the Turks?

Mr. HARTMAN. As an aid to the negotiating process?

Senator KENNEDY. That is right.

Mr. HARTMAN. Yes, and I think, as a matter of fact, that gesture might be more difficult if they thought they were being called upon to do that under pressure. I think their reaction would be to decline to make a gesture of reduction, to perhaps reconsider that now, so that it does not look as if they are doing it under pressure.

Senator KENNEDY. Are not the Greeks under a lot of pressure, too? What about the pressure on all of those refugees? People cannot go home. That is pressure on them.

Mr. HARTMAN. That is right.

Senator KENNEDY. They are being pressured, too—I imagine every day they are denied the right to go home or see their friends. That is what I do not understand—pressure is a one-way street, evidently.

We are reluctant to say very much about the refugees. . . .

Well, are we calling on the Turks to make a gesture? What are we calling on them to do? You say on the one hand it may very well be advantageous for us to continue our military assistance, because then we have some degree of influence.

What are we trying to influence them on, rather than the general kind of vague hopefulness for some fruitful negotiation that you say will will help resolve the conflict? Other than those generalities, what do you expect? What can we look forward to? What have we asked Ankara to do?

Mr. HARTMAN. It seems to me that we must start with what the parties themselves are now prepared to discuss, and that is changing as time goes on. . . .

The real questions that must be decided in the negotiations, and we are discussing these with all parties, are the questions of the degree of separation of the communities, with the Turkish government taking the position that it should be almost a complete separation. . . . And another significant feature of the negotiations will be what are the powers if they move toward a Federal solution? What are the powers of the Federal authority? The refugee question will be one of the most important issues, and here again you have a difference of view as to whether or not there should be a major movement of population to accomplish this virtual separation of the populations of the communities, or whether it should be voluntary with some people going north or some people coming south, but not a completely exclusive two zonal concept with no Greek Cypriots in the north and no Turkish Cypriots in the south.

So the issues in the negotiation are the form of government, the territorial agreements, the withdrawal of foreign forces, and the guarantee for the eventual outcome.

Those are really the four major issues and what we are talking to the parties about is trying to find out what their positions are and whether we can see any common ground that can be suggested. That has been the purpose of our talks with all of the parties. . . .

Senator KENNEDY. But I would hope, as you can well understand, that our government will consider the pressure on these refugees, when the Administration is considering what our public posture is going to be—that their interests and their well-being will be put high on the roster of priorities in terms of any of these negotiations.

I can think of no more important item on any agenda than the well-being of the people of Cyprus who have been absolutely devastated and in many respects decimated on that island.

But "common ground" between Greece and Turkey that the Administration says it is trying to find to facilitate a resumption of negotiations—let alone a final settlement—must be more than finding "flexibility" in the Turkish position, or some way to take "into full account Greek honor and national dignity". And if we can publicly meet Turkish sensitivities over the need for a "demarcation line" across Cyprus, the least we can do is publicly recognize Cypriot and Greek sensitivities over the importance of the refugee problem and the need for a return of refugees to their homes. And silence on this later point, is an inexcusable omission in American policy toward Cyprus.

The Administration, undoubtedly, feels it is doing enough for the Greek refugees. As in the earlier case of Bengali refugees in India, Administration spokesmen point with pride to America's relief efforts and projected increases in contributions to international relief agencies. And most Americans will strongly encourage and support our country's humanitarian leadership on Cyprus.

But some of the policy considerations behind this humanitarian leadership, raise troubling questions over the intent of our humanitarian assistance. In fact a good case can be made that this assistance is closely tied to our political and diplomatic objectives in the Cyprus issue and our policy "tilt" toward Turkish interests. For example, evidence available to the Study Mission, including conversations with American officials, suggest that some of the policy considerations, in giving humanitarian aid to Greek refugees, included the need to improve the political/diplomatic climate. It included the need to show the Greek and Cypriot Governments that we are following a balanced policy. It included the need to keep the refugee problem contained, so as to buy time to assist Ankara in consolidating its position on the island. Indeed, it was intended as well to help refurbish Turkey's international image, thereby strengthening its bargaining position in pursuing its bi-regional objectives on Cyprus.

Further evidence of the cynicism with which elements of our government have viewed the refugee crisis on Cyprus, is suggested in an August cable sent from the Department of Agriculture here in Washington to the United States Embassy in Nicosia. A few days after the second phase of the Turkish "peace operation", the Agriculture Department wanted to know if it were true that the Cyprus citrus crop would be lost this year to Turkey, and therefore probably unavailable for export to England and France. The Department hoped the United States could secure early confirmation of this report, so that American interests could beat the competition in filling the gap.

The above notes on American policy toward Cyprus speak for themselves. They help to confirm some of the worst fears of Congress and many Americans over our "tilt" toward Turkey, and over the failure of our efforts to help bring peace and relief to the people of Cyprus.

As indicated earlier, in response to this kind of conclusion, all quarters in the Administration flatly deny any "tilt" toward the Turkish position in American policy toward Cyprus. Officials in the Department of State and elsewhere suggest instead that the United States is following a policy of "neutrality" in the Cyprus problem. These officials assert that, initially, nothing short of sending in the Marines or using the Sixth Fleet would have kept Ankara from carrying out its plans for Cyprus; for we had no other leverage. And because we are not the world's policeman, our only alternative was what these officials call "neutrality".

These same officials now argue, however, that the United States should not tamper with or cut off military aid to Turkey, because that would reduce new found "leverage" with the Turkish government, and would not be "helpful" to our objective of seeking a negotiated settlement on Cyprus. Furthermore, it would destroy our "neutrality". But the Administration's record on Cyprus confirms that such a policy of "neutrality", in the face of aggression against an independent country, not only tolerates but implicitly aids and abets that aggression, and does, in fact, constitute a "tilt". And this stance by our government—in the face of the human and political tragedy of Cyprus, and in the face of the dismemberment of a small and defenseless nation—should be rejected by all Americans who care deeply about our country's role in the world, and our national efforts to help build a meaningful structure of peace.

Finally, a great deal of speculation is seen in the press and heard among American officials over the impact of Watergate and impeachment proceedings on our policy making toward Cyprus.

It has been argued by some observers that senior officials of our government were so preoccupied during the collapse of the Nixon Presidency, that American policy toward Cyprus hung suspended during the most crucial days of late July and early August. Many omissions in American policy and the bad timing of public statements, for example, were due, these observers say, to a preoccupation by our national leadership with domestic considerations.

Only history can judge the validity of this line. Whether Turkey would have, or could have, seized the military initiative it did in the face of more active American diplomacy prior to August 9th—especially if there had been clear signals of disapproval from a White House that was a full-time White House—history will tell. It will tell if the failure of United States policy towards Cyprus was a casualty of the failing Nixon Presidency.

But if this is really true, to the degree suggested by some observers, it leaves unanswered a basic question: why, then, have not the fundamentals of American policy toward Cyprus changed since?

SUMMARY OF FINDINGS

The longer the time required to achieve a resolution of the crisis on Cyprus, the greater will be the suffering of the people of the island. And it is the tragedy of Cyprus today that time is not on the side of peace.

It is the peculiar tragedy of Cyprus that its fate, now, as in the past, rests less upon solutions to be found among the Cypriots themselves—Turks and Greeks—than it does upon a resolution of outside forces and factors. It is to this extent that the tragedy of Cyprus will now be compounded by the current political instability in Greece and Turkey. No final solution to Cyprus can be anticipated until both Greece and Turkey are able to put their houses in order, to hold elections, and to establish governments with firm political foundations. This, it appears, cannot be expected until the end of 1974.

Meanwhile, the situation on Cyprus festers. And, as in the past, such frustrations will undoubtedly spawn more violence and even greater human suffering, with no end in sight. Until the central issue of the return of the refugees to their homes is resolved, there will be no peace for Cyprus.

I. SEEDS OF CONFLICT

1. Communal tensions began to build in modern Cyprus history during the British rule, as the majority Greek Cypriot community organized guerrilla war to violently end British colonialism on the island. To the Turkish Cypriot minority the spectre of an end to British rule under these circumstances would threaten a union of Cyprus with the Greek motherland—an ancient objective of the Greek Cypriots. The Turkish Cypriots sided with the British and organized themselves into a counter political force, which they remain today.

2. The establishment of an independent Republic of Cyprus in 1960, with constitutional guarantees for the minority, and international guarantees for the integrity of the island, was intended to end the threat of enosis and reduce communal polarization. Through the 1960's, communal tensions mounted, however, as the constitutional provisions designed to minimize conflict between the two communities achieved the opposite: governmental dualism and further ethnic separatism between Greek and Turkish Cypriots.

3. The communal conflict of 1963–64 brought United Nations intervention, and the formation of the U.N. Peace-Keeping Forces (UNFICYP) on the island. A second major crisis in 1967 ended in a humiliating defeat for the Greek colonels and with the withdrawal of 9,000 Greek troops from Cyprus. In both crises the United States played an active and helpful diplomatic role vis-a-vis Greece and Turkey, and the preservation of Cypriot independence.

(53)

4. Communal tensions continued after 1967, but under the U.N. auspices a series of communal talks began in 1968 between Clerides and Denktash, representing the Greek and Turkish communities respectively. Moderate, but frustrating, progress was made.

II. CYPRUS, 1974 : SCENARIO FOR TRAGEDY

5. A growing strain in relations between Athens and President Makarios over the presence of 650 Greek mainland officers, and the underlying issue of enosis with Greece, culminated in a violent coup against Makarios on July 15, 1974.

6. The U.S. learned of the coup in advance, warned Makarios of it, but it was not taken seriously—although the CIA in Athens must have known better. Makarios escaped death and was evacuated to London by the British. American policy appeared to place in the best light events in Nicosia and the intervention of the Greek junta; no official statement was made condemning the coup and supporting Makarios.

7. Turkey appears to have interpreted U.S. policy at that time as a signal of tacit acceptance by the U.S. of the Nikos Sampson military clique. Ankara perhaps felt it had no alternative (as well as a great opportunity) to take the military option it had long planned, ostensibly in behalf of the Turkish Cypriots whose security they felt threatened. Thus, on July 20, five days later, Turkey invaded Cyprus, and within two days established a firm beachhead in Kyrenia before the first of several ceasefires were announced.

8. The Turkish invasion and the ensuing possibility of war with Greece, undermined what credibility the Athens junta had, and it was forced to recall civilian leadership. On the same day, July 23rd, Clerides replaced Sampson as acting President of Cyprus.

9. The restoration of democracy in Greece and the return of constitutional government in Cyprus, raised hopes that a negotiated settlement might be achieved. The guarantor powers met in Geneva on July 26, and negotiations began. They reached an impasse two weeks later when the Turkish proposals for a federal system under which Turkish Cypriots would have a separate administrative area in 38% of the island, and a second proposal for a cantonal system, were received cooly by the Greeks. A 36-hour Greek request to study the proposals was met by the launching of the second phase of the Turkish invasion—achieving on the battlefield what they had not been given at the negotiating table.

III. CONSEQUENCES OF THE INVASION

10. Within a week, 40,000 Turkish troops swept across and occupied over 40% of Cyprus. In the process, some 282,000 Cypriots—both Greeks and Turks—became refugees, detainees, prisoners of war, or cut-off and in need of relief assistance.

11. The humanitarian consequence of the invasion was the creation of a massive refugee problem, the resolution of which has, in turn, become crucial to a resolution of the political problems created by the Turkish action.

12. With the exception of the area around the first Turkish landing in the Kyrenia-Nicosia enclave, there is minimal bomb or structural damage. However, widespread looting has occurred.

13. The impact of the invasion upon the Cyprus economy has been more devastating. The Government estimates that some $4.5 million is lost each day in production. Agriculture, which comprises half the island's economy, is dying—both crops and animals. The vast citrus crop rots on the trees.

14. The political impact of the invasion was to destroy the constitutional and political framework of the Government of Cyprus as it was established in 1960. The future of Cyprus will be a future governed by a new and different governmental and political structure. There are currently a number of options; most frequently mentioned in Ankara and Washington is some form of territorial separation of the two communities. Whatever name is used, it is tantamount to partition.

15. Arranging some form of "bi-regionalism," or "zonal" division, or "federal" structure on Cyprus, may seem to outsiders as only a question of where the line will finally be drawn. But it is questionable whether a Greek Cypriot government can be found which would accept such solutions under the current threat of arms. Subject to negotiations, the current stalemate risks *de facto* partition—double enosis—of an administrative and economic union of the two separate parts of Cyprus with Greece and Turkey. A drift in this direction is already apparent on the Turkish occupied side, with the introduction of mainland Turkish currency, Turkish supplies, Turkish labor, etc. If this is allowed to continue for long, Cyprus will cease to exist.

16. The impact of partition along the Turkish Attila line, which Turkey has demanded, will have serious human and economic consequences. It will require moving and resettling half the population in order to create majority Turkish Cypriot areas above the line. It could involve moving 40,000 families and it would significantly alter the population density and characteristics of the island. Impact upon land ownership would be equally severe and extremely difficult to divide equitably. Impact upon the island's homogeneous economy would be to cut it in an inequitable half, with most of the foreign exchange earning portions of the economy left on the Turkish side.

17. The costs to Turkey from its military activity on Cyprus has been considerable. The actual costs of the invasion—military equipment lost, supplies, etc.—when added to the growing costs of military occupation, suggests that the cost to Turkey will total $1 billion by the end of the year.

IV. HUMANITARIAN NEEDS AND INTERNATIONAL ASSISTANCE

18. Massive humanitarian relief needs were created by the Turkish invasion. Within a month, some 40% of the Greek Cypriot population was rendered homeless, and the need for shelter, blankets, medicine, food, and other supplies, was immediate and serious. The Government of Cyprus estimates that to establish refugee camp sites for all those who are now in need of shelter, will cost over $22 million.

19. The Cypriot administration has demonstrated a commendable capacity to undertake relief programs and to absorb outside relief assistance. A "Special Services for the Relief and Rehabilitation of Displaced Persons" was established in late July, and has—under the

most difficult circumstances—provided emergency relief aid, as well as longer-term assistance.

20. Although there was a commendable and early response from many nations to the plight of Cyprus—especially the International Committee of the Red Cross, Greece, European Economic Community, and the United States—the appeals of both the ICRC and the U.N. High Commissioner for Refugees have only received token amounts to date. Of the UNHCR appeal for $22 million for relief to the end of the year, only $6.2 million has been received or pledged from all sources—less than a third of the sum required.

21. The United States has allocated, as of October 10, $4.6 million for Cyprus relief, with another $1.6 million pledged to the UNHCR in the coming weeks.

22. The needs of the refugees of Cyprus will escalate until a negotiated settlement is achieved, even as the initial enthusiasm and support for Cyprus relief within the international community now threatens to dry up. Massive relief needs remain to be met.

23. The role of the United Nations on Cyprus remains crucial. The UNFICYP forces, although restricted in their movement in the Turkish occupied areas, play an important humanitarian role. The newly augmented 4,292-man UNFICYP force is attempting to generate a feeling of confidence and to obtain information concerning the local situation, particularly in areas where humanitarian and relief measures, including the security of population, are required. They provide logistical support to the UNHCR, which has become the focal point for international relief assistance.

24. The work of the UNHCR has been constrained to primarily the Greek Cypriot refugees in the southern part of the island, in part because they form the bulk of the refugee problem, but also because the UNHCR has not been granted free and unrestricted access to Turkish occupied areas.

V. UNITED STATES POLICY

25. Although flatly denied in all quarters of the Administration, the evidence in the field suggests a perceptible "tilt" in American policy toward Turkey during the Cyprus crisis. In the early days, U.S. policy seems to have been one of hasty improvisation, coldly calculated to minimize disturbances within NATO. This not only achieved the opposite result, but, in the end, it failed the defenseless people of Cyprus.

26. The substance of the American "tilt" towards Turkey can be seen in the long list of omissions in United States diplomacy—in our apparent approval of, and "understanding" over, the Turkish invasion; in our tacit recognition of a Turkish *fait accompli* through the force of arms; in our clear association with the fundamentals of the Turkish negotiating position; and in our cynical use of humanitarian aid for Greek Cypriot refugees to further our political and diplomatic ends.

27. Available evidence suggests that some of the policy considerations in giving humanitarian aid to Greek refugees included the need to improve the political/diplomatic climate, to show the Greek and Cypriot governments that we were following a "balanced" policy, to

keep the refugee problem contained, so as to buy time to assist Ankara in consolidating its position, and to help refurbish Turkey's international image, thereby strengthening its bargaining position. All this evidence confirms the worst fears of Congress and many Americans over the "tilt" towards Turkey and over the failure of American efforts to help bring peace and relief to the people of Cyprus.

RECOMMENDATIONS

Over the coming weeks and months—as they have since the beginning of the Cyprus crisis—the Chairman and members of the Subcommittee will continue to be as tenacious in their concern and suggestions for action as they feel the important situation on Cyprus warrants.

For the purposes of this report, however, the Chairman and the Study Mission make the following recommendations, relating to diplomatic and political problems and humanitarian needs.

1. RESTORING THE FULL INDEPENDENCE AND SOVEREIGNTY AND TERRITORIAL INTEGRITY OF CYPRUS

Restoring the full independence, sovereignty and territorial integrity of Cyprus must be a clearly understood and primary objective in American policy and diplomacy over Cyprus. No other goal better satisfies justice or the bringing of peace and relief to the people of Cypruᵉ.

As in past crises, Cyprus today is a pawn in international politics— caught in an extremely complex network of conflicting interests involving Greece, Turkey, the United Kingdom, the United States, the Soviet Union, other countries, NATO, the United Nations, and, most important of all, the divided people of Cyprus. Viewed in this perspective, the Greek junta's engineered coup on Cyprus last July was a clear attempt to impose an unacceptable solution on the festering communal conflict between the Greek and Turkish communities. So too, was the subsequent military intervention of Turkey, which now threatens a partition of the island.

Perhaps a new constitutional structure and more equitable arrangements between the Greek and Turkish communities are needed on Cyprus; but responding to Cypriot aspirations for maintaining an independent country should be central to the policies and actions of all parties concerned. New guarantees for the future independence and territorial integrity of Cyprus must be achieved through the early resumption of the Geneva negotiations or appropriate alternative arrangements.

2. SUPPORT FOR THE INTER-COMMUNAL TALKS BETWEEN ACTING PRESIDENT CLERIDES AND VICE-PRESIDENT DENKTASH

The periodic talks, on humanitarian and related problems, between Acting President Clerides and Vice President Denktash, the respective leaders of the Greek and Turkish Cypriot communities, must be given the time and chance to succeed. Despite difficulties, these talks, under the auspices of the United Nations, have already produced agreements on the repatriation and exchange of prisoners of war. The talks could be crucial ingredients in helping to resolve Cyprus problems, and they must be very actively encouraged and supported by the United States and all parties concerned. For in the final analysis it will be the Cypriots themselves who will contribute the most toward restoring the mutual trust and harmony which can rescue this island from the tragedy now present.

3. IMPLEMENTING U.N. RESOLUTIONS AND THE GENEVA DECLARATION ON THE REDUCTION AND WITHDRAWAL OF TROOPS

The United States Government, and all parties concerned, must very actively support repeated calls by the United Nations—as well as the Geneva declaration of July 30, agreed to by Greece and Turkey—for the orderly reduction and withdrawal of foreign troops from Cyprus. A viable solution to the Cyprus problem, much less peace on the island, cannot be imposed by the force of arms. Many observers are particularly concerned that the continuing presence of foreign troops on Cyprus threatens guerrilla-style warfare that would probably turn the entire island into a battlefield once again. Steps must be taken to disarm Cyprus.

4. RETURN OF REFUGEES TO THEIR HOMES

Some observers feel that, under a negotiated settlement of the Cyprus problem, the exchange of some population between Greek and Turkish areas of control may be necessary and, indeed, desirable. Nevertheless, a viable solution to the Cyprus problem, much less peace on the island, will not be accomplished unless and until a significant number of Greek Cypriot refugees are permitted to return safely to their lands and homes in areas currently occupied by Turkish forces.

In this regard, the United States must finally use its vast influence and good offices with Turkey to persuade Ankara of the need for a "gesture of goodwill", which includes the withdrawal of occupation forces and the return of refugees to their homes. Such a "gesture of goodwill"—involving perhaps the orderly return of refugees to the Famagusta and Morphou areas of the island—could break the deadlock over the resumption of negotiations and serve as a meaningful first step toward a negotiated settlement of the Cyprus problem.

5. GREATER AUTONOMY AND SECURITY FOR THE TURKISH CYPRIOT COMMUNITY

There is little doubt that the Turkish invasion and occupation of Cyprus has forever destroyed the present constitutional framework and political structure of the island. Given a negotiated settlement of the Cyprus problem, the future clearly includes new arrangements.

It is equally clear that any new arrangements must enhance the Turkish Cypriot community's security, autonomy, and participation in the economic and social and political life of the country. Their grievances over the past decade have, in the main, been legitimate and serious. If there is to be any peace on Cyprus, these grievances must be answered.

Proposals aimed at achieving greater autonomy and security for the Turkish Cypriots were already well advanced in the inter-communal talks before the latest crisis. And there was substantial recognition of this during the Geneva talks after the Turkish invasion. These proposals must now be reactivated, and worked out in practical and useable form for immediate and permanent application. If the Turkish invasion serves to side-track this process, it will have defeated its own stated goals.

6. STRENGTHENED UNITED NATIONS PRESENCE ON CYPRUS

Previous crises on Cyprus have involved and brought forth constructive responses from the United Nations. And over the past decade UNFICYP has played a useful and important role. But there can be little doubt today that the current Cyprus crisis has called into question the effectiveness of the United Nations. Recently, for example, Secretary General Kurt Waldheim warned the Security Council, that the situation on Cyprus raises questions about "the very essence of the United Nations Charter, weighing upon the credibility of the organization and its future effectiveness."

United Nations problems on Cyprus involve both its peace-keeping functions and its humanitarian purposes.

In part, the present difficulties or failure of the United Nations is due to the severe limitations of the UNFICYP mandate, which is outdated and unrelated to the current situation—the presence of a foreign occupying army. In this connection, the United States, in concert with others, should actively support efforts to strengthen and broaden the mandate of UNFICYP, so it can better perform its peace-keeping mission on the island.

The United Nations humanitarian purposes on the island have been seriously compromised, mainly because of the very restrictive access international personnel and relief convoys have to the Turkish occupied areas. Humanitarian needs, especially among the remaining Greek population, have been substantial in some areas, and all reports suggest the condition of these people is deteriorating. This is deplorable, and the United States must urgently lend its diplomacy to remedy the situation and facilitate United Nations' humanitarian efforts on Cyprus.

7. THE UNITED STATES MUST ESCALATE HUMANITARIAN AID TO CYPRUS

Our government—both the Executive Branch and the Congress—should escalate its concern and efforts on behalf of relief and rehabilitation programs among the refugees and others in need on Cyprus.

In the early days of the Cyprus conflict the United States responded commendably to international emergency appeals for humanitarian aid by the ICRC. In late August the UNHCR assumed, from the ICRC, the responsibility for international humanitarian assistance and appealed for $22,000,000 through the end of 1974. To date, the United States has committed $2,000,000—of which only $1,400,000 has been allocated and the remaining $1,600,000 pledged. This is a small commitment, compared to what we can and should do. Tokenism must be replaced with generosity and compassion. An increased commitment of up to $10 million—now, not later—to the UNHCR's emergency program would be consonant with our general contribution to relief efforts elsewhere, and would hopefully encourage other nations to respond more generously as well. In this connection, pending foreign aid legislation—introduced by the Chairman and other members of the Senate—to establish a Cyprus Relief Fund should be enacted at the earliest opportunity.

Apart from making a more meaningful contribution to the current emergency relief program of the UNHCR, the United States must also be prepared to continue providing humanitarian relief and rehabilitation assistance well into 1975. Among the anticipated needs are food supplies, as well as support for various public works and other projects, being initiated by the Cyprus Government, to employ idle refugees.

The United States should support, hopefully through international channels, a variety of programs to help meet these needs. Public Law 480 "food for work" and related food programs, for example, could help meet both food and unemployment problems. In consultation with the Cyprus government, the American Embassy in Nicosia has recommended such programs, and they should be accepted in Washington. Additional kinds of assistance should also be considered by our government.

8. UNITED STATES DIPLOMATIC SUPPORT TO BREAK RELIEF BOTTLENECKS

There are at least two bottlenecks, involving humanitarian relief, that some greater measure of United States diplomatic concern might help to break.

Since the second phase of the Turkish invasion, the island's only major airport in Nicosia has been closed, due to bomb damage but more importantly to diplomatic deadlock. The Turkish army attempted to take the airport during the invasion, but was stymied by the stiff resistance of the Greek Cypriots. Turkish forces now surround the airport on three sides, with the other side held by the Government. UNFICYP forces hold the airport proper. All sides, except Turkey, have agreed to the speedy restoration and opening of the Nicosia airport under United Nations control. Among other things, observers agree that it would greatly facilitate international relief operations, which now must use the overtaxed British air field in the south.

Similarly, the Government of Turkey has unilaterally declared the sea lanes surrounding Cyprus to be "dangerous" because of a state of war. The result has been the cessation of regular sea shipments to Cyprus, in part because of prohibitive insurance costs. This has had a serious impact upon relief shipments, both discouraging foreign ship owners to allow the use of their vessels for Cyprus, as well as adding greatly to the costs of those relief ships which do travel to the island.

Both these restraints on the international relief effort for Cyprus—the closed Nicosia Airport and the restricted sea lanes—must be items high on the diplomatic agenda, and the United States should be doing considerably more in trying to remove these restraints. Progress towards peace and relief on Cyprus will be undertaken in steps, and there can be no better steps than removing bottle-necks to humanitarian relief.

APPENDIX

APPENDIX I

The following is the text of an address made by Senator Edward M. Kennedy before a commemorative dinner in New York City at the Waldorf Astoria on October 20, 1974, in honor of Archbishop Iakovos, Primate of the Greek Orthodox Church in the Americas. Proceeds from the dinner went to the Cyprus Relief Fund.

TEXT OF SENATOR KENNEDY'S ADDRESS

I am grateful for the privilege to join in this tribute to His Eminence, and to share your concern over the human suffering and political tragedy on Cyprus.

The Turkish invasion of Cyprus turned the island into shambles. In political terms, it violated the integrity of an independent state. In economic terms, it shattered the island's flourishing development. And in human terms, it turned half the population into refugees, detainees, or beleagured people caught behind ceasefire lines. Personal tragedy has been the lot of thousands of Cypriot families—many with relatives and friends in the United States.

Since the outbreak of violence on Cyprus—and as Chairman of the Subcommittee on Refugees—I have shared your deep personal concern over the plight of your relatives and friends—and over the suffering of all Cypriots affected by the war. The Subcommittee has held public hearings on this issue, and I have introduced legislation, which calls for the withdrawal of foreign troops, and for a special Cyprus relief fund in our foreign assistance program. I also sent a Study Mission to the island to survey humanitarian needs—and their report was issued just a week ago.

A drive along the roads of Cyprus today quickly tells the tragic tale of the Cypriot people—of the human consequenecs of an armed invasion, of bombing and napalm, of ceasefire violations, of dead-locked diplomacy, of military occupation, and of man's inhumanity to man. In the Turkish occupied areas of the North, only a small percentage of the population remains—including some 8,000 Turkish refugees bombed out of their homes. Desolation and destruction are everywhere. Whole villages and towns and cities—like Famagusta, Kyrenia, and Lapithos—are empty of the Greeks who lived there. In understandable fear, and with only the cloths on their backs, they fled to safety from advancing Turkish forces. But many of their neighbors died.

The Greek Cypriots who remain in the occupied zone face a desperate future. They are a beleaguered and hostage people—prisoners of the Turkish army. Reports from Karpasia and other areas say that the Greeks are confined to their villages—or forcibly detained by Turkish authorities in churches or public buildings. And nearly 500 Greeks—a good share of them elderly people—have been cruelly and needlessly detained in Kyrenia's Dome Hotel—since the early days of the invasion.

The younger men in the occupied zone have been taken away. Food, medicine, and relief goods are in short supply. And international humanitarian agencies are denied regular access, for the purpose of bringing relief to those in need.

Government controlled areas of the island have been inundated with refugees from the North. Over the last three months, more than 200,000 men, women, and children have sought shelter wherever they could find it—under trees, along the roadside, in open fields, in cars, in fragile huts made of pine branches and sticks, and in tents provided by international relief agencies. Schools, monasteries and public buildings have been crammed with refugees—and the population of many towns has suddenly doubled or tripled in size. Only in recent weeks have relief supplies been arriving in significant quantities—mainly from Greece, Western

Europe and the United States. But there is still not enough food and blankets and shelter. Vaccines to ward off epidemics are sometimes difficult to get. And dysentery has stricken children and older people in many areas.

With the onslaught of the rainy season and the winter cold, the condition of the people can only deteriorate—unless adequate resources are made available to the Cyprus government and the relief agencies—or some real progress is made in negotiations, which will permit refugees to return to their homes.

The vast majority of needy people in government-controlled areas are Greek Cypriots. But some 10,000 Turkish refugees also need our help and concern. Human suffering, personal tragedy, and the anguish common to the homeless all over the world, are everywhere present on Cyprus. But like the Greeks of old, Cypriots today are meeting their disaster undefeated. As Pericles put it in his classic Funeral Oration: "We do not have to spend our time practicing to meet sufferings . . . And when they are upon us, we show ourselves just as brave."

And "take heart," wrote Aeschylus. "Suffering, when it climbs highest, lasts but a little time." These lines from a play described his spirit—as it describes today, the spirit of Cyprus.

Our spirit—America's spirit—should be no less. And so we must mobilize our country—and we must do all that we can to assist the children, the orphans, the refugees, and the people in distress on Cyprus. Your efforts here tonight, and those in the weeks to come, reflect America's compassion for people in need. They will surely make an important contribution to the survival and welfare of all the refugees on Cyprus.

Much has been said about America's role in the Cyprus crisis—and about the apparent complicity of our government in the human and political tragedy of the Cypriot people. Our government suggests—and few will disagree—that Americans should recognize and appreciate legitimate Turkish grievances on the island. But our government goes much further. We are told that what has happened on Cyprus is understandable. We are told we must be practical in our approach to the Cyprus issue. And so we must accept the "new realities" on the island.

But what are these "new realities?" And what are we being asked to understand and accept?

Are we to condone the invasion and occupation of Cyprus? Are we to condone the nibbling away of an independent state—and continuing threats of a new offensive in the so-called "Turkish Peace Operation"? Are we to condone the human tragedy brought about with the illegal use of American supplied weapons? Are we to condone a policy of national silence over the fate of refugees on Cyprus? Are we to condone the failure of our government to condemn the invasion, and to try actively to prevent it? Are we to condone the omissions in our diplomacy, and the efforts of our government to cover-up the "tilt" toward Turkey?

I ask you tonight—are we to stand silent in the face of these realities? I believe the American people expect more of their government. This is clearly reflected in your presence here tonight—and in the recent actions of Congress over the issues of military aid to Turkey, and humanitarian contributions to the refugees on Cyprus.

If Cyprus today is on the brink of new conflict and even greater tragedy, our government's policy bears a special responsibility. For the omissions in our diplomacy over Cyprus—our largely uncritical support of the Turkish position—our casual attitude toward human need—and the President's insistence on maintaining a business-as-usual attitude toward military shipments to Turkey. All of these acts only encourage Ankara's intransigency. And they feed frustrations on Cyprus, and among our friends in neighboring Greece. The time is past due for us to rescue our foreign policy from a course that ignores our best traditions as a nation, and threatens our broader interests in the Eastern Mediterranean.

American goals on Cyprus, and the implications for our foreign policy, are clear. *First*, restoring the full independence, sovereignty and territorial integrity of Cyprus must be a clearly understood and primary objective of our diplomacy. No other goal will satisfy the demands of justice—or really bring peace and relief to the people of Cyprus.

Second, the President must finally show some real evidence of concern for the humanitarian needs and fate of the refugees. The policy of silence on this issue, at the highest levels of our government, is an affront to common human decency, and the moral sensibilities of all Americans. Spokesmen for our government speak of the "new realities" on Cyprus, and freely talk about bi-regionalism and a "demarcation line" for the de facto partition of the island. But what about the "new reality" of homeless people brought about by the Turkish invasion, and the yearning of refugees to return to their families and homes?

I submit tonight that the fate of these people is central to the Cyprus issue, and to any negotiations over the future of the island. The time is long overdue for a "tilt" in American policy toward the people of Cyprus—toward the men and women and children who are suffering on that tortured island, especially the refugees, both Turkish and Greek. The time is long overdue for our country to put the problem of Cypriot refugees at the top of our agenda for Cyprus. And I call upon the President to publicly show that America cares about their plight—and that we will do everything we can to help them lead normal lives.

The Administration says it is trying to find some "common ground" between Greece and Turkey to facilitate a resumption of negotiations over Cyprus. But finding "common ground" must be more than finding what officials call "flexibility" in the Turkish position—or some way to take "into full account Greek honor and national dignity." If we can so freely meet Turkish sensibilities over the need for what Secretary Kissinger calls a "demarcation line" on Cyprus—the least we can do is publicly recognize the importance of refugees, and also recognize Greek and Cypriot sensitivities over the need for a return of refugees to their homes. And the President's continuing silence on this issue is an inexcuseable omission in American policy toward Cyprus.

We must finally recognize that the lives of people caught in the crunch of disaster and war are important in any effort to build a structure for peace—especially when these problems are immediately central to resolving the issue at hand. In this connection, the United States must finally use its vast influence and good offices with Turkey, to persuade Ankara that a gesture of goodwill is needed to break the dead-lock in negotiations. The orderly withdrawal of Turkish forces from the Famagusta and Morphou areas, for example, would permit the return of many refugees to their homes, and be a real first step toward a negotiated settlement of the Cyprus problem.

The President argues strongly that continuing military aid to Turkey is not only important to our national security, but also gives us some leverage to constructively influence Ankara's policy on Cyprus. The President now has this so-called leverage, for 60 days more. So let him use it—in the interests of bringing peace and relief to the people of Cyprus. There may be national security interests at stake—but there is also human suffering on Cyprus. To protect the one—and to prevent or remedy the other—there is no effort too great for us to make.

And, finally, our government must make a dramatic increase in its humanitarian concern over Cyprus, and fully encourage and support private relief efforts among our citizens on behalf of Cyprus.

Conditions among Greek Cypriots in the Turkish-occupied areas, and the heavy restrictions placed upon the movement of international relief personnel, are deplorable, and we must urgently lend our diplomacy to remedy this situation.

Also, generosity and compassion must replace the tokenism and casualness of our support for relief programs by the United Nations and the Cypriot government. There is no excuse to be lax on this issue—especially in light of the millions of dollars we freely spend in military shipments to Turkey. The legislation I introduced for this purpose passed the Senate nearly two weeks ago. And I pledge my best efforts for the full enactment of this bill when Congress returns in November.

On Cyprus today we are seeing a very important struggle, by a courageous and spirited people, for self-preservation and the maintenance of national independence. Despite the presence of a well equipped occupation army, and despite continuing threats from Ankara of new military operations, the Cypriot people are standing their ground. They have not lost hope, and their spirit serves as an inspiration for free peoples around the globe. They love their country and their freedom—and they are patriots in the cause of Cyprus. But what is love of country? And what is patriotism?

Several years ago, my brother, Senator Robert Kennedy, asked these questions, and gave this answer:

"[Love of country and patriotism] is more than merely the physical attributes of the nation in which we live. It is the mountains, the seas, the streams and lakes, the forests, the villages, the cities, the farms—it is all these but it is much more. . . . It is a feeling for a system which recognizes the individual, where the individual can fulfill himself, where the opportunity of progress, of hope, is always present. The Greeks said 'happiness is the exercise of vital powers along the lines of excellence, in a life affording them scope.' "

That should be true today, for Cyprus. So let us dedicate ourselves "to tame the savageness of man and make gentle the life of the world." Let us dedicate ourselves to that goal on Cyprus—and say a prayer for our country, for Cyprus, and the world.

APPENDIX II

[From the Congressional Record, Senate, Aug. 8 and 13, 1974]

Humanitarian Problems on Cyprus

Mr. Kennedy. Mr. President, events on Cyprus have been a source of deep concern for many Americans and people around the world. But after days of intense violence and political turmoil, reports now suggests some hopeful signs that at least the violence is subsiding—and that additional efforts will now be made by all parties concerned to effect a meaningful separation of forces under United Nations auspices. Hopefully, as well, new efforts to resume negotiations on a political settlement of the conflict will be diligently pursued—and will not only restore the security of civilians and constitutional rule to all of Cyprus, but also the island's territorial integrity and full independence.

In pursuing these objectives, however, the parties concerned—and all men of good will—should not lose sight of the human tragedies which have hit the people of Cyprus. Regrettably, their situation has taken second place to the military and political issues at stake—and to the special interests of those who have much to lose, or to gain, by the outcome of the conflict. But the civilians of Cyprus—both Greeks and Turks—also have interests. And for many thousands, apparently—especially among the Greek population in the Turkish salients—recent weeks have been a nightmare of death and horror and grief.

Reports from the area—including official reports to our own Government and elsewhere—fully confirm the human tragedy of Cyprus. Tens of thousands of women and children have been forcibly expelled from their villages—especially in Turkish occupied areas—or have fled their homes as refugees. Thousands of able-bodied men have disappeared—and some apparently have been deported to camps or prisons in southern Turkey. Refugees tell of "much suffering" and "systematic" arson, looting, murder, and rape. And civilian casualties—both wounded and dead—number in the hundreds, if not the thousands.

Mr. President, I do not rise to offer any magic solution for meeting the immediate political and humanitarian problems of Cyprus. But I do rise to express a deep personal concern over the plight of Cypriot civilians—and especially over the continuing violations of human rights and the rules of common human decency which are evidenced in Turkish occupied areas. A spokesman for our own Government suggests that "some very rough stuff" continues. This is a deplorable situation, and I appeal to the Turkish Government and all parties involved to make every effort in behalf of bringing peace and relief to Cyprus.

Apart from securing a meaningful separation of forces and a political settlement at the conference table in Geneva, there are three items of immediate concern to me as chairman of the Subcommittee on Refugees:

First, the emergency relief needs of refugees and others in distress—including food, water, shelter, medicine, and protection;

Second, the condition, treatment, and release of civilian detainees—including those who may have been deported to Turkey or other areas; and

Third, the free movement of international relief convoys and humanitarian personnel from the United Nations or the International Committee for the Red Cross—ICRC—including the free access of Red Cross personnel to detention centers on both sides.

The United Nations and the ICRC are the primary international agencies charged with the care and protection of Cypriot civilians. Reports from the U.N. and elsewhere suggest, however, that difficulties continue in all three areas of my immediate concern—especially in the Turkish salients of the country.

The humanitarian services of the U.N. and the ICRC have been indispensable in helping to bring peace and relief in many areas of the world. And today in Cyprus the services of these organizations deserve the full support of the parties to the conflict, our own Government, and others as well.

In conclusion, let me express some concern over the course of U.S. policy toward Cyprus. We have heard a great deal about the travels of our diplomats to the area, but we have heard very little about the substance and objectives of American policy toward developments on Cyprus and related issues.

I fully appreciate the immense difficulties in the Cyprus issue. It is a complex matter for diplomats and humanitarians alike. But should not our Government give more evidence of concern? What are American policy objectives? What is the substance of our activities? What have we done to help restrain Turkish forces? And how are we responding to help meet humanitarian needs among the Cypriot civilians who are refugees or detainees on either side?

The American people and their representatives in Congress deserve some answers, and should not be in the dark over United States policy toward Cyprus. I am extremely hopeful, Mr. President, that the administration will finally give some additional evidence of a very active concern over the needed efforts to bring peace and relief to the people of Cyprus.

SENATE CONCURRENT RESOLUTION 110—SUBMISSION OF A CONCURRENT RESOLUTION RELATING TO THE SITUATION IN CYPRUS

(Referred to the Committee on Foreign Relations.)

Mr. KENNEDY submitted the following concurrent resolution:

S. CON. RES. 110

Resolved by the Senate (the House of Representatives concurring),

Whereas a settlement of the present conflict in the Republic of Cyprus is vital to the peace and security of the eastern Mediterranean and is in the best interests of world peace and stability; and

Whereas a settlement depends upon the right of the Cypriot people to determine their own destiny and the efforts of the United Nations to act as a negotiating body; and

Whereas Resolution 2077 (xx)) adopted by the General Assembly on December 8, 1965, "calls upon all states . . . to respect the sovereignty, unity, independence and territorial integrity of the Republic of Cyprus and to refrain from any intervention directed against it"; and

Whereas the continued presence of foreign troops in Cyprus undermines the ability of the Cypriot people to resolve their own crisis and the efforts of the United Nations to restore peace; and

Whereas Resolution 353 adopted by the Security Council on July 20, 1974, "demands an immediate end to foreign military intervention in the Republic of Cyprus" and "requests the withdrawal without delay from the Republic of Cyprus of foreign military personnel present otherwise than under the authority of international agreements . . ."; and

Whereas the declaration on Cyprus signed by the foreign ministers of Britain, Turkey, and Greece, in Geneva on July 30, 1974, calls for a "timely and phased reduction of the number of armed forces" from Cypriot soil; and

Whereas the continued presence of foreign troops in Cyprus violates international agreements and United Nations resolutions threatens the independence and territorial integrity of the island, jeopardizes peace and stability in the eastern Mediterranean, and imperils the very existence of NATO; Now, therefore, be it

Resolved by the Senate (the House of Representatives concurring),

That all foreign troops currently involved in Cyprus be withdrawn immediately so that the United Nations and the International Committee of the Red Cross may be permitted to restore peace to the island, and to guarantee the protection and civil rights of all persons and communities and the right of the Cypriot people working together to determine their own destiny.

APPENDIX III

Text of Senator Kennedy's Amendment for Relief and Rehabilitation Assistance to Cyprus, Africa, and Bangladesh

[Adopted in the Senate, Oct. 2, 1974: introduced on Sept. 17, 1974]

Foreign Assistance Act of 1974—Amendment

AMENDMENT NO. 1878

(Ordered to be printed and to lie on the table.)

Mr. Kennedy (for himself and Mr. McGee) submitted an amendment intended to be proposed by them jointly to the bill (S. 3994), supra.

RELIEF AND REHABILITATION FUNDS FOR AFRICA, BANGLADESH, AND CYPRUS

Mr. Kennedy. Mr. President, I am submitting today an amendment to S. 3394, the pending Foreign Assistance authorization bill. The amendment provides special funds for disaster relief and rehabilitation programs in the drought-stricken areas of Africa, for flood relief in Bangladesh, and for refugee assistance in Cyprus.

The amendment authorizes the use of existing funds—an estimated $119,000,-000 available under scheduled loan repayments administered by AID—to permit our Government to respond to the massive human tragedies in these areas, and to possible disasters in other parts of the world.

The current crisis in Cyprus, the massive flooding in Bangladesh, and the spreading drought and famine in Africa, are only the latest links in the chain of ravaged populations which have circled the globe in recent years. Such humanitarian crises have always brought forth an immediate response from the American people—in fulfillment of our Nation's longstanding leadership in helping, to the extent we can, all people in need. Just last spring the Congress responded to the famine needs of Africa, and the disaster relief requirements of Pakistan and Nicaragua, by enacting the Foreign Disaster Assistance Act. And, during consideration of the foreign assistance bill last year, the Congress enacted section 639B, which provided substantial famine and disaster relief to the African Sahel for the first time.

The amendment I am introducing today continues our country's record of concern for our fellow man, and the longstanding support of Congress for disaster relief overseas. The amendment was prepared in very close cooperation with AID, and carries with it the support of the Ford administration.

For the people of Cyprus, Mr. President, this is especially a perilous time—as it is also for the renewal of democracy and freedom in Greece, and for the future of peaceful relations in the Eastern Mediterranean. Regrettably, the plight of Cypriot civilians has taken second place to the military and political dimensions of the Cyprus problem—and to the special interests of those who have much to lose or to gain by the outcome of the conflict on the island. But the civilians of Cyprus—both Greeks and Turks—also have interests. And for tens of thousands, the past weeks have been a nightmare of death and tragedy and grief.

1. CYPRUS

This week I received a preliminary report from a special study mission to Cyprus, which visited the area on behalf of the Subcommittee on Refugees, which I serve as chairman. The study mission visited refugees in all parts of the island, including the Turkish occupied areas. The study mission met with both Greek and Turkish Cypriot leaders and United Nations relief officials, and also held extensive conversations on humanitarian and related problems with officials in Ankara and Athens.

(71)

The study mission reports that nearly 300,000 Cypriots—mostly Greeks—are now refugees. They fled the advancing Turkish Army, leaving their homes and nearly all of their belongings behind. This is close to half the island's population—without sufficient food and medicine, with little shelter, with few clothes and blankets, and with increasingly little hope for an early return to their villages and homes.

A drive along the highways of Cyprus, especially in the southern zone, quickly tells the tragic tale of the events of July and August—of the human consequences of an armed invasion, of constant ceasefire violations, of military occupation, and of man's inhumanity to man.

Refugees are still fleeing down the roads of Cyprus. During the team's recent visit some 20,000 people fled the town of Athna, in advance of what the Turkish Army calls "armed reconnaissance in force"—or what simple language would label a ceasefire violation. These thousands of refugees, like the tens of thousands before them, are today seeking protection and safety in the towns of southern Cyprus, swelling the local population in some areas by at least 500 percent. They are seeking shelter wherever they can find it—in open fields, under trees, along the roadsides, and in schools, churches, and civic buildings. In the first days they had no shelter, and few blankets. And only in the past 2 weeks have relief supplies begun to arrive in meaningful quantities, and clusters of tents are beginning to sprout around towns and cities in the government controlled areas of the island. The overwhelming majority of those in need are Greek Cypriots, but significant numbers of Turks also command our help and concern.

The economy and life of Cyprus has been shattered by the Turkish invasion, with some 80 percent of the economic base located in the occupied areas which now have less than 10 percent of the population. The vast citrus industry rots on the trees. Farms on the plain lie idle, as cattle and other livestock die from lack of food and water. The tourist center of Kyrenia has been looted beyond recognition, and the city of Famagusta—a city of over 40,000 people—is now a ghost town, with empty streets, houses, and hotels. The population of whole cities have become refugees.

For many refugee families, the tragedy is still too fresh, their flight to safety too recent, for them to realize fully what has happened. And few in the international community have recognized the full tragedy of Cyprus. Our Government's role during the crisis—our early silence and later vacillation toward the political and military problems of the island—must not characterize our Nation's attitude or response to the escalating human crisis which has gripped all of Cyprus.

The study mission reports that important relief efforts have now been undertaken, in cooperation with Cypriot authorities, by the United Nations High Commissioner for Refugees and the International Committee of the Red Cross, among others. But these initiatives, and programs for humanitarian relief in Cyprus, are just getting off the ground and need the immediate support of the United States—support which this amendment will provide. It is estimated that the United Nations High Commissioner for Refugees will alone need some $22 million for emergency relief through the end of this year, and that an additional sum will be required for returning the refugees home or resettling them elsewhere on the island. Our Government must be in a position to actively encourage and generously support this important humanitarian work of the United Nations and the Cypriot authorities. Peace and relief for all Cypriots in need must be our goal on Cyprus.

2. BANGLADESH

In Bangladesh, there can be no doubt today that great tragedy has once again hit the Bengali people. A recent hearing before the Subcommittee on Refugees indicated that flood refugees number in the millions, as the worst floods in over 20 years have inundated the land and people of Bangladesh. Crops have been destroyed, and food reserves have been lost. Housing, schools, health clinics and other facilities have been swept away. And all reports confirm that this latest disaster seriously compounds existing economic and social problems brought about by the dislocations of the 1971 war for independence.

In testimony before the Refugee Subcommittee recent travelers to the area report that there is more human suffering than ever before, that the country stands on the brink of starvation, and that epidemic and disease threaten the well-being and lives of millions, and, perhaps, the nation as a whole. In purely human terms, there is great suffering today in Bangladesh, 'which must call forth a greater response from the United States—out of humanitarian concern, as well as concern for the stability and peace of South Asia. The United States cannot assume the full responsibility for meeting the massive human needs in Bangladesh. The United Nations and other governments must help. But we, too, must do what we can with what we have.

3. AFRICA

And in the Sahel and other parts of Africa, the food situation continues to deteriorate as famine conditions spread across the continent. Contrary to our Government's general optimism over the past year, recent reports, even within the government, tell of catastrophic consequences from the Sahelian drought, and that the situation among the people is precarious in some areas. The number of famine refugees is growing. Relief camps are over-burdened. Last year's logistical bottlenecks and administrative delays in the movement of food and 're-lief supplies continues. Malnutrition and disease still threaten the lives of many thousands, and unless something more is done the death rate will continue to climb.

Mr. President, it is the purpose of this amendment to make available already appropriated funds to support international relief and rehabilitation programs in Cyprus, Bangladesh, Africa, and other areas of possible need over the coming year. This amendment authorizes the Agency for International Development—AID—to use 50 percent of the fiscal year 1975 scheduled loan repayments, which now revert to the Treasury, to be used for the relief, rehabilitation, and reconstruction purposes mandated in the amendment—especially in Cyprus, Bangladesh, and Africa. Current estimates by AID suggest that some $119 million is immediately available. And by using the loan repayments, under specific Congressional authorization, it will not be necessary to appropriate a new obligational authority this fiscal year.

The humanitarian concerns today—in Cyprus, Bangladesh, and Africa—illustrate-once again that those foreign policy variables involving people are crucial elements in our foreign policy. Little will be achieved in building a structure of peace unless governments place a higher priority on the welfare and real-life problems of people—whose neglect fosters instability and spawns conflict around the globe.

Political wisdom and simple humanity demands of our country that we do more to help the critical humanitarian needs in today's world. The extraordinary needs in Cyprus and elsewhere demand that we take extraordinary steps to utilize all readily available sources of funds—including those scheduled loan repayments which will revert to the Treasury, unless Congress and the administration act to use them for humanitarian purposes in the interest of world stability and peace. The amendment I introduce today will help accomplish this end.

Mr. President, I ask unanimous consent that the text of the amendment, as well as a section-by-section analysis of its provisions, be printed at this point in the Record.

There being no objection, the amendment and analysis were ordered to be printed in the Record, as follows:

AMENDMENT No. 1878

At the end of the bill, add the following new section:

RECONSTRUCTION, RELIEF, AND REHABILITATION

SEC. 33. (a) Section 203 of the Foreign Assistance Act of 1961 is amended by inserting immediately after "of this part." the following: "The balance of such receipts for fiscal year 1975 is authorized to be made available for the purposes of sections 639B, 639C, and 639D of this Act."

(b) Section 639B of the Foreign Assistance Act of 1961 is amended by adding at the end thereof the following: "Notwithstanding any prohibitions or restrictions contained in this or any other Act, the President is authorized to furnish assistance, on such terms and conditions as he may determine, for reconstruction and economic development programs in the drought-stricken nations of Africa.

Such assistance shall be furnished solely out of funds made available under section 203 of this Act to carry out this section."

(c) The Foreign Assistance Act of 1961 is amended by adding after section 639B a new section 639C as follows:

"Sec. 639C. Relief and Rehabilitation in Bangladesh and Cyprus.—(a) The Congress finds that the recent flooding in the People's Republic of Bangladesh, and the civil and international strife in the Republic of Cyprus, have caused great suffering and hardship for the peoples of the two Republics which cannot be alleviated with their internal resources. The President shall make every effort to develop and implement programs of relief and rehabilitation, in conjunction with other nations providing assistance, the United Nations, and other concerned international and regional organizations and voluntary agencies, to alleviate the hardships caused in these two nations.

"(b) Notwithstanding any prohibitions or restrictions contained in this or any other Act, the President is authorized to furnish assistance, on such terms and conditions as he may determine, for disaster relief, rehabilitation, and related programs in the People's Republic of Bangladesh and the Republic of Cyprus. Such assistance shall be furnished solely out of funds made available under section 203 of this Act to carry out this section."

(d) The Foreign Assistance Act of 1961 is amended by striking after section 639C, as added by subsection (c) of this section, the following new section:

"Sec. 639D. Disaster Relief and Rehabilitation.—Notwithstanding any prohibitions or restrictions contained in this or any other Act, the President is authorized to furnish assistance, on such terms and conditions as he may determine, for disaster relief, rehabilitation and related programs in the case of disasters that require large scale relief and rehabilitation efforts which cannot be met adequately with the funds available for obligation under section 451 of this Act. Such assistance shall be furnished solely out of funds made available under section 203 of this Act to carry out this section."

(e) The Foreign Assistance Act of 1961 is amended by adding after section 639D, as added by subsection (d) of this section, the following new section:

"Sec. 639E. Internationalization of Assistance.—Assistance for the purposes set forth in Sections 639A, 639B, 639C, and 639D shall be distributed wherever practicable under the auspices of and by the United Nations and its specialized agencies, other international organizations or arrangements, multilateral institutions, and private voluntary agencies."

Section-by-Section Analysis of the Amendment

The purpose of this amendment is to permit the President to respond to the disasters in Cyprus and Bangladesh, to have the authority to respond to future disasters of a like nature, and to permit him to complement disaster relief for the drought-stricken nations of Africa with long-term development and reconstruction assistance which will facilitate a reorientation of the Sahelian and Ethiopian economies and will halt the advance of the desert. Absent such efforts, the African nations are likely to endure a perpetual and ever-growing disaster.

This amendment also directs that both reconstruction and relief assistance be undertaken with other donors, international organizations, and voluntary agencies.

Subsection (a): This subsection provides a funding source for the Sahelian and Ethiopian development authority, the Bangladesh and Cyprus relief authorizations and future large scale disasters which other portions of this amendment create. Presently, A.I.D. may use 50% of the scheduled loan repayments for new loans under its regular development accounts. The balance reverts to the Treasury. This subsection makes the 1975 balance available for loans or grants for the purposes set forth below. A.I.D. estimates that this balance will total 119 million. Although only 1975 receipts will be used, the funds need not be used during this fiscal year but will remain available for use as multilateral programs for the Sahel, Bangladesh and Cyprus develop. By using the loan repayments, it will not be necessary to appropriate now obligational authority.

Subsection (b): Last year the Congress enacted Section 639B which urged the Executive to develop, in conjunction with other donors and international organizations, long-range development plans in the drought-stricken African nations. Congress indicated its belief that the short-range reaction to the disaster (authorized by Section 639A) must be followed by reconstruction and development that will halt or reverse the advance of the desert, if the inhabitants of the area are ever to overcome their misfortune and participate in a self-sustaining economy. This subsection complements that directive by authorizing the President to furnish such assistance. There are some restrictions in the Act that will work against this effort, however. One example is the 25% local participation requirement of Section 110(a). The drought-stricken regions of Africa are confronted with such enormous problems that their scant resources cannot provide even 25% of the cost of reconstruction. For this reason, the language "notwithstanding any prohibitions or restrictions . . ." is included. The amendment's sponsors believe that this authorization will greatly facilitate the executive Branch's attempts to involve other nations and organizations in development plans by showing the seriousness of our commitment.

Subsection (c) : This subsection responds to the misfortunes of the people of Cyprus and Bangladesh. In both cases, events beyond the control of the local populace—armed conflict in one case and devastating flooding in the other—have caused great suffering and hardship to the respective populations. Emergency relief and rehabilitation in large but still undetermined amounts is needed in both situations. The Congress recognizes this need and authorizes and encourages the President to make every effort to work in concert with other concerned nations and organizations to provide assistance to these two areas. As in subsection (b), a waiver of the restrictions of the Act is necessary. Such restrictions as sections 620(a)(3) and (n), which prohibit assistance to countries whose ships carry cargoes to Cuba and North Vietnam respectively, must be overcome. Other disaster relief provisions of the Foreign Assistance Act contain similar language which permit the Act's prohibitions to be overridden.

Subsection (d) : Rather than reacting to disasters some time after they occur, this subsection will give the President the authority to respond quickly to large-scale disasters the nature and consequence of which cannot yet be foreseen. Drawing on the same funding source as the other portions of this disaster oriented provision, this subsection will be available for efforts beyond those possible under the Contingency Fund of Sec. 451. This section will allow response when disasters are so serious and on such a large scale that an extensive effort will be needed. The funds allocated under Sec. 451 are authorized primarily for disaster relief purposes, but are limited to $30 million under current authorizations. This subsection makes it possible for the U.S. to respond promptly to the Sahels, Cypruses and Bangladeshes of the future without obtaining new authorizing and appropriating legislation. Since this subsection does focus on a need that will transcend normal policy restrictions, this provision includes a waiver of the restrictions of this and other laws. Such a waiver is consistent with the other disaster relief provisions of the Foreign Assistance Act.

Subsection (c) : Stipulates that the assistance provided under all the above sections "shall be distributed wherever practicable under the auspices of and by the United Nations and its specialized agencies, other international organizations or arrangements, multilateral institutions, and private voluntary agencies."

APPENDIX IV

TEXT OF SECRETARY OF STATE KISSINGER'S NEWS CONFERENCE OF AUGUST 19, 1974, AND OFFICIAL STATEMENTS ON THE CYPRUS ISSUE BEFORE THE UNITED NATIONS SECURITY COUNCIL

SECRETARY KISSINGER'S NEWS CONFERENCE OF AUGUST 19, 1974

Secretary KISSINGER. I would like to begin with a few observations about the tragic death of Ambassador [Rodger P.] Davies.

Ambassador Davies has been a close associate for all the years that I have been in Washington. He worked closely with me on Middle East problems when he was Deputy Assistant Secretary. His performance after he was appointed Ambassador in Cyprus has been outstanding. I think I can do no better than to read to you two cables which I sent to him, one on July 22, the other on August 10.

On July 22 I sent him the following cable:

"I would like to express my thanks for your performance and that of your staff during the last week. I relied heavily on your good judgment and on the excellent reporting from Nicosia. The steadiness and courage displayed by you and your staff under dangerous conditions were exemplary. The Embassy's overall performance deserves the highest commendation. Please convey my congratulations and profound thanks to all members of your staff. Hopefully, and in great measure due to your efforts, the situation will calm in Cyprus."

Then on August 10 I sent him another cable:

"Art Hartman [Arthur A. Hartman, Assistant Secretary for European Affairs] has just reported to me in some detail on the magnificent performance of all of you under the most dangerous and trying circumstances. Your courage under fire, your accurate, perceptive and calm reporting, and your continued efforts to further our policy and protect American citizens with a reduced and overworked staff are a credit to you and are in the finest tradition of the Service."

My associates will tell you that the highest praise they usually get from me is the absence of criticism. And I want to call your attention to these two cables which express the extraordinary performance of Ambassador Davies. Those of us who have known him will miss him for his outstanding human qualities.

The Foreign Service, which is often criticized, has produced no better representative. And his work is in the best traditions of a Service to which dedication and the performance of a national duty are the principal objectives.

I have sent the following message to Ambassador Davies' children:

"You both have my deepest sympathy in this tragic time. While there is little that anyone can say at a moment such as this to lessen the sorrow, I want you to know that we share your deep sense of loss. Your father was loved, respected and admired by all of his colleagues in the Foreign Service and the State Department. You should be very proud of him; we are. Mrs. Kissinger and I stand ready to do anything we can to help in the difficult months ahead."

You know that the White House has already announced that the President has ordered that a plane be sent for the children. I have asked our Deputy Under Secretary of State, [L. Dean] Brown, whose distinguished service includes service as Ambassador in Jordan in very difficult circumstances, to go out with this plane, to represent the United States in Cyprus until we can appoint an Ambassador and get him in place. The designation of an officer of the distinction of Ambassador Brown leaves no doubt of the importance we attach to a speedy and peaceful resolution of the Cyprus issue.

This morning also, President Clerides called me to express his personal sorrow at the loss of Ambassador Davies, whom he described as a close personal and very trusted friend. I assured President Clerides that the United States fully understood the lack of responsibility of the Cyprus Government for this tragic event. I assured him that the United States would continue a major effort to bring about peace, and he urged us to make such an effort. I emphasized to him, however, that these efforts would not be helped by anti-American demonstrations that were unjustified by the record and that could only create conditions to hamper these efforts.

I also have had an opportunity this morning to speak with President Ford about the situation in the eastern Mediterranean. We were in close touch by telephone yesterday, and we have met personally several times in the preceding days. President Ford has asked me to make the following statement on behalf of the United States:

First, the United States shall insist on the strict maintenance of the cease-fire on Cyprus.

Second, the imperative and urgent need is to begin negotiations.

Third, we will continue to support efforts to bring the parties to the negotiating table.

Fourth, the United States will play any role requested by the parties. We are also prepared to support the able efforts of the British Foreign Secretary, [James] Callaghan, in this regard.

Fifth, in these negotiations, we believe it wil be necessary for Turkey, as the stronger power on the ground, to display flexibility and a concern for Greek sensitivities, both in terms of territory and the size of military forces on the island. I have made this point directly this morning to the Prime Minister of Turkey. I have been assured that the Turkish Government considers the demarcation line negotiable and that it will carry out the provisions of the Geneva agreement calling for phased reductions of troops on Cyprus.

Sixth, the United States greatly values the traditional friendship of Greece. It has the highest regard for Prime Minister Karamanlis and wishes every success to his democratic government. We will use our influence in any negotiation to take into full account Greek honor and national dignity. At the same time, we assume that all of our allies, including Greece, join in collective defense in their own interests. We are willing to strengthen these common alliance ties and to help the Greek Government in any way possible. We will not be pressured by threat of withdrawal from the [NATO] alliance, or anti-American demonstrations, which in any event are totally unjustified by our record.

I repeat that this statement has been gone over by President Ford.

Question. Will we get a copy?

Secretary KISSINGER. You will have a copy—I suppose we will have a copy available.

Question. May I ask, has the President been in touch with Prime Minister Ecevit?

Secretary KISSINGER. I have been in touch with him, and I affirm that the answer is "Yes."

Question. Will you take questions?

Secretary KISSINGER. Reluctantly.

Question. Last week, one of your associates described as plain "baloney" suggestions that the United States has tilted toward Turkey. Do you share in that view? And can you tell us specifically the consideration that was given to cutting off arms to Turkey and why arms were not cut off during the building crisis?

Secretary KISSINGER. With the speaker sitting here and looking balefully at me, my options, as they say, are severely limited—I completely support the statement of Mr. McCloskey [Ambassador at Large Robert J. McCloskey].

The situation on Cyprus tilted toward Turkey not as a result of American policy but as a result of the actions of the previous Greek Government which destroyed the balance of forces as it had existed on the island.

The United States did not threaten the cutoff of military aid to Turkey, for these reasons: First, it was considered that such an action would be ineffective and would not prevent the threatening eventuality; secondly, as was pointed out in this statement, we are giving economic and military aid as a reflection of our common interest in the defense of the eastern Mediterranean. Once such a decision is taken, it will have the most drastic consequences and not just over a period of time covering a few days but over an extended period of time.

For all these reasons, it was judged that the United States would be both ineffective and counterproductive to threaten the cutoff of aid.

Short of this, however, we made the most repeated and urgent representations to Turkey in order to prevent the military action that happened. We have criticized the action, and we believe also that the inflexibility of all of the parties in Geneva contributed to it.

Question. Mr. Secretary, I don't know the exact wording, but back earlier you said, "The United States will play"—this is in the President's statement—"The United States will play any role requested by the parties." Is that correct? You will await some request from them, or do you have any initiatives to take on your own?

Secretary KISSINGER. First of all, I think the exact status of the statement I read is that it is not a statement "by" the President. It is a statement approved and directed by the President—and I don't know what the distinction is but generally, Presidential statements are made at the White House.

But the practical consequences are the same, because it has been gone over with the President, and he has asked me to make it in his name.

Now on "Have practical steps been proposed?"—it is my understanding that the British Government is considering an initiative, which we shall support. We have also made clear to the parties that we are prepared to use any alternative method that promises results.

As you know, during the last week, we offered to all of the parties a more active American role, and it is up to them to avail themselves of it.

We have not yet made any specific proposal as to a particular solution, but you will see in the statement that I have just read our view as to the direction in which the negotiations should go.

Question. Can I follow that up, Mr. Secretary? Has there been any request by the parties to get you more personally involved by either going there personally—and what would be the reaction if you were asked?

Secretary KISSINGER. There has not been any formal request, and our first effort now is to get the parties to the conference table.

We would be prepared to entertain any request that offered a prospect of success.

Question. Mr. Secretary, there has been widespread criticism around the world from diplomats, as well as from public demonstrators, that the United States used "quiet diplomacy" which was so quiet during the past four weeks that it was ineffective. Can you address yourself to whether the United States at an earlier point might have done what it has done today, if it had issued a firm, specific statement?

Also, you have been burned in effigy on Lafayette Square, I believe for the first time.

Secretary KISSINGER. Well, I am honored—is it really only the first time? [Laughter.]

Question. In Lafayette Square, I believe.

Secretary KISSINGER. I hope you all realize that half of the demonstrators were State Department employees. [Laughter.]

Let us understand the context within which the negotiations have taken place.

Until early August, until in fact August 8, it was the general judgment of all those dealing with the negotiations, including specifically that of the United Kingdom, that the conference in Geneva would lead to a settlement and that in fact it would, after an initial phase which would be conducted by Foreign Ministers, break up into working groups that would settle the issue.

Under those circumstances, it would have been highly inappropriate for the United States to make a public statement of the solution that it advocated.

After it became apparent that the negotiations in Geneva were heading for a stalemate, the United States, first, responded to every request by the principal mediator, the British Foreign Secretary, for specific assistance and specific proposals. In addition, the United States made many demarches to Turkey to prevent the threatened military action.

And it [the United States] would have preferred if, perhaps, some more flexibility could have been shown by all of the parties in Geneva.

Our judgment was that a public statement would freeze the positions and that it would not achieve the objective of thwarting a military attack.

After the event, it is never possible to prove whether some other course might not have been successful. Our judgment was that under the circumstances quiet diplomacy would lead to these results. But there is a limit to what diplomacy can achieve. It cannot substitute for an existing relationship of forces.

We understand the frustrations of the Greek community. We understand also the frustrations and disappointments of the Greek Government—but it is important to remember that the original dislocations were not of our own making and that the United States, while it will try to be helpful, cannot solve all problems around the world.

With respect to the demonstrations, it is worth while to remember that a few years ago the demonstrators were complaining about excessive American involvement. Now the complaint seems to be the opposite.

Question. Mr. Secretary, has the perception of the United States as "tilting toward Turkey," regardless of whether it's correct or incorrect, in any way hampered your efforts to serve as an effective mediator between the two sides?

Secretary KISSINGER. I think that it is understandable that Greek emotions run very deep at this moment.

I believe that upon calmer reflection the responsible Greek leaders will recognize that the United States has shown deep sympathy for the Greek Government, that we welcome the present democratic government in Greece, and that within the limits of what was possible we have attempted to pay a constructive role.

I think the Greek Government will also realize that the U.S. roles can be very important in bringing about a result consistent with the dignity and honor of all of the parties—and we hope it will realize that anti-American demonstrations and anti-American gestures do not contribute to our effectiveness.

Question. Mr. Secretary, yesterday, Secretary [of Defense James R.] Schlesinger talked about the arms embargo and the continued Turkish advances, and it sounded like it was still an active possibility if the Turks continued their military operations on Cyprus. Is it? And to what point do we invoke some form of embargo?

Secretary KISSINGER. I do not wish to speak of circumstances that have not arisen. We have been given assurances by the Turkish Government that it would strictly abide by the cease-fire—and these assurances were reiterated in my conversations with Prime Minister Ecevit this morning.

I do not want to consider what our point of view would be if it turned out that these assurances weren't correct.

Question. Mr. Secretary, on the question about military assistance, please, the Foreign Assistance Act stated—

Secretary KISSINGER. Where is the question?

Question. I am asking the question from back here. The Foreign Assistance Act states—

Secretary KISSINGER. I thought I was looking at Bernie Gwertzman.

Question. That defense services to any country shall be furnished solely for internal security and for legitimate self-defense. It also states that any country which uses articles which we have given them in substantial violation of the act shall be immediately ineligible for further assistance.

The question that I am asking is whether or not, what your understanding of the legal terms of the act are, whether or not we are not required under the terms of the act to cut military assistance to Turkey?

Secretary KISSINGER. Well, I will have to get a legal opinion on that subject, which I have not done. The considerations from a policy point of view that were at the mind of the President and myself have been stated here.

Question. In your conversation with the Prime Minister of Turkey today, just to broaden one of your points, do you have the understanding that the one-third of Cyprus which is now under Turkish control can be significantly reduced in size?

Secretary KISSINGER. I have the understanding that it can be reduced in size.

Question. But not significantly.

Secretary KISSINGER. I did not go into that much detail.

Question. Mr. Secretary, in view of the crisis in Cyprus, can you assess, or could you reassess, the capability of the United States to stop or limit local wars between smaller states?

Secretary KISSINGER. Well, the United States has never claimed, and could not accept the proposition, that it must stop every local war between smaller states wherever they occur.

Secondly, it is also clear that the United States cannot be asked to redress any upset in any balance, regardless of how it has occurred and where it has occurred, by its own military forces.

We are disappointed by the outcome, by the actions of various of the parties at various times on Cyprus.

We chose—in order not to internationalize the issues too much—to support Britain, which had a legal position as a guaranteeing power in its mediating effort. We are prepared to continue to do this, and we are prepared also to make other efforts.

I do not think it is fair to generalize from this one event, which had a long and complicated history, on a global basis.

Question. Mr. Secretary, earlier you spoke about a new British initiative. Could you give us an idea as to what it would be, what would be the direction of it?

Secretary KISSINGER. I saw a ticker before I came here in which this had allegedly been announced by the British Foreign Office, and I do not want to go into the details of it, because it has been the subject of confidential discussions over the weekend. I simply wanted to indicate the U.S. support for it.

Question. Mr. Secretary, on the one hand, just a couple minutes ago, you did not rule out totally the cutting off, or the possible cutting off, of military aid. You merely said you didn't want to discuss circumstances which have not yet arisen. But on the other hand, you gave us two very good reasons why the cutoff of military aid would not be effective anyway. Why can you not rule it out?

Secretary KISSINGER. The cutoff of military aid was judged not to be effective in the circumstances existing last week. It is a step we would take only in very extreme circumstances which, I repeat, have not arisen, and which I do not foresee. We cannot rule it out for all time, but we do not foresee it, and we are not threatening with it now.

Question. Mr. Secretary, what is happening on the negotiations on the Jackson amendment? Where does that stand? When do you expect that that will come to a fulfillment?

Secretary KISSINGER. As the three Senators said after the meeting with President Ford the other day, we made good progress in the negotiations. We hope that we can make further progress during this week.

Question. Mr. Secretary, in your conversations with the parties involved in the Cyprus situation, would you care to characterize the situation now as a winding down, or do you expect it to go on indefinitely?

Secretary KISSINGER. No, my impression is that the military operations have substantially wound down. It is of course a serious problem for Greece whether and under what circumstances it will enter negotiations. We favor early negotiations because we do not believe that the stiuation will improve. Indeed, the status quo will tend to be confirmed the longer the negotiations are delayed.

I have stated the American position with respect to the negotiations and with respect to the role we would play in a negotiation, and we expect to have clearer responses about that in the next few days.

Question. Mr. Secretary, could you explain the American position on the next step in the diplomatic dialogue in the Middle East? Yesterday's U.S.-Jordanian communique said that at an appropriately early date there should be a Jordanian-Israeli disengagement agreement. Does this now mean that the United States sees the next step being between Israel and Jordan?

Secretary KISSINGER. First of all, let me say that there are many versions of disengagement schemes between Jordan and Israel, and the United States did not imply by this statement that it backed any particular scheme between Jordan and Israel.

As to which negotiation should be next, I think we cannot decide until the round of discussions is completed which involves the Foreign Minister of Syria, who is arriving this week, the Foreign Minister of Saudi Arabia, who is arriving next week; and we have also invited the Prime Minister of Israel to come here in the first half of September for discussions with the President. It is only after all of these discussions are completed that we can make a judgment as to what the next move should be.

Question. Following up on that, do you expect on your scheduled trip to India to stop off in the Middle East to possibly begin some shuttle diplomacy between Amman and Jerusalem?

Secretary KISSINGER. I think that as a general practice a foreign government must not expect that every time there is a crisis the Secretary of State will come rushing into the area and spend all of his time settling that particular crisis. On that basis we could never conduct a consistent American foreign policy. And it cannot become the rule that every issue is settled by the personal shuttle diplomacy of the Secretary of State.

I'm prepared to go to the Middle East for a specific trip. And I may, if there is an especially critical point, engage in a brief shuttle diplomacy. But I do not think it is in the U.S. interests nor in the interests of other countries to expect me personally to settle every ssue no matter where it arises.

So we will support further diplomatic moves, but one must not expect the same degree of extended absences from Washington which characterized the last negotiations.

Question. Thank you very much, Mr. Secretary.

U.S. HUMANITARIAN ASSISTANCE TO CYPRUS

Following is a statement read to news correspondents on August 20 by Robert Anderson, Special Assistant to the Secretary of State for Press Relations.

The Secretary has authorized an additional cash grant of $500,000 to the International Red Cross to meet urgent needs that that group is in the process of identifying on the island of Cyprus.

This is in addition to a previous grant of $225,000 that was made available through the American Red Cross to the ICRC [International Committee of the Red Cross].

In addition, the United States has made available from its AID regional disaster stockpile in Leghorn, Italy, over $600,000 worth of tents, blankets, water containers, and other material which have been requested by the Red Cross.

The Secretary also instructed Ambassador [L. Dean] Brown, who is proceeding to Cyprus as his personal representative, to assess current needs urgently with the aid of a disaster relief expert from AID and report urgently on these needs.

The Secretary also welcomed U.N. Secretary General Waldheim's decision to ask the United Nations High Commissioner for Refugees to use his best efforts to actively pursue a humanitarian relief effort to help the people of Cyprus.

The Department is contacting representatives of European governments to encourage them to make a greater effort to meet what we are certain will be additional requirements for food, shelter, and medical supplies.

UNITED NATIONS CALLS FOR CEASE-FIRE IN CYPRUS: STATEMENTS BY THE U.S. DELEGATE

Following are statements made in the U.N. Security Council by U.S. Representative John Scali on July 16, 19, and 20 and by U.S. Deputy Representative W. Tapley Bennett, Jr., on July 22 and 23.

AMBASSADOR SCALI, JULY 16

USUN press release 88 dated July 16

The United States strongly deplores the violence which has upset the delicate balance on the island of Cyprus. Unhappily, such violence and bloodshed have all too often influenced the fate of this Republic.

We have listened with keen attention to the report of the Secretary General on recent developments there. I am sure that all of us share a common sense of relief that Archbishop Makarios is alive and free. Unfortunately, there is much more we still do not know about the emerging situation on Cyprus, and it is difficult at this moment to see clearly whether and how the Council can make a positive contribution.

We continue to support the independence and territorial integrity of Cyprus and its existing constitutional arrangements. We urge all other states to support a similar policy. We wish to urge in particular that all interested parties exercise the utmost restraint and statesmanship and avoid actions which might further worsen the situation.

AMBASSADOR SCALI, JULY 19

[USUN press release 91 dated July 19]

We are gathered at a moment when peace is clearly threatened in the eastern Mediterranean. As responsible members of the Security Council I believe that we all have an obligation to ask ourselves what is the most useful contribution we can make to avoid conflict and to stabilize peace.

We have listened with great attentiveness to the words of Archbishop Makarios. We join in the sense of relief that all of us feel that he is able to be with us today and to express his views so eloquently.

My government looks forward to welcoming President Makarios in Washington to discuss with him what additional steps can be taken to resolve this crisis and to help end the suffering and the agony of the Cypriot people.

Let there be no misunderstanding about the attitude of the U.S. Government in this situation. As I stated in the Council on Tuesday, the U.S. Government continues to support the independence, the sovereignty, and the territorial integrity of Cyprus and the existing constitutional arrangements.

Further, I would like to emphasize a fundamental point. The United States does not consider *enosis*, or union between Greece and Cyprus, as an acceptable solution of the Cyprus problem. The United States continues to believe in the future of a free and independent Cyprus as a sovereign nation capable of making its own decisions in full equality with the rest of the independent countries of the world.

We do not consider military intervention by any party for any reason to be justified in the present situation. In our view, Mr. President, the first and very important step is that all interested parties continue to exercise the utmost restraint and good judgment to prevent this crisis from taking further unfortunate turns. In particular, the U.S. Government is firmly opposed to any attempt to bring about a military solution to the present problem. Such attempts would severely, perhaps irretrievably, set back the negotiating process, which alone can bring about the peaceful and constitutional solution which we all desire.

Therefore we most earnestly appeal to all governments concerned to resist the temptation to settle this issue by force. We ask them instead to pursue the much harder but wiser course of negotiation.

Having said this, however, I am sure that all of us around this table will recognize that there are many critical uncertainties in the present situation. We are gratified to note that the fighting on the island apparently has ceased. Yet the threat of military action in this area remains a grim prospect.

I note with considerable interest that the Representative of the Soviet Union is impressed by the fact that American citizens have sent messages to his Embassy expressing their view on this crisis. I am not surprised that he is impressed; American citizens have the right to communicate with anyone, regardless of the point of view they wish to express.

We are all aware of the special treaty provisions which govern the relationships of the governments concerned in Cyprus and the historically unique constitutional arrangements which were established to provide an acceptable basis of association between the Greek and Turkish communities.

Given the forcible overthrow of the existing government, it is quite understandable that strong emotions are widely felt about how to resolve the problem. It is also quite natural that many members feel compelled to pronounce themselves quickly on some of the very complicated issues involved.

At the same time, the Security Council does have very definite responsibilities which we must always keep clearly in mind. Our obligation is first and foremost to contribute to a peaceful resolution of disputes. Thus in considering what action we should take, we should ask ourselves precisely what it is that we are trying to achieve. What we clearly should not be seeking are pronouncements which serve only propaganda purposes or are without practical effect or which because of their nature would serve to inflame an already aggravated situation.

For example, one suggestion proposed in informal consultations is to have the Council demand that Greece remove its officers in the Cypriot National Guard. At this point I merely suggest that if such a proposal is pursued, members of the Council should carefully weigh the implications. Would it perhaps lead to an even more unstable situation? What would be the prospects of compliance with such an appeal? I raise these questions without foreshadowing or prejudicing my government's ultimate position on this matter.

And lest there be any misunderstanding about the general attitude of the United States, my government has always opposed intervention in the internal affairs of one country by another, and to the extent that this may be the case in Cyprus, I repeat we deplore it. We believe that this Council is unanimous in its view that the Cyprus crisis demands a peaceful and constitutional solution. But what we need to search for, of course, before we can pronounce wisely, is the best way to achieve this result.

In our view, it can only be accomplished through discussions among the parties who are themselves directly involved. These discussions are already underway. Intensive consultations have been taking place in London between the British and Turkish Governments and a representative of my own government. Other consultations are taking place urgently in the area.

Under these circumstances, the United States considers it to be a serious error to rush to judgment on an issue of this gravity. We have an obligation to peace, to statesmanship, to allow enough time for a peaceful resolution of this crisis, no matter how difficult or insurmountable the deadlock may seem.

My government has had some experience in bridging differences which have defied solution in this part of the world. Let us not at this stage permit over-hasty actions in another crisis in this important region complicate and delay efforts and processes outside this chamber. Together, we can achieve what neither can achieve alone. Let us give peace a chance.

AMBASSADOR SCALI, JULY 20

First Statement

[USUN press release 92 dated July 20]

We convene here today in the wake of open military action in the eastern Mediterranean. To our deep regret, Turkish troops have landed on Cyprus. This Council, all too familiar with the antagonisms which have shaped Greek-Turkish relations on Cyprus, needs no reminder of what the Turkish landing forebodes for the stability of the island and what a serious threat is posed for peace in the area. Regrettably the process of diplomacy was not given a chance to run its course. The people of Cyprus are the tragic losers, once more overtaken by events sadly beyond their capability to control. Indeed, Mr. President, we are all losers as international peace hangs most precariously and dramatically in the balance.

My government deplores the pressures and interventions which contributed to the Turkish action on Cyprus and for which Greece must bear a heavy share of the responsibility. However, this invasion in no way serves the hopes for peace of the Turkish community on Cyprus or, indeed, the cause of peace in the world. Neither can we be convinced that foreign military intervention in Cyprus, from whatever quarter and by whatever means, has at any time been justifiable.

We oppose any intervention in the internal affairs of a member state of these United Nations.

My government has worked untiringly these past days in an attempt to forestall the escalation toward intervention in the eastern Mediterranean. Tragically, with the Turkish intervention last night, another step has been taken toward exactly that which we have attempted to forestall.

Turkey is and will remain an ally of the United States; Greece is and will remain an ally of the United States.

It is in the interest of the people of Greece and the people of Turkey to insure that Greece remains the ally of Turkey. As friends for a generation, both peoples have made giant strides; as enemies, they stand to lose all.

It is in the interest of the people of Cyprus as well as those of Greece and Turkey and all members of this Council that Cyprus not become a Mediterranean battleground.

The United States will continue to work with its friends toward this goal. We urge the Governments of Greece and Turkey to display to the members of this Council the maximum spirit of restraint and compromise in the interest of peace.

We believe that with good will, common sense, and extraordinary statesmanship by all concerned, it is still not too late to avert major tragedy.

We appreciate that all members of the Security Council have joined in calling for an immediate cease-fire. We owe the embattled people of Cyprus no less.

All the members of this Council have wisely joined with us in a request to the Governments of Greece and Turkey to accept immediately the United Kingdom proposal for negotiations among the guarantor powers. We believe that at this time the Security Council can make no greater contribution to the cause of peace and constitutional government in Cyprus.

Second Statement

[USUN press release 93 dated July 20]

Again the Representative of the Soviet Union has peeked into some mysterious corner and discovered that it is really NATO, the North Atlantic Pact, which is instigating the tragic developments on Cyprus. It seems to be a curious recurring nightmare, a sort of James Bond-ish twist of the real facts.

The NATO allies who have spoken up at this Council table have deplored all violations of the independence, the sovereignty, and the territorial integrity of the Republic of Cyprus.

Along with the United Kingdom and France, we have sought to promote and encourage negotiations in London for the purpose of restoring peace and the return of constitutional government to the island of Cyprus. If this is plotting, I submit to you perhaps the world needs more of it.

AMBASSADOR BENNETT, JULY 22

[USUN press release 94 dated July 22]

It is indeed high time that the cease-fire take effect. My government, as is well known, has taken a very active part in trying to supplement the work of this Council and to arrange a cease-fire, with very active diplomacy in the capitals concerned.

All parties in the fighting, certainly the two governments away from Cyprus, have publicly accepted the cease-fire. Now, the firing did not immediately cease at 10 o'clock. I believe that is fairly usual in such circumstances. There are many technical complications. But I would call on the parties to give their best efforts, and I would call on the population of Cyprus similarly. To the best of our most recent information, the two armed forces involved, Greece and Turkey, have begun to observe the cease-fire. There is still communal fighting going on. That may be the most difficult to stop. But I would hope that we can, before this day is over, have a genuine cease-fire.

Let the killing cease! It seems to me that is our priority and primary purpose and objective at this time. And then let us go forward with the negotiations, as our British colleague has described them, negotiations which hold such tremendous importance for the future, if we are going to have some resolution of this age-old problem and allow the decent people of Cyprus, whatever their historical or ethnic origin, to have a life of their own and to live in peace in their own way.

The Secretary General has described to us the extreme tests which are being imposed on UNFICYP [United Nations Peace-keeping Force in Cyprus]. My government has always supported UNFICYP. It continues to do so, and if more men are needed there, as circumstances would seem to dictate, then we would support what the Secretary General has outlined as the means of supplementing the present force.

And so, Mr. President, despite the tragedy through which we have been living—the people of Cyprus living it most intensely of all—this past week, I would agree with our British colleague that this is a time for looking forward. Let us bind up the wounds of war. Let us try to look at this in an objective way to give to each side of this communal situation its own right to exist. We can look forward to an independent and single Cyprus. Let us go forward toward a better fate for Cyprus.

AMBASSADOR BENNETT, JULY 23

[USUN press release 95 dated July 23]

I think that little needs to be said here. The facts as we know them and as we have just heard them from the Secretary General speak for themselves, and they are somber enough for all of us. The cease-fire in Cyprus agreed to yesterday by all the parties is not being observed. The guns are still firing; the innocent are still dying.

The resolution which this Council has just adopted, as the resolution we adopted on the 20th, was unanimously adopted. The new resolution is short and to the point. In this resolution we demand that the parties, all the parties, comply immediately with the cease-fire provisions of Resolution 353 and cease the hostilities in Cyprus, hostilities which have brought suffering and death to countless innocent people and which so clearly threaten international peace and security.

The United States has joined in supporting the resolution adopted by this Council because of our determination that the cease-fire ordered by the Council on July 20 should be made fully effective at the earliest possible moment. My government believes that the governments and peoples of Cyprus, Greece, and Turkey, as well as all the rest of us, want an end to the fighting and that they want it now.

Nothing is more difficult, Mr. President, nothing requires greater political leadership and courage, than to stop hostilities once they have started. I call on the parties to exercise that leadership and that courage now. I call on the parties to stop the blood-letting and turn to the negotiating table. The cease-fire has to be the first step toward peace. It must be the basis for other efforts toward conciliation and for other developments which can lead on to a brighter future for the people of Cyprus.

STATEMENT BY AMBASSADOR BENNETT

[USUN press release 97 dated July 31]

The United States is deeply gratified by the agreement reached in Geneva among the Foreign Ministers of Greece, Turkey, and the United Kingdom. In that connection, Mr. President, I should like to read a statement issued yesterday by the White House in Washington:

"The United States welcomes the announcement in Geneva of the agreement reached by the Foreign Ministers of the United Kingdom, Greece, and Turkey. We consider this an important step toward the restoration of peace and stability in Cyprus.

We commend the intensive and patient efforts of the three governments concerned which brought about this achievement. In particular, we wish to pay tribute to the skill and persistence of Mr. Callaghan, the Minister of State of Great Britain, who, as leader of the conference, deserves great credit for its success, and to the Foreign Ministers of Greece and Turkey."

We believe this agreement justifies the wisdom of this Council in adopting Resolution 353 and thereafter in supporting the intensive efforts at Geneva to negotiate the serious issues involved in this Cyprus crisis.

I want to reiterate the view of my government that we consider this agreement an important step toward the restoration of peace and stability in Cyprus.

We particularly welcome the recognition by the three Foreign Ministers of the "importance of setting in train, as a matter of urgency, measures to adjust and regularize within a reasonable period of time the situation in the Republic of Cyprus on a lasting basis," having regard to the international agreements of 1960 and Resolution 353 of the Security Council. My government wants to see strict maintenance of the cease-fire in the area and the prompt implementation of other portions of the agreement signed in Geneva. My government very much hopes that this agreement foreshadows a quick return to more normal conditions in Cyprus, conditions which will bring to all the people of Cyprus a return to constitutional government and a new measure of political stability and general well-being.

We note that the United Nations Peace-keeping Force in Cyprus is asked to undertake certain responsibilities under the terms of the agreement of July 30. UNFICYP has been on duty now for more than 10 years. And we may recall that Security Council Resolution 186 of March 4, 1964, recommended in paragraph 5 "that the function of the Force should be, in the interest of preserving international peace and security, to use its best efforts to prevent a recurrence of fighting and, as necessary, to contribute to the maintenance and restoration of law and order and a return to normal conditions." We consequently believe it appropriate to urge the Secretary General to take immediately any necessary steps to this end. Consistent with this view, my delegation supports the resolution before the Council requesting the Secretary General to take appropriate action, and we urge its approval without delay.

Mr. President, an important first step has been taken toward the normalization of conditions in Cyprus, and it points the way toward the full implementation of Security Council Resolution 353 of July 20. We believe it is now the obligation of this Council to maintain and encourage the momentum toward peace which has now been generated. We strongly urge members of this Council to support the efforts of the parties and to place no doctrinal or procedural barriers in their way. Our individual and collective support for this Geneva agreement and its continuing implementation will be our most important contribution to the maintenance of international peace and security in the area.

Mr. President [Yakov A. Malik]: I salute you as you return refreshed and relaxed from the Soviet Union in time to assume the Presidency of the Security Council. I express the hope that with your broad experience we can all join together in this month to help promote the peace. I wish to pay particular tribute to the skill and the wisdom with which Ambassador [Jovier] Perez de Cuellar has guided our deliberations in this past rather difficult month. This Council has seen many distinguished Presidents, but I am sure that the performance and the gentle wisdom of the Ambassador of Peru will rank among the very highest.

I am glad that we have done today what we should have done yesterday.

As Ambassador Bennett told this Council last night, the U.S. delegation believes it entirely appropriate to urge the Secretary General to take immediately any steps necessary to fulfill the recommendation in paragraph 5 of Security Council Resolution 186 of March 4, 1964. It reads as follows: "that the function of the Force should be, in the interest of preserving international peace and security, to use its best efforts to prevent a recurrence of fighting and, as necessary, to contribute to the maintenance and restoration of law and order and a return to normal conditions."

Mr. President, in voting the two previous resolutions which this Council has considered in the past few days, some important first steps already have been taken to normalize conditions on Cyprus. In approving today's resolution, we can speed up the full implementation of Security Council Resolution 353 of July 20. The Council has now acted to maintain and to encourage the momentum toward peace which has been generated. We are confident that all parties involved in the complex Cyprus situation will do their utmost to keep the peace, to maintain the cease-fire without which prospects for negotiation toward a just and durable settlement would remain dim.

As we have done throughout these debates, we urge all members of this Council to support the efforts of the parties and to place no barriers of doctrine or procedure in their way. Our individual and collective support for the resolutions of the Security Council and the Geneva declaration—a roadmap for peace—will be a most important contribution to the maintenance of international peace and security in the area.

Mr. President, like the majority of the Council, my delegation was disappointed and concerned when it proved impossible yesterday to take prompt action of the kind needed to help make the cease-fire effective and thus to enhance the prospects for peace. We are concerned that delay offered opportunity for further violence. Today we have acted, and I believe we can congratulate ourselves that the Security Council has again acted as it should in a moment of crisis.

RESUMPTION OF CYPRUS NEGOTIATIONS URGED IN U.N. SECURITY COUNCIL

My delegation deeply regrets that almost a month after the approval of Security Council Resolution 353, we have found it necesary to meet once again in this hall to consider new steps to end violence on the island of Cyprus. We regret this all the more because this return of violence was so unnecessary. Promising negotiations had been going forward in Geneva pursuant to Resolution 353 and in keeping with the Charter of the United Nations and treaties of guarantee establishing the state of Cyprus. But, unhappily, in the absence of a conciliatory spirit at the conference table, these negotiations have been interrupted and the guns of war are speaking again.

The United States, Mr. President, is convinced that only through such negotiations can a settlement emerge which will restore constitutional government to Cyprus and peace and stability in the eastern Mediterranean. As this Council is aware, the United States has lent its total support to this process. My government did this because of its close relations with its allies Greece and Turkey, because of its commitment to the independence and territorial integrity of Cyprus, because of its concern for the welfare of the Cypriot people of both communities, and also, but not least, because of its overriding concern for peace in the area.

We have given our full support to the valiant and tireless efforts of the United Kingdom, a guarantor power under the London-Zurich agreement, to bring about a measure of common understanding at Geneva which would point the way toward a new constitutional arrangement in Cyprus which takes into account the new realities. In this role we have been in constant touch with all of the parties to do whatever we could to encourage the negotiating process.

The United States has taken heart from the restoration of constitutional government in Greece so ably led by Prime Minister Karamanlis. The Greek Government has pursued with diligence the search for arrangements to restore constitutional government in Cyprus. As a guarantor power, Greece has legitimate interests which must be fully recognized.

We also pay tribute to the people of Cyprus of both communities, who have endured many hardships in the past month. The Acting President of Cyprus, Mr. Clerides, and the Turkish Vice President, Mr. Denktash, have both made major contributions in this complicated process of negotiation.

Turkey also has legitimate interests which must be fully recognized. My government made clear yesterday in a public statement its view that the position of the Turkish community on Cyprus requires considerable improvement and protection as well as a greater degree of autonomy [1]

My government, Mr. President, considers that it is the duty of this Council to do everything in keeping with Resolution 353 to aid in bringing the parties back to the negotiating table. It is only at that table that a consensus can emerge leading to a settlement which will be satisfactory to all the parties and which will bring peace and stability once again to this area.

The duty of this Council tonight is simply this : We must call for an immediate end to the fighting, and we must call for the earliest resumption of negotiations. My government pledges that it will continue its own efforts toward the end that the voice of reason will again be heard and the voice of the cannons once more stilled.

Statement of August 15

[USUN press release 107 dated Aug. 15]

It is with a sense of deep appreciation to those who seek to keep the peace on behalf of the United Nations that we have voted for this resolution [359] tonight, which was sponsored by five member countries. It is also with a sense of grief, however, because of the tragic news that three Austrian members of UNFICYP [United Nations Peacekeeping Force in Cyprus] have been killed while carrying out their duties on Cyprus. Our government extends its profound condolences to the Austrian Government and to the families of these brave men who have sacrificed their lives for the peace which is the goal of us all.

We further note with a feeling of deepest sorrow that an additional number of UNFICYP troops have been wounded in the fighting, 27 by the latest count of the Secretariat. These men are international heroes. They deserve not only our gratitude but our support so that their task can be facilitated, not hampered, as they carry out their tasks far from home, like other United Nations peacekeepers in the Middle East and in other areas. We, the representatives of our governments, who sit here in the safety of this chamber, must remember them because, regardless of nationality, they are our sons. We must make sure that they and their successors patrolling distant battlefields have the capacity and the mandate to carry out their dangerous assignments without requiring of them that they give up their lives.

---

[1] In a news briefing on Aug. 13, Robert Anderson, Special Assistant to the Secretary of State for Press Relations, said :
"The U.S. position is as follows :
"We recognize the position of the Turkish community on Cyprus requires considerable improvement and protection. We have supported a greater degree of autonomy for them.
"The parties are negotiating on one or more Turkish autonomous areas. The avenues of diplomacy have not been exhausted. And therefore the United States would consider a resort to military action unjustified.
"We have made this clear to all parties."

Statement of August 16

[USUN press release 108 dated Aug. 16]

We can all take satisfaction from the Secretary General's report that at long last the guns are stilled on Cyprus. The cease-fire seems finally to be in effect. Regrettably, the U.N. peace forces, UNFICYP, have suffered further casualties. We extend our deepest sympthy to the Danish Government and to the bereaved families of these soldiers of peace who have given their lives selflessly in the service of others.

Mr. Prsident, with the cease-fire now taking hold, we must also turn our attention to forging the peace, to establishing conditions under which the good people of Cyprus may live undisturbed and walk in paths of their own choosing.

My delegation hopes that, on reflection, all parties to the Cyprus dispute will decide it is in their own national interests to move on to Geneva without delay to resume the peace negotiations suspended earlier this week.

The success of these talks, under the chairmanship of the distinguished British Foreign Secretary, involves the peace of the eastern Mediterranean. The world is watching. The participants have an obligation to mankind to enter into negotiations in a spirit of conciliation and fairminded compromise to reach an understanding which will renew and indeed reinforce the historic friendship of the peoples of the area.

U.S. Calls for International Action To Assist Refugees in Cyprus

STATEMENT BY AMBASSADOR SCALI

[USUN press release 111 dated Aug. 30.]

First I would like to express to the Secretary General the thanks of my delegation and my government for his recent visits to Cyprus, Greece, and Turkey to discuss the situation on that island. In particular, we commend him for his statesmanlike role in bringing about a meeting on humanitarian questions in which Acting President Clerides, Vice President Denktash, and the [U.N.] High Commissioner for Refugees have participated. The value of such talks between the leaders of the Greek Cypriot and Turkish Cypriot communities cannot be overemphasized.

For the sake of all of the people of Cyprus, we urge the international community to make every effort to help create a negotiating climate which can produce constructive solutions, particularly of humanitarian questions.

Mr. President, we have heard at length today from one delegate of a special formula for peace which his government is going to sell. To persuade others to accept it, we have heard some fairy tales from another era—the bold charges of mysterious machinations by unidentified members of NATO. Mr. President, these stories might amuse or titillate the readers of summertime fiction on the beaches of the Crimea, but such fairy tales will not help us solve the real problems of Cyprus. I think in this regard that we can all agree that an absolute prerequisite for solving the critical humanitarian problems on Cyprus is strict compliance with the cease-fire as called for in previous Security Council resolutions.

The United States shares the concern of the Secretary General and the parties for the plight of the refugees from both communities who have been made homeless. We commend the International Committee of the Red Cross and the U.N. High Commissioner for Refugees, as well as other humanitarian organizations, for their outstanding efforts to give emergency assistance particularly to those whose lives have been dislocated. We urge all of the parties concerned to adhere scrupulously to international agreements concerning the human rights of civilians during times of conflict.

Upon the recommendation of the late American Ambassador to Cyprus, Rodger Davies, the United States has responded to appeals from the International Committee of the Red Cross for emergency humanitarian assistance. We have donated $3.1 million as of now. This sum includes a cash contribution of $725,000 plus airlifts of relief supplies, and emergency equipment such as tents, blankets, and other provisions. The United States stands ready to provide additional assistance based on recommendations from the International Red Cross and the U.N. High Commissioner for Refugees. It is our view that such assistance goes to the heart of the issues before the Council today. We therefore appeal to the international community to join with us in responding to this humanitarian effort.

The United Nations Peace-keeping Force in Cyprus (UNFICYP) has performed courageously in assisting the parties and international relief agencies in carrying out their crucial humanitarian responsibilities. The United States underscores its support for Security Council Resolution 359, which demands that all parties cooperate with UNFICYP in carrying out all of its tasks, "including humanitarian functions, in all areas of Cyprus and in regard to all sections of the population."

The effort to render assistance to the people of Cyprus is a necessary emergency measure. However, the imperative and urgent need is to resume negotiations. A negotiated settlement of the Cyprus dispute offers the best hope for all of the people on the island to live in peace and security.

The U.S. delegation supports the resolution before this Council and commends the spirit of compromise with which various points of view converged to produce it. Perhaps each delegation—and I would not exclude my own—would have preferred some variations in the text. Nonetheless, in our view, passage of this resolution can make positive contributions to easing the plight of refugees and should pave the way for further efforts to get broader negotiations under way again.

In closing, Mr. President, may I say a simple but no less heartfelt "thank you" to those who have spoken words of condolence on the memory of Ambassador Rodger Davies.

SECRETARY OF STATE KISSINGER'S COMMENT ON CYPRUS IN HIS ADDRESS BEFORE THE 29TH SESSION OF THE UNITED NATIONS GENERAL ASSEMBLY, NEW YORK, SEP-*tember* 23, 1974 [excerpt from his address printed below]

CYPRUS

The tormented island of Cyprus is another area where peace requires a spirit of compromise, accommodation, and justice. The United States is convinced that the sovereignty, political independence, and territorial integrity of Cyprus must be maintained. It will be up to the parties to decide on the form of government they believe best suited to the particular conditions of Cyprus. They must reach accommodation on the areas to be administered by the Greek and Turkish Cypriot communities as well as on the conditions under which refugees can return to their homes and reside in safety. Finally, no lasting peace is possible unless provisions are agreed upon which will lead to the timely and phased reduction of armed forces and armament and other war material.

The United States is prepared to play an even more active role than in the past in helping the parties find a solution to the centuries-old problem of Cyprus. We will do all we can, but it is those most directly concerned whose effort is most crucial. Third parties should not be asked to produce miraculous outcomes not anchored in reality, Third parties *can* encourage those directly involved to perceive their broader interests; they can assist in the search for elements of agreement by interpreting each side's views and motives to the other. But no mediator can succeed unless the parties genuinely want mediation and are ready to make the difficult decisions needed for a settlement.

The United States is already making a major contribution to help relieve the human suffering of the people of Cyprus. We urge the international community to continue and, if possible, to increase its own humanitarian relief effort.

APPENDIX V

United Nations Security Council Resolutions on Cyprus, 1974

(Security Council Resolutions of 1974, Nos. 353, 354, 355, 357, 358, 359, 360, and 361)

RESOLUTION 353, JULY 20

The Security Council, having considered the report of the Secretary-General at its 1779th meeting about the recent developments in Cyprus,

Having heard the statement made by the President of the Republic of Cyprus and the statements by the representatives of Cyprus, Turkey, Greece and other member countries,

Having considered at its present meeting further developments in the island,

Deeply deploring the outbreak of violence and continuing bloodshed,

Gravely concerned about the situation which led to a serious threat to international peace and security, and which created a most explosive situation in the whole Eastern Mediterranean area,

Equally concerned about the necessity to restore the constitutional structure of the Republic of Cyprus, established and guaranteed by international agreements,

Recalling Security Council resolution 186 (1964) of 4 March 1964 and subsequent resolutions of the Security Council on this matter,

Conscious of its primary responsibility for the maintenance of international peace and security in accordance with Article 24 of the Charter of the United Nations,

1. Calls upon all States to respect the sovereignty, independence and territorial integrity of Cyprus;

2. Calls upon all parties to the present fighting as a first step to cease all firing and requests all States to exercise the utmost restraint and to refrain from any action which might further aggravate the situation;

3. Demands an immediate end of foreign military intervention in the Republic of Cyprus that is in contravention of operative paragraph 1;

4. Requests the withdrawal without delay from the Republic of Cyprus of foreign military personnel present otherwise than under the authority of international agreements including those whose withdrawal was requested by the President of the Republic of Cyprus, Archbishop Makarios, in his letter of 2 July 1974;

5. Calls on Greece, Turkey and the United Kingdom of Great Britain and Northern Ireland to enter into negotiations without delay for the restoration of peace in the area and constitutional government in Cyprus and to keep the Secretary-General informed;

6. Calls on all parties to co-operate fully with UNFICYP to enable it to carry out its mandate;

7. Decides to keep the situation under constant review and asks the Secretary-General to report as appropriate with a view to adopting further measures in order to ensure that peaceful conditions are restored as soon as possible.

RESOLUTION 354, JULY 23

The Security Council, reaffirming the provisions of its resolution 353 (1974) of 20 July 1974,

Demands that all parties to the present fighting comply immediately with paragraph 2 of Security Council resolution 353 (1974) calling for an immediate cessation of all firing in the area and requesting all States to exercise the utmost restraint and to refrain from any action which might further aggravate the situation.

TEXT OF RESOLUTION 355 [1]

The Security Council, recalling its resolutions 186 (1964) of 4 March 1964, 353 (1974) of 20 July 1974 and 354 (1974) of 23 July 1974,

Noting that all States have declared their respect for the sovereignty, independence and territorial integrity of Cyprus,

Taking note of the Secretary-General's statement made at the 1788th meeting of the Security Council,

Requests the Secretary-General to take appropriate action in the light of his statement and to present a full report to the Council, taking into account that the cease-fire will be the first step in the full implementation of Security Council resolution 353 (1974).

STATEMENT BY SECRETARY GENERAL WALDHEIM

As members of the Council are aware, at 5 p.m. New York time on July 30, that is, yesterday, I received a communication from Mr. Callaghan, the Secretary of State for Foreign and Commonwealth Affairs of the United Kingdom, on behalf of the three Foreign Ministers who had been negotiating in Geneva, communicating to me the text of the declaration and statement which have been agreed to by the Foreign Ministers of Greece, Turkey, and the United Kingdom. The texts of the declaration and statement have been circulated as an official document (S/11398). I am sure the members of the Council will wish to give their urgent consideration to that document. I hope that the agreement reached in Geneva on the cease-fire will be a first step to the full implementation of Security Council Resolution 353 (1974).

Members of the Council will note that the declaration invisages certain tasks for UNFICYP. In particular, the declaration calls for action in consultation with UNFICYP to determine the size and character of the security zone, which will be entered by no forces other than those of UNFICYP. Other important functions are also foreseen for UNFICYP.

I wish to inform the Council that I have requested my Special Representative and the Force Commander of UNFICYP to give me a preliminary assessment of the practical implications of the declaration as far as UNFICYP is concerned. I shall report to the Council on the practical consequences involved.

The total strength of UNFICYP as of July 31 is 3,484 men. That total comprises 3,332 military personnel and 152 civilian police. By August 7 the total strength of UNFICYP will, it is estimated, be 4,238 men. When all the reinforcements currently pledged have arrived—by about August 12—the total strength of UNFICYP will be approximately 4,443.

I take this opportunity to draw the attention of members of the Council to the question of the nature of UNFICYP's continued presence in the Turkish area of control, which I mentioned to the Council on July 29 and which needs clarification. As you know, UNFICYP has been playing, and should continue to play, a most useful humanitarian role in all parts of the island of Cyprus in assisting the civilian population—Turkish and Greek Cypriots alike—who have been afflicted by the recent hostilities. This matter is now under discussion by UNFICYP with the Turkish Military Command in Cyprus. I am confident that these discussions will enable UNFICYP to continue to perform its role in all parts of the island with the full agreement of all the parties concerned.

I think that is as much as I should say at this stage. I am sure that the members of the Council are fully aware of the complexity of the situation. I do not have to say that I and my colleagues in the Secretariat, both here and in Cyprus, are prepared fully to cooperate with the parties in order to restore peaceful conditions in the island, so that negotiations can continue and Security Council Resolution 353 (1974) can be fully implemented.

RESOLUTION 357, AUGUST 14 [2]

The Security Council, recalling its resolutions 353 (1974) of 20 July 1974, 354 (1974) of 23 July 1974, and 355 (1974) of 1 August 1974.

Deeply deploring the resumption of fighting in Cyprus contrary to the provisions of its resolution 353 (1974),

---

[1] U.N. doc. S/RES/355 (1974) ; adopted by the Council on Aug. 1 by a vote of 12 (U.S.) to 0, with 2 abstentions (Byelorussian SSR, USSR) and with the People's Republic of China not participating in the vote.

[2] Adopted by the Council unanimously on Aug. 14.

1. Reaffirms its resolution 353 (1974) in all its provisions and calls upon the parties concerned to implement those provisions without delay;

2. Demands that all parties to the present fighting cease all firing and military action forthwith;

3. Calls for the resumption of negotiations without delay for the restoration of peace in the area and constitutional government in Cyprus in accordance with resolution 353 (1974);

4. Decides to remain seized of the situation and on instant call to meet as necessary to consider what more effective measures may be required if the cease-fire is not respected.

RESOLUTION 358, AUGUST 15 [3]

The Security Council, deeply concerned about the continuation of violence and bloodshed in Cyprus,

Deeply deploring the non-compliance with its resolution 357 (1974),

1. Recalls its resolutions 353 (1974), 354 (1974), 355 (1974) and 357 (1974);

2. Insists on the full implementation of the above resolutions by all parties with the immediate and strict observance of the cease-fire.

RESOLUTION 359, AUGUST 15 [4]

The Security Council, noting with concern from the Secretary-General's reports on developments in Cyprus, in particular S/11353/Add.24 and 25, that casualties are increasing among the personnel of the United Nation's Peace-keeping Force in Cyprus as a direct result of the military action which is still continuing in Cyprus,

Recalling that the United Nations Peace-keeping Force in Cyprus was stationed in Cyprus with the full consent of the Governments of Cyprus, Turkey and Greece,

Bearing in mind that the Secretary-General was requested by the Security Council in resolution 355 (1974) of 1 August 1974 to take appropriate action in the light of his statement made at the 1788th meeting of the Council in which he dealt with the role, functions and strength of the United Nations Peace-keeping Force in Cyprus and related issues arising out of the most recent political developments in respect of Cyprus.

1. Deeply deplores the fact that members of the United Nations Peace-keeping Force in Cyprus have been killed and wounded;

2. Demands that all parties concerned fully respect the international status of the United Nations Peace-keeping Force in Cyprus and refrain from any action which might endanger the lives and safety of its members;

3. Urges the parties concerned to demonstrate in a firm, clear and unequivocal manner, their willingness to fulfil the commitments they have entered into in this regard;

4. Demands further that all parties co-operate with the United Nations Peace-keeping Force in Cyprus in carrying out its tasks, including humanitarian functions, in all areas of Cyprus and in regard to all sections of the population on Cyprus;

5. Emphasizes the fundamental principle that the status and safety of the members of the United Nations Peace-keeping Force in Cyprus, and for that matter of any United Nations peace-keeping force, must be respected by the parties under all circumstances.

RESOLUTION 360, AUGUST 16 [5]

The Security Council, recalling its resolutions 353 (1974), 354 (1974), 355 (1974), 357 (1974) and 358 (1974).

Noting that all States have declared their respect for the sovereignty, independence and territorial integrity of the Republic of Cyprus,

Gravely concerned at the deterioration of the situation in Cyprus, resulting from the further military operations, which constituted a most serious threat to peace and security in the Eastern Mediterranean area.

[3] Adopted by the Council unanimously on Aug. 15.
[4] Adopted by the Council on Aug. 15 by a vote of 14 (U.S.) to 0, with the People's Republic of China not participating in the vote.
[5] Adopted by the Council on Aug. 16 by a vote of 11 (U.S.) to 0, with 3 abstentions (Byelorussian S.S.R., Iraq, U.S.S.R.), with the People's Republic of China not participating in the vote.

1. Records its formal disapproval of the unilateral military actions undertaken against the Republic of Cyprus;

2. Urges the parties to comply with all the provisions of previous resolutions of the Security Council, including those concerning the withdrawal without delay from the Republic of Cyprus of foreign military personnel present otherwise than under the authority of international agreements;

3. Urges the parties to resume without delay, in an atmosphere of constructive co-operation, the negotiations called for in resolution 353 (1974) whose outcome should not be impeded or prejudged by the acquisition of advantages resulting from military operations;

4. Requests the Secretary-General to report to it as necessary with a view to the possible adoption of further measures designed to promote the restoration of peaceful conditions;

5. Decides to remain permanently seized of the question and to meet at any time to consider measures which may be required in the light of the developing situation.

RESOLUTION 361 (1974)

Adopted by the Security Council at its 1795th meeting, on August 30, 1974

The Security Council, conscious of its special responsibilities under the United Nations Charter,

Recalling its resolutions 186 (1964) 353 (1974), 354 (1974), 355 (1974), 357 (1974), 358 (1974), 359 (1974) and 360 (1974),

Noting that a large number of people on the island have been displaced, and are in dire need of humanitarian assistance,

Mindful of the fact that it is one of the foremost purposes of the United Nations to lend humanitarian assistance in situations such as the one currently prevailing in Cyprus,

Noting also that the United Nations High Commissioner for Refugees has already been appointed as Co-ordinator of United Nations Humanitarian Assistance for Cyprus with the task of co-ordinating relief assistance to be provided by United Nations programmes and agencies and from other sources,

Having considered the report of the Secretary-General contained in document S/11473,

1. Expresses its appreciation to the Secretary-General for the part he has played in bringing about talks between the leaders of the two communities in Cyprus;

2. Warmly welcomes this development and calls upon those concerned in them to pursue the talks actively with the help of the Secretary-General and in the interests of the Cypriot people as a whole;

3. Calls upon all parties to do everything in their power to alleviate human suffering, to ensure the respect of fundamental human rights for every person and to refrain from all action likely to aggravate the situation;

4. Expresses its grave concern at the plight of the refugees and other persons displaced as a result of the situation in Cyprus and urges the parties concerned, in conjunction with the Secretary-General, to search for peaceful solutions of the problems of refugees, and take appropriate measures to provide for their relief and welfare and to permit persons who wish to do so to return to their homes in safety;

5. Requests the Secretary-General to submit at the earliest possible opportunity a full report on the situation of the refugees and other persons referred to in paragraph 4 of this resolution and decides to keep that situation under constant review;

6. Further requests the Secretary-General to continue to provide emergency United Nations humanitarian assistance to all parts of the population of the island in need of such assistance;

7. Calls upon all parties, as a demonstration of good faith, to take, both individually and in co-operation with each other, all steps which may promote comprehensive and successful negotiations;

8. Reiterates its call to all parties to co-operate fully with UNIFCYP in carrying out its task;

9. Expresses the conviction that the speedy implementation of the provisions of this resolution will assist the achievement of a satisfactory settlement in Cyprus.

APPENDIX VI

REPORTS OF THE SECRETARY-GENERAL ON DEVELOPMENTS IN CYPRUS AND THE FIRST ASSESSMENT OF THE U.N. HIGH COMMISSIONER FOR REFUGEES

REPORT OF THE SECRETARY-GENERAL ON DEVELOPMENTS IN CYPRUS

Since I reported to the Council on 20 July on developments in Cyprus, I have continued to receive regular reports from my Special Representative in Cyprus and from the Force Commander of the United Nations Peace-keeping Force in Cyprus (UNFICYP) on developments in the Island. The following information is based on three reports describing the situation at 0500, 0900 and 1100 hours local time on 21 July.

2. The fighting on the Island, which had died down during the night, grew in intensity during the morning of 21 July and was accompanied by air attacks by high-performance Turkish aircraft. There were reports of atrocities in scattered locations throughout the Island. Steps were being taken to evacuate foreign civilians to the British Sovereign Base areas. According to a later report, UNFICYP assisted the United Kingdom and United States authorities in the implementation of the scheme, which applied to all foreign nationals. More than 4,000 persons, including the persons trapped in the Ledra Palace Hotel, were collected, with no casualties reported, from various localities in Nicosia between 1200 and 1600 for dispatch to the British Sovereign Base area of Dhekelia.

3. In the Nicosia district, a truce arranged along the Green Line went into effect at 0630 hours local time, but at 1100 hours it was reported that fighting had broken out again along the Green Line. The United Nations has retained control of the Ledra Palace Hotel area, where 386 civilians remained. Despite this, the hotel came under heavy fire from mortars. The Canadian contingent is withdrawing its personnel to Camp Cronberg. A further Canadian soldier was reported wounded, bringing the total to seven.

4. There have been heavy air attacks by Turkish planes with bombs and rockets against the International Airport area. At 1010 hours local time, rounds were falling in the vicinity of UNFICYP headquarters and camp and 60 Turkish helicopters were overflying the airport area.

5. In the Kyrenia district, heavy fighting which occurred during the evening of 20/21 July for control of Kyrenia pass was reported to have died down by the the next morning. On 21 July, National Guard troops were reported retreating towards Bellapais in United Nations landrovers with United Nations flags, said to have been captured from a Finnish patrol. The 12 members of the patrol are believed to be in National Guard hands. The National Guard garrison at Bellapais was attacked by aircraft and napalm was reported to have been used. Kyrenia was said to be quiet and believed to be in National Guard hands. During early firing, artillery fire from National Guard hit the United Nations Tjiklos Camp and two United Nations soldiers were wounded. At last reports, the camp and three OPs were still manned.

6. In the Famagusta district, there were reports of sporadic small-arms fire throughout the district and of National Guard artillery fire on the old city and of Turkish aircraft bombing Famagusta, with the use of napalm reported. One United Nations OP was withdrawn.

7. In the Larnaca district the Danish civilian police and outlying UNFICYP posts were withdrawn. Negotiations for a cease-fire broke down at 0335. Heavy fighting began with artillery and mortar fire by the National Guard. UNFICYP tried to reinstate the cease-fire but the National Guard resumed the attack at 0900. In the ensuing heavy fire, National Guard fired mortar bombs in the direction of United Nations Camp Leopold and Turkish Cypriots fired mortars from vicinity of the Camp. At 1030, Turkish Cypriots in Larnaca were reported to have begun surrendering.

8. In the Limassol district, 1100 Turkish Cypriots were reported to be in National Guard hands at 2250 on 20 July. They were to be allowed to return to the Turkish quarter after surrendering their arms. One UNFICYP soldier of the British contingent was accidentally killed while unloading a surrendered Turkish weapon. All British personnel in Limassol were concentrated in the Polemidhia Camp.

9. In the Paphos district, a large number of refugees are being held at St. Patrick's Camp. In Paphos town a cease-fire was reported to be in existence at 0900; and at 1100, all resistance by Turkish Cypriots there appeared to have stopped. UNFICYP was continuing to man three OPs in the district. The National Guard was reported to have attacked Mandria village with mortar fire; fighting continued at 0900.

10. In the Lefka district, the Limnitis enclave was surrounded by the National Guard. Firing with mortars and heavy machine guns was reported at Lefka town at 0445, followed at 0845 by an attack with high-level bombing, rockets and shelling. Sporadic fighting was also reported in Xeros. UNFICYP OPs were being maintained in two outlying locations.

11. UNFICYP received a protest from National Guard headquarters that the Turks were bombing indiscriminately civilian targets including the hospital in Famagusta. They said that if it was not stopped immediately there would be very strong retaliation, which could lead to a lot of bloodshed. According to UNFICYP information the hospital had been bombed but it appears to have been evacuated on 21 July.

12. UNFICYP later reported that they had obtained the agreement of the Turkish Ambassador that if anti-tank guns, artillery and mortars were removed from Nicosia city, the city would not be attacked by the Turkish Air Force. The Commander of the National Guard also agreed and UNFICYP was hopeful that both sides would comply.

13. On the morning of Sunday, 21 July, I issued the following statement:

"The Secretary-General welcomes the decision concerning the Cyprus question taken unanimously by the Security Council on 20 July. He expresses the hope that the authorities concerned will implement this important decision with the least possible delay.

"However, as long as the Council's demand for a cease-fire is not complied with and fighting continues, the situation remains extremely serious.

"The Secretary-General is appealing to all concerned to bring the fighting to an immediate end and to begin forthwith negotiations for a peaceful settlement in line with the resolution of the Security Council.

"The United Nations Peace-keeping Force in Cyprus has been doing all it can, especially in the humanitarian field, and will continue to do its utmost to limit the fighting and to protect the civilian population."

In this connexion, I have addressed appeals to the Prime Ministers of Greece and Turkey.

14. In view of reports reaching me from Cyprus, I have made the following appeal:

"Reports reaching me from Cyprus indicate that the fighting is extremely violent and bitter and that the civilian population in many parts of the Island is living in grave danger, fear and great suffering.

"I appeal most urgently to all the parties involved in the fighting, pending the achievement of a cease-fire, to exercise extreme restraint, and to respect the accepted international rules for the treatment of civilian populations in time of war. I urge them to take every possible measure to avoid actions which may cause further suffering to the civilian population and which can only further embitter the already tragic situations."

I have asked my representatives in Cyprus to make all possible efforts to communicate this appeal to all of the parties concerned.

INTERIM REPORT OF THE SECRETARY-GENERAL PURSUANT TO SECURITY COUNCIL RESOLUTION 355 (1974)

A. INTRODUCTION

1. At the 1788th meeting of the Security Council on 31 July 1974, I drew the attention of the members of the Council to the communication I had received on the previous day from the Secretary of State for Foreign and Commonwealth Affairs of the United Kingdom, on behalf of the three Foreign Ministers who

had been negotiating in Geneva, transmitting the text of the Declaration and statement which had been agreed to by the Foreign Ministers of Greece, Turkey and the United Kingdom (S/11398). I expressed the hope that the agreement reached in Geneva on the cease-fire would be a first step to the full implementation of Security Council resolution 353 (1974). I also referred to the functions which the Declaration envisaged for UNFICYP.

2. On 1 August 1974, the Security Council adopted resolution 355 (1974) in which, taking note of the Secretary-General's statement made at the 1788th meeting, it requested the Secretary-General "to take appropriate action in the light of his statement and to present a full report to the Council, taking into account that the cease-fire will be the first step in the full implementation of Security Council resolution 353 (1974)".

3. This interim report gives an account of the action taken as of 9 August 1974 in pursuance of resolution 355 (1974). A full report will be presented to the Council in due course.

4. Immediately after the adoption of resolution 355 (1974), I instructed my Special Representative in Cyprus and the Commander of UNFICYP to proceed, in co-operation with the parties, with the full implementation of the role of UNFICYP as provided for in Security Council resolution 355 (1974).

5. The Special Representative and the Force Commander have since been in close touch with the parties and have indicated to them that UNFICYP stands ready to carry out all the functions devolving upon it under resolution 355 (1974) of the Security Council. In particular, UNFICYP has repeatedly appealed to the parties to observe the cease-fire called for by the Security Council in its resolutions 353 (1974) and 354 (1974).

B. OBSERVANCE OF THE CEASE-FIRE CALLED FOR BY SECURITY COUNCIL RESOLUTIONS 353 (1974) AND 354 (1974)

6. Since the outbreak of hostilities in Cyprus and especially since the adoption of Security Council resolution 353, in accordance with my instructions, UNFICYP has made every effort to secure an effective cease-fire. In addition, UNFICYP has carried out continuous observation and reporting on the status of the observance of the cease-fire. This has provided the basis for my regular reports to the Security Council on developments in Cyprus (S/11353/Add. . . . series).

7. In general, the fighting diminished substantially and ceased in some areas after the agreement announced on 22 July that Greece and Turkey had agreed on a cease-fire to be implemented at 1600 hours. Since that time, although the cease-fire by and large has been observed by the parties throughout most of the island, intermittent fighting and some forward movement has continued in the area west of Kyrenia, along the coast and on the southern slopes of the Kyrenia mountains. There has also been some movement on the eastern side of the main Turkish enclave, especially in the Bellapais area. Exchanges of fire and minor movements also occurred in the western and eastern outskirts of Nicosia. In the Famagusta harbour area, UNFICYP has had to interpose itself between the Turkish Cypriots and the National Guard.

C. ACTION TAKEN PURSUANT TO SECURITY COUNCIL RESOLUTION 355 (1974)

8. The military representatives of Greece, Turkey and the United Kingdom, together with a representative of UNFICYP, began meeting in Nicosia on 2 August 1974. The communiqués issued by the military representatives have been reproduced in the Secretary-General's further reports on developments in Cyprus (S/11353, Add.13, para. 4; Add.15, para. 5; Add.16, para. 6; Add.17, para. 6; Add. 18, para. 7). On 9 August the military representatives signed the agreement on the demarcation line, which has been submitted to the Foreign Ministers meeting at Geneva.

9. The military representatives have not as yet determined the size of the security zone to be established at the limit of the areas occupied by the Turkish armed forces on 30 July 1974 at 2200 hours Geneva time. Accordingly, the action of UNFICYP in relation to paragraph 3 (a) of the Geneva Declaration has been limited thus far to the participation of a representative of UNFICYP in the deliberations of the military representatives.

10. Concerning the provision of paragraph 3 (b) of the Geneva Declaration which provides for the immediate evacuation of "all the Turkish enclaves occupied by Greek or Greek Cypriot forces", the Special Representative and the Force Commander have reported that on 2 August 1974 Vice-President Denktash ad-

dressed a letter to Acting President Clerides requesting that this evacuation should be carried out. It does not appear that Mr. Clerides has replied to that letter, but it is understood that the question of the implementation of paragraph 3 (b) will be discussed at the negotiations which were resumed in Geneva on 8 August. My Special Representative and the Force Commander have discussed this matter with the authorities on both sides of Nicosia. UNFICYP stands ready to assume its function of protecting the Turkish enclaves as soon as the essential preliminary step, namely, evacuation of the "Greek or Greek Cypriot forces", has been carried out.

11. Pending the evacuation of Greek or Greek Cypriot forces, UNFICYP protective functions in respect of Turkish enclaves have continued. UNFICYP is regularly patrolling all the villages and areas occupied by the National Guard, as reported in my regular reports. Generally, UNFICYP assists the population by ascertaining needs, providing convoys for relief supplies, escorting persons to buy supplies and where possible providing water and medicaments. The able-bodied males from many of these villages have either been removed to prisoner-of-war camps or have been disarmed and released. Those under detention have had their names listed and are regularly visited by UNFICYP and the ICRC to ensure that their treatment is satisfactory.

12. The protective and humanitarian functions described above are also carried out in the "other Turkish enclaves" referred to in paragraph 3(b) of the Geneva Declaration, as well as in mixed villages. Some of the enclaves are surrounded by the National Guard; others have not been affected by the hostilities. Some of the mixed villages have come under National Guard control; others are untouched. UNFICYP visits all these villages regularly and has provided relief convoys in the same way as for the villages referred to in paragraph 11. I shall report further on measures taken regarding UNFICYP security zones and the assumption of security and police functions in mixed villages by UNFICYP in my next report.

D. EXCHANGE OR RELEASE OF DETAINED MILITARY PERSONNEL AND CIVILIANS

13. The International Committee of the Red Cross has informed me that on 3 August 1974 it received a note from the Turkish Government on the subject of the release of civilians and exchange of prisoners-of-war. The note reads as follows:

"1. With a view to implement without delay Article 3, paragraph d of the Geneva Declaration, the Turkish Government is prepared to release regardless of numerical reciprocity Greek Cypriot and Greek civilians who happen to be in the Turkish regions in Cyprus if the interested parties are willing to do the same. The Turkish Government deems it necessary that the parties concerned should also make declaration to the effect that they are ready to release civilians and the International Committee of the Red Cross undertake to carry out its obligations towards both parties concerning these declarations. As can be seen from the above, the Turkish Government attaches priority to the release of civilians.

"2. In conformity with the Geneva Declaration and the Geneva conventions of 1949, after the release of civilians the Turkish Government will be ready with the least possible delay to undertake the exchange of the prisoners-of-war. In order to determine the plan for the exchange, a list of prisoners-of-war in Turkish hands will be duly notified."

A similar communication was passed to UNFICYP on 4 August by the Turkish Embassy. At the Embassy's request, that communication was transmitted to the Greek Cypriot authorities (S/11353/Add.15, para. 11).

14. The ICRC addressed the following reply to the Government of Turkey on 5 August:

"The ICRC has received the text of a declaration, concerning the release and exchange of military and civilian detainees in Cyprus and Turkey, from the Turkish Government. According to information given to the ICRC, the same communication has been addressed to the Governments of Cyprus and Greece.

"The ICRC repeats that it is prepared to assume the tasks envisaged in the Geneva Tripartite Declaration of 30 July regarding the exchange and release of civilian and military detainees. The ICRC proposes the following measures:

"(a) Exchange of data regarding the numbers of, and names of, detained persons;

"(b) The drawing up of a concerted exchange and release plan by the three Governments, or their representatives on the spot, in co-operation with the ICRC;

"(c) In the waiting period before the exchange and release, the ICRC will visit the detainees, and will be given the opportunity to assist them;

"(d) As regards civilian detainees, the establishment of a procedure whereby they may freely choose the place or zone where they wish to be released;

"(e) No detainee should be obliged to return to his habitual place of residence, nor, on the other hand, to leave such habitual place of residence, against his will.

"The ICRC is prepared to co-operate on the humanitarian level to the various exchange and release operations. Should circumstances so require, the ICRC could take part in any transport operations necessary.

"The ICRC calls to mind that the repatriation of prisoners envisaged by the Third Geneva Convention, and the release of civilians envisaged in the Fourth Geneva Convention, are two different operations envisaged in two distinct conventions. Consequently, neither of these operations depends on the accomplishment of the other: the two operations should be carried out simultaneously."

15. On 7 August, Acting President Clerides sent the following communication to representatives of the ICRC in Cyprus:

"In conformity with the provisions of the Geneva cease-fire Agreement, article 3(d):

"1. The Government of Cyprus is prepared to liberate immediately all Turkish civilian detainees in its hands, without regard to number, provided that the other side is prepared to do the same.

"2. The operation should be carried out under the supervision of the International Committee of the Red Cross. This should be done on the basis of detailed nominative lists which should be handed over to the International Committee of the Red Cross forthwith by both sides.

"3. It should be made absolutely clear that all civilian detainees thus liberated shall return with their families to their homes and be given all facilities to do so immediately. Permanent security of life and property should be assured to Greek Cypriots living in Turkish controlled areas to the satisfaction of the Government of Cyprus, as is assured for Turkish Cypriots living outside Turkish controlled areas.

"4. With regard to the prisoners-of-war, the Government of Cyprus is prepared to exchange these under the supervision of the International Committee of the Red Cross according to arrangements to be made after detailed lists shall have been handed over by both sides. The Government of Cyprus is ready to hand over forthwith the lists of prisoners-of-war."

E. METHOD OF OPERATION OF UNFICYP

16. UNFICYP's current operations are based on a framework of static posts, which have been established wherever possible at specially sensitive places, supplemented by frequent mobile patrols, both military and UNCIVPOL, to all parts of districts lying outside the Turkish controlled area. The main purposes of this activity are to generate a feeling of confidence and to obtain information concerning the local situation, not least in order to ascertain those areas where humanitarian and relief measures are required. A special problem exists in Nicosia city, where a close military confrontation exists and UNFICYP is endeavouring to interpose itself to prevent a recurrence of fighting and, in particular, to prevent shooting incidents, of which there continue to be many, from spreading throughout the city. This has required the establishment of a large number of United Nations posts along the area of confrontation and very active patrolling between them.

17. Within the Turkish controlled area, UNFICYP activities are centred on humanitarian and relief measures in Kyrenia and certain surrounding villages, especially Bellapais. These activities include the delivery of food to a considerable number of small isolated groups.

18. In all areas outside the Turkish controlled area UNFICYP is making special efforts to prevent looting and harassment of civilians, especially in the major towns, although UNFICYP resources do not permit complete surveillance over all the areas concerned.

19. A special humanitarian economics branch was set up at UNFICYP Headquarters on 22 July 1974 to deal specifically with problems of this nature. That branch, which is staffed by both military personnel and UNCIVPOL members, has been most active in organizing and co-ordinating a wide range of humanitarian and relief measures for both communities. The branch operates in close

co-operation with the ICRC representatives in Cyprus. At the present time all food relief convoys to all parts of the island are organized by this branch, which also engages in many other humanitarian tasks such as arranging the evacuation to hospital of urgent medical cases, both by United Nations helicopter and by road ambulance.

F. UNFICYP STRENGTH

20. At the 1782d meeting of the Security Council, I explained that the present strength of UNFICYP was obviously not sufficient for it to ensure effectively the maintenance of the cease-fire. I therefore stated my intention, in compliance with Security Council resolution 186 (1964) of 4 March 1964 and as a first step, to ask the contributing countries urgently to reinforce their contingents which have been serving with UNFICYP.

21. In response to my request, the following pledges of military personnel to strengthen UNFICYP were received by me from the contributing countries:

Austria, 60; Canada, 460; Denmark, 200; Finland, 400; Sweden, 350; and United Kingdom, 611.

22. The table below indicates the projected military strength of UNFICYP by 14 August 1974 when the pledged reinforcements will have arrived in the island:

Austria	300
Canada	950
Denmark	432
Finland	626
Ireland	4
Sweden	575
United Kingdom	1,391
Subtotal	4,278
Hospital unit (Austria)	14
Total	4,292

23. The Force Commander has assessed the desirable strength of UNFICYP in the light of UNFICYP's present and future tasks. As a result of his assessment the Force Commander has informed me that the reinforced strength of UNFICYP as described above is sufficient in terms of military personnel. However, he has recommended that the civilian police element of UNFICYP (UNCIVPOL) should be increased from 153 to 200. Accordingly, I have requested the Governments providing civilian police to UNFICYP to increase their police contingents in order to reach this figure.

G. OBSERVATIONS

24. In the days since the adoption of resolution 355 (1974) some progress has been achieved towards bringing peace to Cyprus. However, despite the efforts of the United Nations, of interested Governments and of the parties directly concerned, the cease-fire is not yet secure in all parts of the island; there have been forward movements of troops in some areas, and enclaves continue under occupation in other areas.

25. As indicated elsewhere in this report, UNFICYP has stood ready, since the adoption of resolution 355, to carry out the functions devolving upon it under that resolution, and it has repeatedly urged the parties to take the necessary actions to that end, beginning with the full observance of the cease-fire. Nevertheless, the full implementation of Security Council resolutions 353 (1974) and 355 (1974) is still in its first stages.

26. In effectively carrying out its task of assisting the parties in implementing the resolutions of the Security Council, UNFICYP needs their full co-operation, as called for in paragraph 6 of resolution 353. There has been a measure of co-operation in recent days, but a greater degree of co-operation is required if further progress is to be made in implementing resolutions 353 and 355, and if UNFICYP's efforts are to achieve their maximum effect. This particularly applies to the consolidation of the cease-fire, the establishment of UNFICYP supervised security zones and the evacuation of occupied Turkish enclaves. I have had the opportunity to discuss these problems in Geneva with all of the parties concerned.

REPORT OF THE SECRETARY-GENERAL PURSUANT TO SECURITY COUNCIL
RESOLUTION 361 (1974)

1. This report is submitted in pursuance of paragraph 5 of resolution 361 (1974), which the Security Council adopted on 30 August 1974. In that resolution, the Council expressed its grave concern at the plight of the refugees and other persons displaced as a result of the situation in Cyprus, requested the Secretary-General to continue to provide emergency United Nations humanitarian assistance to all parts of the population in need of such assistance and to report to the Council at the earliest possible opportunity.

2. On 20 August 1974, I announced the appointment of the United Nations high Commissioner for Refugees as co-ordinator of United Nations humanitarian assistance for Cyprus. The High Commissioner visited the island from 22 to 27 August 1974 to study the problem at first hand.

3. In the light of the Security Council resolution, I requested the High Commissioner to submit to me a report on humanitarian problems in Cyprus with special reference to the plight of the refugees. The High Commissioner prepared his report in close co-operation with the Special Representative of the Secretary-General in Cyprus and the Commander of the United Nations Peace-keeping Force. The text of that report is attached.

4. The High Commissioner has informed me that, in order to meet the immediate needs, he has been in touch with the representatives of potential donor Governments. However, the problems left in the wake of the recent hostilities in Cyprus are of such magnitude that substantial resources will be required if the Secretary-General, and the High Commissioner in his capacity as co-ordinator for humanitarian assistance, are to be in a position to continue to provide emergency assistance as requested by the Security Council in paragraph 6 of its resolution 361 (1974). I therefore intend to make, before the end of this week, an appeal to Governments, non-governmental organizations and individuals to support the United Nations effort to assist the afflicted population of Cyprus, to provide relief and to endeavour to find a peaceful solution to the problem of refugees.

ANNEX: REPORT OF THE UNITED NATIONS HIGH COMMISSIONER FOR REFUGEES TO THE SECRETARY-GENERAL ON HUMANITARIAN ASSISTANCE IN CYPRUS

INTRODUCTION

1. On August 20, 1974 the Secretary-General appointed me co-ordinator of United Nations humanitarian assistance in Cyprus. Preceded by two UNHCR officials, I arrived in the island on 22 August 1974 and remained there until 27 August.

2. During my stay in the island I had several occasions to meet with Acting President Clerides and with Vice-President Denktash. I also attended on 26 August the joint meeting on humanitarian questions presided over by the Secretary-General with the Acting President and the Vice-President. In addition, I had consultations with the Special Representative of the Secretary-General in Cyprus and the Commander of the United Nations Peace-keeping Force in Cyprus and met with senior members of the Red Cross and the Red Crescent, the chief delegate of the International Committee of the Red Cross (ICRC) as well as with representatives of potential donor Governments.

3. Thanks to the co-operation received from the authorities and the logistic support provided by UNFICYP, I visited by car and helicopter the British Sovereign Base Areas of Dhekelia and Episkopi where there are considerable numbers of displaced persons. I also toured the areas of Kyrenia, Kythrea, Larnaca, Limassol, the Troodos Mountains and Paphos and stopped to see some villages on the way. In the course of these visits, I had occasion to gather first-hand impressions of human sufferings and the extent of disruption.

THE PROBLEM

4. A large number of Greek Cypriot displaced persons, estimated to be 163,800, have fled their homes in the northern part of the island and are now in the south. There are also an estimated 34,000 Turkish Cypriots in the south. Of these numbers, some 50,000 Greek Cypriots and some 7,800 Turkish Cypriots are in the British Sovereign Base Areas. In the south there is, therefore, a total of some

197,800 persons in need. In the north there are an estimated 20,000 Greek Cypriots who did not or could not leave and a further 7,800 Turkish Cypriots who are homeless, making a total of 27,800 persons in need in the north and a total of 225,600 in the whole island. These figures were given locally to UNHCR by the Red Cross and the Red Crescent. It should be noted that not all 225,600 are displaced, as most of the Greek Cypriots in the north are still in their own homes, but deprived of their livelihood. The great majority of these are or shortly will be in need of assistance.

5. Related to the present situation are also other problems such as the care of large numbers of livestock left behind on Greek Cypriot farms in the north and the maintenance of the irrigation of the citrus plantations.

ASSISTANCE ALREADY PROVIDED

6. The immediate assistance is already being provided from several sources, both bilateral and multilateral. Since the second half of July, the International Committee of the Red Cross (ICRC) has played a vital role not only in its traditional context of the Geneva Red Cross conventions but also in the provision of relief. Indeed, the ICRC has some 40 delegates on the island distributing relief assistance in close co-operation and in many instances with the logistical support of UNFICYP.

7. Since the beginning of the hostilities in Cyprus in July 1974, UNFICYP has made all possible efforts to assist the afflicted population. UNFICYP activities in support of the humanitarian relief programme have included information gathering on conditions in towns and villages, providing supply convoys, giving medical assistance and escorts for medical and casualty evacuations, escorting work parties to repair power lines, transformers, generators and other essential services, assisting in tracing missing persons and protection, where necessary, of Turkish Cypriot villages.

8. Supplies for Turkish Cypriots come through the Red Crescent and for Greek Cypriots either through the Cyprus Government Welfare Department or the Red Cross. Four UNFICYP trucks are allocated permanently to move food and supplies to areas in need. Vehicles are allotted on a daily basis in response to requests from the agencies involved, and the supplies are delivered to their destination under UNFICYP escort. To date, 121 loads have been delivered, 92 to Turkish Cypriots and 29 to Greek Cypriots.

9. UNFICYP provides medical assistance to the sick and infirm in isolated villages and co-operates in the evacuation of seriously ill patients by providing escorts by road, and if required, by helicopter.

10. Specific instances of successful UNFICYP intervention as regards public facilities include Pyroi, where the badly damaged transformer has now been repaired, and the power line from Nicosia to Kyrenia, which was broken at Kaimakli, and where work is proceeding under UNFICYP protection. A joint meeting of Greek Cypriot and Turkish Cypriot technicians is being arranged under UNFICYP auspices to consider the repair of the electricity supply to Lefkoniko.

11. The UNFICYP Civilian Police (UNCIVPOL) too is actively engaged in the humanitarian relief efforts. In addition to the tracing service established by the ICRC in line with its traditional work, a special UNFICYP missing persons bureau has been set up since 15 July 1974. About 2,180 persons have been reported missing, of whom 580 were located. It must be mentioned, however, that UNCIVPOL investigations in this regard and other related matters are hampered in the north owing to restrictions of movement. UNCIVPOL co-operation with the ICRC is excellent and it is supporting the Red Cross efforts by visiting prisons and refugee camps.

CONCLUSIONS AND FUTURE ACTION

12. The economic and social disruption caused by the recent upheavals in Cyprus constitutes a serious obstacle to the efforts of local authorities to bring life back to normal. More than one third of the total population has been affected by the events. The condition of nearly a quarter of a million persons requiring humanitarian assistance has been mentioned in the above paragraphs. These groups include not only those homeless and uprooted who have had to leave one zone of control for another, but also sizable groups of Greek Cypriots in the Turkish zone and Turkish Cypriots in the Greek zone. They are mostly concen-

trated in identified areas where all protective measures possible under the circumstances are being taken. However, they are deprived of their livelihood and, in terms of assistance required, their situation is comparable to that of displaced persons.

13. Pending an amelioration of the over-all situation leading to some measure of socio-economic stability and enabling populations in rural and urban areas to pursue their normal means of livelihood, considerable efforts would be required of the international community to provide adequate humanitarian assistance in Cyprus. The assessment of requirements made on the spot calls for (i) immediate assistance required in coming days and weeks to save human lives and alleviate hardship; (ii) short-term assistance required over a period of several months, depending on the evolution of the over-all situation.

14. During the first phase, the United Nations efforts are to be concentrated on supplementing the humanitarian work already being carried out, on providing such basic assistance as medicaments, food, blankets, shelter, etc., and on preventing duplication of relief to the extent possible, both through bilateral and multilateral channels. The need for such assistance is immediate and, given adequate means, may be completed in the next few weeks.

15. Concurrently, efforts have to be made to provide assistance required over a longer period. The necessary planning for timely provision of required material assistance is being carried out. It is felt, in this respect, that the full extent of disruption will be more acutely felt by the population of Cyprus in general as the existing meagre stocks run out.

16. The co-ordinator is represented in both zones. A satisfactory mechanism of consultation and co-ordination has been established both at UNHCR headquarters level in Geneva and at the local level in Nicosia. In my capacity as United Nations co-ordinator of humanitarian assistance to Cyprus I have already approached Governments for contributions in cash and kind amounting to $US 9 million, in order to meet the immediate requirements. At the same time, needs for the short-term phase are being identified and costed and it is expected that the United Nations Secretary-General will be in a position during this week to appeal to Governments for their support.

17. It is clear that the situation of displaced persons and other elements of the Cypriot population should not be allowed to deteriorate into a more or less permanent burden. The support of the international community over the coming months would be critical in determining the future of these people. It is hoped that, as in the case of similar situations in the past, the international community will rise to this humanitarian challenge and respond generously to the Secretary-General's appeal.

OFFICE OF THE HIGH COMMISSIONER FOR REFUGEES—PRESS RELEASE REF/1178, SEPTEMBER 9, 1974

DETAILS OF $22 MILLION PROGRAMME FOR HUMANITARIAN ASSISTANCE TO CYPRUS ANNOUNCED

Emergency accommodation is the main item in the $22 million programme of humanitarian assistance to Cyprus being co-ordinated by the UN High Commissioner for Refugees. According to the first official breakdown made public today following the appeal of the Secretary-General on September 6, the $8.9 Emergency Accommodation item includes principally tents, beds and blankets, while $8.1 million is earmarked for various types of food including cereals, edible oil, condensed milk, sugar, canned meat, canned fish and pulses.

The other major components in the plan are $2.5 million for transportation including overseas air and sea freight and inland transportation and $850,000 for domestic and community equipment such as stoves, domestic utensils, mobile kitchens and related equipment. An amount of $1.65 million is foreseen as a contingency reserve and programme support.

The High Commissioner, Sadruddin Aga Khan, has pointed out that on the basis of some 226,000 persons, either displaced or isolated, who are estimated to be in need of international assistance on the island, the required $22 million represents an aid amounting to only 80 cents per person per day until the end of the year.

The UN plan is designed to supplement humanitarian work already being done both bilaterally and multiliterally, mainly under the aegis of the International

Committee of the Red Cross. The ICRC's role in providing relief will phase out in due course as the UN humanitarian action takes over. Details of the UN programme are being dispatched to governments today as a follow-up on the Secretary-General's appeal.

The High Commissioner has stated that in order to allow flexibility in planning, cash contributions are preferred. Sources of principal supplies have been found for the most urgently needed items and shipment by air transport will begin as soon as funds are pledged.

UNHCR has already set up an office in Cyprus. A mechanism of co-ordination has been established in Geneva and Nicosia in order to avoid duplication and maximize the effort of multilateral and bilateral humanitarian efforts. Meetings of representatives of the UN bodies involved, including UNFICYP, UNICEF, WFP and WHO are being held regularly to ensure effective co-operation within the UN system. Similar co-ordination is being arranged with nongovernmental organizations.

UNITED NATIONS PRESS SECTION, OFFICE OF PUBLIC INFORMATION—PRESS RELEASE CYP/788, IHA/217, REF/714, OCTOBER 14, 1974

CONTRIBUTIONS FOR HUMANITARIAN ASSISTANCE TO CYPRUS REACHES $7 MILLION

[The following is reproduced as received from the UNHCR, Geneva]

The level of aid channelled through the United Nations system for the programme of humanitarian assistance in Cyprus, being co-ordinated by the United Nations High Commissioner for Refugees (UNHCR), has now reached $7 million, thanks to seven new contributions.

The seven, not previously announced, are: Canada ($51,020), France ($416,667), Federal Republic of Germany ($188,758), Mauritius ($17,544), Monaco ($1,042), Norway ($90,580) and the Philippines ($2,300).

They bring to 17 the number of Governments which have contributed cash or kind in response to the appeal of the Secretary-General and the High Commissioner on 6 September. The largest contributor through the United Nations system remains the United States with $3 million thus far.

RELIEF SUPPLIES POUR IN

Meanwhile, more than half of the 204,000 blankets ordered by the UNHCR, through the United Nations Children's Fund (UNICEF), have been delivered and distributed. UNHCR-chartered planes are moving the blankets from Europe as fast as they are procured. And all but 10,000 of the 40,000 camp beds ordered by the UNHCR will be in Cyprus by 17 October. In addition, the UNHCR has arranged to buy 25,000 from local manufacturers.

Another of the main priorities—tents—is well on the way to being met. The last installment of the 2,500 tents bought with UNHCR funds will leave the United Kingdom by ship on 15 October, with arrival scheduled for 1 November. At that point, almost 15,000 family tents—many made available from bilateral sources—will have been provided to shelter over 70,000 displaced or uprooted persons as the period of cold weather approaches. Family cooking equipment and domestic utensils are being purchased in large quantities through the UNICEF and are being delivered by air.

The three large donations in food commodities made available by Belgium, Denmark and the European Economic Community (EEC), respectively, will begin to move to Cyprus by sea on 25 October. The UNHCR has made available $200,000 to cover the transportation costs involved. The World Food Programme (WFP) is providing technical expertise in arranging the shipment.

The most pressing needs in the medical field at present are ambulances, supplies for environmental sanitation, pharmaceuticals and hospital equipment. With a view to meeting these requirements, the UNHCR has made an initial allocation of $400,000 to the World Health Organization (WHO) and UNICEF.

APPENDIX VII

Documents Relating to the Founding of Cyprus, Including the Treaty of Guarantee, 1959

[From Documents on International Affairs, 1959, edited by Gillian King, Oxford University Press, London, 1963]

1. Documents Regarding Cyprus Signed and Initialled at Lancaster House, London, February 19, 1959 [1]

(A) BASIC STRUCTURE OF THE REPUBLIC OF CYPRUS

1. The State of Cyprus shall be a Republic with a presidential régime, the President being Greek and the Vice-President Turkish elected by universal suffrage by the Greek and Turkish communities of the Island respectively.

2. The official languages of the Republic of Cyprus shall be Greek and Turkish. Legislative and administrative instruments and documents shall be drawn up and promulgated in the two official languages.

3. The Republic of Cyprus shall have its own flag of neutral design and colour, chosen jointly by the President and the Vice-President of the Republic.

Authorities and communities shall have the right to fly the Greek and Turkish flags on holidays at the same time as the flag of Cyprus.

The Greek and Turkish communities shall have the right to celebrate Greek and Turkish national holidays.

4. The President and the Vice-President shall be elected for a period of five years.

In the event of absence, impediment or vacancy of their posts, the President and the Vice-President shall be replaced by the President and the Vice-President of the House of Representatives respectively.

In the event of a vacancy in either post, the election of new incumbents shall take place within a period of not more than 45 days.

The President and the Vice-President shall be invested by the House of Representatives, before which they shall take an oath of loyalty and respect for the Constitution. For this purpose, the House of Representatives shall meet within 24 hours after its constitution.

5. Executive authority shall be vested in the President and the Vice-President. For this purpose they shall have a Council of Ministers composed of seven Greek Ministers and three Turkish Ministers. The Ministers shall be designated respectively by the President and the Vice-President who shall appoint them by an instrument signed by them both.

The Ministers may be chosen from outside the House of Representatives.

Decisions of the Council of Ministers shall be taken by an absolute majority.

Decisions so taken shall be promulgated immediately by the President and the Vice-President by publication in the official gazette.

However, the President and the Vice-President shall have the right of final veto and the right to return the decisions of the Council of Ministers under the same conditions as those laid down for laws and decisions of the House of Representatives.

---

[1] The agreement on Cyprus was approved by the Greek Parliament on 28 February, by 170 votes to 118, by the Turkish Parliament on 4 March, by 347 votes to 138 with 2 abstentions, and by the House of Commons on 19 March, with no division, after an opposition amendment criticizing the Government's policy since 1954, had been defeated by 299 votes to 246. On 10 November 1959 agreement was reached on the question of executive authority in the new constitution. On 13 December Archbishop Makarios was elected first President of the future republic of Cyprus, he received 70 per cent of the votes. The state of emergency on the island ended on 4 December 1959.

6. Legislative authority shall be vested in a House of Representatives elected for a period of five years by universal suffrage of each community separately in the proportion of 70 per cent for the Greek community and 30 per cent for the Turkish community, this proportion being fixed independently of statistical data. (*N.B.*—The number of Representatives shall be fixed by mutual agreement between the communities.)

The House of Representatives shall exercise authority in all matters other than those expressly reserved to the Communal Chambers. In the event of a conflict of authority, such conflict shall be decided by the Supreme Constitutional Court which shall be composed of one Greek, one Turk and one neutral, appointed jointly by the President and the Vice-President. The neutral judge shall be president of the Court.

7. Laws and decisions of the House of Representatives shall be adopted by a simple majority of the members present. They shall be promulgated within 15 days if neither the President nor the Vice-President returns them for reconsideration as provided in Point 9 below.

The Constitutional Law, with the exception of its basic articles, may be modified by a majority comprising two-thirds of the Greek members and two-thirds of the Turkish members of the House of Representatives.

Any modification of the electoral law and the adoption of any law relating to the municipalities and of any law imposing duties or taxes shall require a simple majority of the Greek and Turkish members of the House of Representatives taking part in the vote and considered separately.

On the adoption of the budget, the President and the Vice-President may exercise their right to return it to the House of Representatives, if in their judgment any question of discrimination arises. If the House maintains its decisions, the President and the Vice-President shall have the right of appeal to the Supreme Constitutional Court.

8. The President and the Vice-President, separately and conjointly, shall have the right of final veto on any law or decision concerning foreign affairs, except the participation of the Republic of Cyprus in international organisations and pacts of alliance in which Greece and Turkey both participate, or concerning defence and security as defined in Annex I.

9. The President and the Vice-President of the Republic shall have, separately and conjointly, the right to return all laws and decisions, which may be returned to the House of Representatives within a period of not more than 15 days for reconsideration.

The House of Representatives shall pronounce within 15 days on any matter so returned. If the House of Representatives maintains its decisions, the President and the Vice-President shall promulgate the law or decision in question within the time-limits fixed for the promulgation of laws and decisions.

Laws and decisions, which are considered by the President or the Vice-President to discriminate against either of the two communities, shall be submitted to the Supreme Constitutional Court which may annul or confirm the law or decision, or return it to the House of Representatives for reconsideration, in whole or in part. The law or decision shall not become effective until the Supreme Constitutional Court or, where it has been returned, the House of Representatives has taken a decision on it.

10. Each community shall have its Communal Chamber composed of a number of representatives which it shall itself determine.

The Communal Chambers shall have the right to impose taxes and levies on members of their community to provide for their needs and for the needs of bodies and institutions under their supervision.

The Communal Chambers shall exercise authority in all religious, educational, cultural and teaching questions and questions of personal status. They shall exercise authority in questions where the interests and institutions are of a purely communal nature, such as sporting and charitable foundations, bodies and associations, producers' and consumers' co-operatives and credit establishments, created for the purpose of promoting the welfare of one of the communities. (*N.B.*—It is understood that the provisions of the present paragraph cannot be interpreted in such a way as to prevent the creation of mixed and communal institutions where the inhabitants desire them.)

These producers' and consumers' co-operatives and credit establishments, which shall be administered under the laws of the Republic, shall be subject to the supervision of the Communal Chambers. The Communal Chambers shall also exercise authority in matters initiated by municipalities which are composed of one community only. These municipalities, to which the laws of the Republic shall apply, shall be supervised in their functions by the Communal Chambers.

Where the central administration is obliged to take over the supervision of the institutions, establishments, or municipalities mentioned in the two preceding paragraphs by virtue of legislation in force, this supervision shall be exercised by officials belonging to the same community as the institution, establishment or municipality in question.

11. The Civil Service shall be composed as to 70 per cent. of Greeks and as to 30 per cent. of Turks.

It is understood that this quantitative division will be applied as far as practicable in all grades of the Civil Service.

In regions or localities where one of the two communities is in a majority approaching 100 per cent., the organs of the local administration responsible to the central administration shall be composed solely of officials belonging to that community.

12. The deputies of the Attorney-General of the Republic, the Inspector-General, the Treasurer and the Governor of the Issuing Bank may not belong to the same community as their principals. The holders of these posts shall be appointed by the President and the Vice-President of the Republic acting in agreement.

13. The heads and deputy heads of the Armed Forces, the Gendarmerie and the Police shall be appointed by the President and the Vice-President of the Republic acting in agreement. One of these heads shall be Turkish and where the head belongs to one of the communities, the deputy head shall belong to the other.

14. Compulsory military service may only be instituted with the agreement of the President and the Vice-President of the Republic of Cyprus.

Cyprus shall have an army of 2,000 men, of whom 60 per cent. shall be Greek and 40 per cent. Turkish.

The security forces (gendarmerie and police) shall have a complement of 2,000 men, which may be reduced or increased with the agreement of both the President and the Vice-President. The security forces shall be composed as to 70 per cent. of Greeks and as to 30 per cent. of Turks. However, for an initial period this percentage may be raised to a maximum of 40 per cent. of Turks (and consequently reduced to 60 per cent. of Greeks) in order not to discharge those Turks now serving in the police, apart from the auxiliary police.

15. Forces, which are stationed in parts of the territory of the Republic inhabited, in a proportion approaching 100 per cent., by members of a single community, shall belong to that community.

16. A High Court of Justice shall be established, which shall consist of two Greeks, one Turk and one neutral, nominated jointly by the President and the Vice-President of the Republic.

The President of the Court shall be the neutral judge, who shall have two votes.

This Court shall constitute the highest organ of the judicature (appointments, promotions of judges, &c.).

17. Civil disputes, where the plaintiff and the defendant belong to the same community, shall be tried by a tribunal composed of judges belonging to that community. If the plaintiff and defendant belong to different communities, the composition of the tribunal shall be mixed and shall be determined by the High Court of Justice.

Tribunals dealing with civil disputes relating to questions of personal status and to religious matters, which are reserved to the competence of the Communal Chambers under Point 10, shall be composed solely of judges belonging to the community concerned. The composition and status of these tribunals shall be determined according to the law drawn up by the Communal Chamber and they shall apply the law drawn up by the Communal Chamber.

In criminal cases, the tribunal shall consist of judges beonging to the same community as the accused. If the injured party belongs to another community, the composition of the tribunal shall be mixed and shall be determined by the High Court of Justice.

18. The President and the Vice-President of the Republic shall each have the right to exercise the prerogative of mercy to persons from their respective communities who are condemned to death. In cases where the plaintiffs and

the convicted persons are members of different communities the prerogative of mercy shall be exercised by agreement between the President and the Vice-President. In the event of disagreement the vote for clemency shall prevail. When mercy is accorded the death penalty shall be commuted to life imprisonment.

19. In the event of agricultural reform, lands shall be redistributed only to persons who are members of the same community as the expropriated owners.

Expropriations by the State or the Municipalities shall only be carried out on payment of a just and equitable indemnity fixed, in disputed cases, by the tribunals. An appeal to the tribunals shall have the effect of suspending action.

Expropriated property shall only be used for the purpose for whch the expropriation was made. Otherwise the property shall be restored to the owners.

20. Separate municipalities shall be created in the five largest towns of Cyprus by the Turkish inhabitants of these towns. However :—

(a) In each of the towns a co-ordinating body shall be set up which shall supervise work which needs to be carried out jointly and shall concern itself with matters which require a degree of co-operation. These bodies shall each be composed of two members chosen by the Greek municipalities, two members chosen by the Turkish municipalities and a President chosen by agreement between the two municipalities.

(b) The President and the Vice-President shall examine within four years the question whether or not this separation of municipalities in the five largest towns shall continue.

With regard to other localities, special arrangements shall be made for the constitution of municipal bodies, following, as far as possible, the rule of proportional representation for the two communities.

21. A treaty guaranteeing the independence, territorial integrity and constitution of the new State of Cyprus shall be concluded between the Republic of Cyprus, Greece, the United Kingdom and Turkey. A Treaty of military alliance shall also be concluded between the Republic of Cyprus, Greece and Turkey.

These two instruments shall have constitutional force. (This last paragraph shall be inserted in the Constitution as a basic article.)

22. It shall be recognised that the total or partial union of Cyprus with any other State, or a separatist independence for Cyprus (i.e., the partition of Cyprus into two independent States), shall be excluded.

23. The Republic of Cyprus shall accord most-favoured-nation treatment to Great Britain, Greece and Turkey for all agreements whatever their nature.

This provision shall not apply to the Treaties between the Republic of Cyprus and the United Kingdom concerning the bases and military facilities accorded to the United Kingdom.

24. The Greek and Turkish Governments shall have the right to subsidise institutions for education, culture, athletics and charity belonging to their respective communities.

Equally, where either community considers that it has not the necessary number of schoolmasters, professors or priests for the working of its institutions, the Greek and Turkish Goverments may provide them to the extent strictly necessary to meet their needs.

25. One of the following Ministries—the Ministry of Foreign Affairs, the Ministry of Defence or the Ministry of Finance—shall be entrusted to a Turk. If the President and the Vice-President agree they may replace this system by a system of rotation.

26. The new State which is to come into being with the signature of the Treaties shall be established as quickly as possible and within a period of not more than three months from the signature of the Treaties.

27. All the above Points shall be considered to be basic articles of the Constitution of Cyprus.

E. A.-T.   F. R. Z.

S. L.

† A. M.   F. K.

ANNEX I

A

The defence questions subject to veto under Point 8 of the Basic Structure are as follows :—

(a) Composition and size of the armed forces and credits for them.

(b) Appointments and promotions.

(c) Imports of warlike stores and of all kinds of explosives.
(d) Granting of bases anad other facilities to allied countries.
The Security questions subject to veto are as follows :
  (a) Appointments and promotions.
  (b) Allocation and stationing of forces.
  (c) Emergency measures and martial law.
  (d) Police laws.
(It is provided that the right of veto shall cover all emergency measures or decisions, but not those which concern the normal functioning of the police and gendarmerie.)

(b) *Treaty of Guarantee between the Republic of Cyprus and Greece, the United Kingdom and Turkey*

The Republic of Cyprus of the one part, and Greece, the United Kingdom and Turkey of the other part :—

I. Considering that the recognition and maintenance of the independence, territorial integrity and security of the Republic of Cyprus, as established and regulated by the basic articles of its Constitution, are in their common interest ;

II. Desiring to co-operate to ensure that the provisions of the aforesaid Constitution shall be respected ;

Have agreed as follows :

ARTICLE 1

The Republic of Cyprus undertakes to ensure the maintenance of its independence, territorial integrity and security, as well as respect for its Constitution.

It undertakes not to participate, in whole or in part, in any political or economic union with any State whatsoever. With this intent it prohibits all activity tending to promote directly or indirectly either union or partition of the Island.

ARTICLE 2

Greece the United Kingdom and Turkey, taking note of the undertakings by the Republic of Cyprus embodied in Article 1, recognize and guarantee the independence, territorial integrity and security of the Republic of Cyprus, and also the provisions of the basic articles of its Constitution.

They likewise undertake to prohibit, as far as lies within their power, all activity having the object of promoting directly or indirectly either the union of the Republic of Cyprus with any other State, or the partition of the Island.

ARTICLE 3

In the event of any breach of the provisions of the present Treaty, Greece, the United Kingdom, and Turkey undertake to consult together, with a view to making representations, or taking the necessary steps to ensure observance of those provisions.

In so far as common or concerted action may prove impossible, each of the three guaranteeing Powers reserves the right to take action with the sole aim of re-establishing the state of affairs established by the present Treaty.

ARTICLE 4

The present Treaty shall enter into force on signature.

The High Contracting Parties undertake to register the present Treaty at the earliest possible date with the Secretariat of the United Nations, in accordance with the provisions of Article 102 of the Chapter.

E. A.–T.   F. R. Z.

                 S. L.

†A. M.   F. K.

(c) *Treaty of Alliance between the Republic of Cyprus, Greece and Turkey*

1. The Republic of Cyprus, Greece and Turkey shall co-operate for their common defence and undertake by this Treaty to consult together on the problems raised by this defence.

2. The High Contracting Parties undertake to resist any attack or aggression, direct or indirect, directed against the independence and territorial integrity of the Republic of Cyprus.

3. In the spirit of this alliance and in order to fulfill the above purpose a tripartite Headquarters shall be established on the terrtiory of the Republic of Cyprus.

4. Greece shall take part in the Headquarters mentioned in the preceding article with a contingent of 950 officers, non-commissioned officers and soldiers and Turkey with a contingent of 650 officers, non-commissioned officers and soldiers. The President and the Vice-President of the Republic of Cyprus, acting in agreement, may ask the Greek and Turkish Governments to increase or reduce the Greek and Turkish contingents.

5. The Greek and Turkish officers mentioned above shall be responsible for the training of the Army of the Republic of Cyprus.

6. The command of the tripartite Headquarters shall be assumed in rotation and for a period of one year each by a Cypriot, Greek and Turkish General Officer, who shall be nominated by the Governments of Greece and Turkey and by the President and the Vice-President of the Republic of Cyprus.

E. A.–T.		**F. R. Z.**
	S. L.	
†A. M.		**F. K.**

(d) Declaration by the Government of the United Kingdom, 11 February 1959

DECLARATION BY THE GOVERNMENT OF THE UNITED KINGDOM

The Government of the United Kingdom of Great Britain and Northern Ireland, having examined the documents concerning the establishment of the Republic of Cyprus, comprising the Basic Structure for the Republic of Cyprus, the Treaty of Guarantee and the Treaty of Alliance, drawn up and approved by the Heads of the Governments of Greece and Turkey in Zürich on February 11, 1959, and taking into account the consultations in London, from February 11 to 16, 1959, betwee nthe Foreign Ministers of Greece, Turkey and the United Kingdom

Declare:

A. That, subject to the acceptance of their requirements as set out in Section B below, they accept the documents approved by the Heads of the Governments of Greece and Turkey as the agreed foundation for the final settlement of the problem of Cyprus.

B. That, with the exception of two areas at

(a) Akrotiri—Episkopi—Parmali, and

(b) Dhekelia—Pergamos—Ayios Nikolaos—Xylophagou, which will be retained under full British sovereignty, they are willing to transfer sovereignty over the Island of Cyprus to the Republic of Cyprus subject to the following conditions:—

(1) that such rights are secured to the United Kingdom Government as are necessary to enable the two areas as aforesaid to be used effectively as military bases, including among others those rights indicated in the Annex attached, and that satisfactory guarantees are given by Greece, Turkey and the Republic of Cyprus for the integrity of the areas retained under British sovereignty and the use and enjoyment by the United Kingdom of the rights referred to above;

(2) that provision shall be made by agreement for:—

(i) the protection of the fundamental human rights of the various communities in Cyprus;

(ii) the protection of the interests of the members of the public services in Cyprus;

(iii) determining the nationality of persons affected by tne settlement;

(iv) the assumption by the Republic of Cyprus of the appropriate obligations of the present Government of Cyprus, including the settlement of claims.

C. That the Government of the United Kingdom welcome the draft Treaty of Alliance between the Republic of Cyprus, the Kingdom of Greece and the Republic of Turkey and will co-operate with the Parties thereto in the common defence of Cyprus.

D. That the Constitution of the Republic of Cyprus shall come into force and the formal signature of the necessary instruments by the parties concerned shall take place at the earliest practicable date and on that date sovereignty will be transferred to the Republic of Cyprus.

SELWYN LLOYD.
ALAN LENNOX-BOYD.

E. A.-T.
†A. M.   F. K.   F. R. Z.

ANNEX

The following rights will be necessary in connexion with the areas to be retained under British sovereignty :—

(*a*) to continue to use, without restriction or interference, the existing small sites containing military and other installations and to exercise complete control within these sites, including the right to guard and defend them and to exclude from them all persons not authorised by the United Kingdom Government;

(*b*) to use roads, ports and other facilities freely for the movement of personnel and stores of all kinds to and from and between the abovementioned areas and sites;

(*c*) to continue to have the use of specified port facilities at Famagusta;

(*d*) to use public services (such as water, telephone, telegraph, electric power, &c.) ;

(*e*) to use from time to time certain localities, which would be specified, for troop training;

(*f*) to use the airfield at Nicosia, together with any necessary buildings and facilities on or connected with the airfield to whatever extent is considered necessary by the British authorities for the operation of British military aircraft in peace and war, including the exercise of any necessary operational control of air traffic;

(*g*) to overfly the territory of the Republic of Cyprus without restriction;

(*h*) to exercise jurisdiction over British forces to an extent comparable with that provided in Article VII of the Agreement regarding the Status of Forces of Parties to the North Atlantic Treaty, in respect of certain offenses committed within the territory of the Republic of Cyprus:

(*i*) to employ freely in the areas and sites labour from other parts of Cyprus;

(*j*) to obtain, after consultation with the Government of the Republic of Cyprus, the use of such additional small sites and such additional rights as the United Kingdom may, from time to time, consider technically necessary for the efficient use of its base areas and installations in Cyprus.

(e) *Additional article to be inserted in the Treaty of Guarantee*

The Kingdom of Greece, the Republic of Turkey and the Republic of Cyprus undertake to respect the integrity of the areas to be retained under the sovereignty of the United Kingdom upon the establishment of the Republic of Cyprus, and guarantee the use and enjoyment by the United Kingdom of the rights to be secured to the United Kingdom by the Republic of Cyprus in accordance with the declaration by the Government of the United Kingdom.

S. L.   E. A. T.   F. R. Z.
       † A. M.   F. K.

APPENDIX VIII

MEMORANDUM

INTRODUCTION :

As it is known on the 20th of July forty thousand Turkish forces assisted by Turkish air and naval forces, in violation of the Charter of the United Nations and all principles governing international relations, invaded the small Island State of Cyprus.

The Turkish air-force systematically bombed inhabited areas, including hospitals and hotels, thus killing civilians and forcing thousands of others to flee away to safer areas.

The Turkish army on invading Cyprus started occupying Greek-inhabited areas and systematically looted and plundered the properties of the inhabitants, arrested men, molested women, children and elderly people and indulged in repeated rapes, arsons, cold-blooded murders of hundreds of civilians and finally forced expulsion of the inhabitants from their homes.

According to foreign press reports, Turkey, in an effort to artificially change the population ratio, which in this century has always been 82% Greeks, 18% Turks, started to transport to the Island Turks from Turkey.

Thus Turkey is trying to change the Greek character of the Island, which was preserved for some 4,000 years, as evidenced by History, the people and the many monuments which are now being systematically destroyed by the Turkish Forces.

EFFECTS OF THE TURKISH INVASION ON THE COUNTRY AND ITS ECONOMY

It is very difficult at this juncture to quantify all damage and future repercussions on the Cyprus economy as a result of the Turkish invasion of Cyprus. It is even more difficult to estimate accurately the damage incurred in the areas controlled by the Turkish invading forces in terms of residential buildings, hotels, factories, etc., bombed or of other properties already lost. What follows is a first attempt to estimate the economic consequences of the invasion on the economy.

Since the invasion, the whole economy has been disrupted. It is estimated that the country is foregoing about 2 million pounds worth of production every day. So far, more than 60 million pounds of production has been lost because of the standstill in economic activity. Virtually the whole of the labour force is unemployed or seriously underemployed, compared with the state of full employment which existed before the invasion.

About 200,000 persons, representing about 40 per cent of the Greek population of the Island, have been displaced from their homes and peaceful occupations to refugee camps, living under lamentable conditions, underfed and facing the serious problem of survival, owing to malnutrition and hygenic hazards.

It is estimated that about 40,000 households have been broken up and forcibly expelled, leaving behind all their properties. The household movable properties alone are estimated to be of the order of 50–100 million pounds. Out of these properties, even those which may not be further looted, will be destroyed by time. In addition, goods left in warehouses, fields, factories and shops in the Turkish controlled areas amount to many millions of pounds. Another serious damage which cannot be expressed in pecuniary terms is the destruction by bombings of an area of 100 square miles of pine-wood forests, which represents about one fifth of the main state forests. Tourist activities, which was expected to fetch more than 30 million pounds of foreign exchange earnings this year, suffered the worst blow of all sectors and the negative consequences are expected to last for a number of years.

Hundreds of thousands of animals are dying because of lack of food and veterinary care or are slaughtered of feed the invading army. Citrus orchards worth millions of pounds and other plantations fetching more than 10 million pounds of income every year are in danger of irreparable destruction because of not being watered.

An off-hand estimate places the damage at 350 million pounds, a sum which most probably will prove to be inferior to the real financial damage. This same amount should also be considered not as an absolute figure but within the context of the Cypriot economy and in comparison with its potentialities.

In order to underline the importance of the disaster that this figure represents for a small country like Cyprus, it should be remarked that the amount of 350 million pounds corresponds to 11 years of expenditure in the Cyprus general budget (1970: 32 million pounds) which for the United States, for example, would be 2.1 trillion dollars.

The above-estimated figure does not include other damage that will unavoidably result in the future from the Turkish invasion, such as:

(a) Livestock belonging to Greek-Cypriots and left in occupied areas without water or food die in masses every day. Turkish military authorities do not permit the Greek-Cypriots to approach their livestock, with the pretext that they will be taken care of by the Turkish authorities;

(b) In the orange plantations of the Morphou region, the trees are not being watered and in the midsummer if this situation lasts for a few more days, the entire system of plantations, which has been created after many years of work and with considerable expenditure, will be completely lost;

(c) The Turkish occupation has already covered 40 per cent of the Cypriot territory which, however, corresponds to 70 per cent of the agricultural production and to the same percentage of the whole economic life of the country, for the following reasons:

Turkish forces control the most fertile areas of Messaoria and Morphou, the lemon plantations of Lapithos and Karavas, the olive plantations of the Kythrea, Kyrenia and Solea, the orange plantations of Morphou and Famagusta, the water resources of Lapithos and Kythrea, the tourist installations of Kyrenia and Famagusta, a great part of various industrial areas of Nicosia, etc.

The territory controlled by Turkish forces at present is about 40 percent of the total area of the Island. In this area the inhabitants were 82 percent Greeks and 18 percent Turks. The area comprised almost all the Messaoria plains, east and west, the Kyrenia District and the Karpass Peninsula. It is the almost exclusive cereal, carob-producing and the main citrus, vegetable, meat-, milk and egg-producing area of Cyprus. It contains two-thirds of the tourist activities, 55–60 percent of the industrial activity, 65 percent of the cultivated land, 60 percent of the underground water resources, 60 percent of the mining and quarrying activities (almost 100 percent of the quarrying activities), the main port of Cyprus at Famagusta, through which 83 percent of the general cargo was handled, and the main specialized port of Karavostassi, through which 85 percent of the minerals were handled. In other words, the economic significance of this area is much more important than its size. It is estimated that about 70 percent of total gross production from all sources emanates from this area, not to mention the immense wealth of physical assets, resources and structures situated there in the form of hotels and hotel apartments, houses, factories, orchards, arable and irrigated fertile land, mineral and quarrying resources, water resources and high valued tourist land.

From the above figures, it can be concluded that in 1974 the gross national product of the whole Island will be significantly reduced to perhaps half of its average size, whereas investment and other physical wealth has been badly damaged with negative consequences for years to come.

The Turkish Cypriots, despite their share of 18 percent in total population, were contributing less than 10 percent to the gross domestic product. The land registered in the names of Turkish people and organizations represents only 12.8 percent of the total area of Cyprus compared to 58.8 percent registered in the names of the Greeks and 1.4 percent in others. Even if the remaining 27 percent of forest, state and communal land is distributed between the Greeks and the Turks in accordance with the population proportions, the Turks are entitled to only 17.9 percent of the total area of Cyprus.

The refugee problem

(a) The whole of Cyprus has been turned into a vast refugee camp. Forty percent of the Greek population of the island have been turned into refugees and what is worse as a result of the most relentless and organised persecution. Consequently, they moved in panic and at the beginning without of course any preplanned aim. If this is coupled with the fact that the displaced persons abandoned their homes without being able to take anything with them, and that 70% of the general stores of food, livestock and agricultural and industrial products remained in the cut-off areas and, are therefore, inaccessible, one can easily assess the magnitude of the enormous problem of sheltering and maintaining these unfortunate people, who are not being allowed to return to their homes.

(b) A number of refugees at first sought shelter where they thought they would be safe. Subsequently some moved to towns and villages where they had relatives or friends or to the British base areas, while the majority were forced to remain in forests and hills. The total number, estimated at 191,259 (about 40,000 families) is believed to be distributed as follows:

Town	Urgently needing accommodation	Temporary accommodations	Accommodation with relatives	Total
Nicosia	5,162	2,858	24,559	32,579
Larnaca	57,900	3,800	28,100	89,800
Limassol	18,300	4,767	20,389	43,456
Kakopetria-Pedoulas area	750	2,760	18,095	21,605
Paphos		373	3,446	3,819
Total	82,112	14,558	94,589	191,259

Of these people, only 27,496 could be regarded as being able to maintain themselves. The remaining 163,763 are in need of constant care and assistance. Their subsistence alone requires an expenditure which at the most conservative estimate amounts to 400 mils per day per person.

(c) As regards clothing and elementary domestic and other equipment, it is estimated that about 12 million pounds will be needed.

(d) Concerning immediate requirements (the constant supply of foodstuffs of all kinds is of primary importance) there is an urgent need to secure:

30,000 tents and another 100 large ones capable of being used as common spaces.

630,000 blankets.

150,000 campbeds and other bedding.

33,000 heating sets.

320 mobile kitchens.

a sufficient number of mobile bakeries to cater for about 100,000 persons.

other elementary installations particularly in open-air camps such as sanitary and electric installations, water supply, telephone communications, transportation etc.

CONCLUSIONS

There is no doubt whatsoever that the aim of the Turkish Government is simply to destroy the territorial integrity of the Republic of Cyprus by military force in order to promote Turkey's expansion. For the success of this aim they have used means and methods not only in absolute disregard of the 1949 Geneva Conventions and of fundamental human rights but such that remind the most dark pages of human history. Turkey's purpose went far beyond the scourge of war. It is an attempt to use force to deface the Island and break up its economic and cultural continuity and its development. By intensive napalm bombing of defenseless villages Turkey aimed at spreading death and destruction. For the first time since World War II the invaders were pursuing their determined policy of expelling Cypriots from their ancestral homes. They had entered Cyprus with the set purpose of conducting a policy of expulsion by blood and iron and of geographic and demographic dismemberment.

It should be noted that the orgy of destruction by Turkey had begun at the very time the Prime Minister of Turkey was broadcasting to the World that "our mission is peaceful". It should also be noted that Turkey acted under the guise of a guarantor of the independence and territorial integrity of Cyprus.

What can be done now?

(1) First and foremost there must be implementation of the Agreements reached recently in Geneva between the United Kingdom, Greece and Turkey. At the same time there must be implementation of the Security Council Resolutions. Both the Geneva Agreements and the Security Council Resolutions provide for the withdrawal of the Turkish invading force from Cyprus.

(2) Secondly, there should be return of the 200,000 Greek Cypriot refugees, to their homes, who have been expelled from their houses by the invading forces for the reasons that have already been explained.

(3) Thirdly, there should be exchange of prisoners of war and hostages.

With all these vital and fundamental problems remaining unresolved any negotiations for the future of the Island will be carried out under pressure and blackmail, as it happened at Geneva. Cyprus expects from the whole international community and especially from the countries that have the power to do so to exert their influence in the right direction in order to secure for Cyprus its independence, sovereignty and territorial integrity and for the consolidation of peace not only in Cyprus itself but in the whole region.

MINISTRY OF FOREIGN AFFAIRS.

Nicosia, 4th September, 1974.

HUMANITARIAN PROBLEMS ON CYPRUS
PART II

HEARING

BEFORE THE

SUBCOMMITTEE TO INVESTIGATE PROBLEMS CONNECTED WITH REFUGEES AND ESCAPEES

OF THE

COMMITTEE ON THE JUDICIARY
UNITED STATES SENATE

NINETY-THIRD CONGRESS

SECOND SESSION

PART II

CONTENTS

Statements of:

His Eminence, Archibishop Iakovos, Primate of the Greek Orthodox Church in the Americas_____ Page 4

William G. Chirgotis, Supreme President, Order of AHEPA, and William P. Tsaffaras, cochairman, AHEPA Justice for Cyprus Committee_____ 13

APPENDIX

I. AHEPA Report: Humanitarian Mission to Cyprus, November 1974_____ 23

II. Text of subcommittee's correspondence with Secretary of State Henry Kissinger on U.S. policy toward Cyrpus___ 37

III. Selected press reports and commentaries on the Cyprus situation_____ 45

APPROXIMATE AREA OF TURKISH MILITARY OCCUPATION OF CYPRUS AS OF DECEMBER

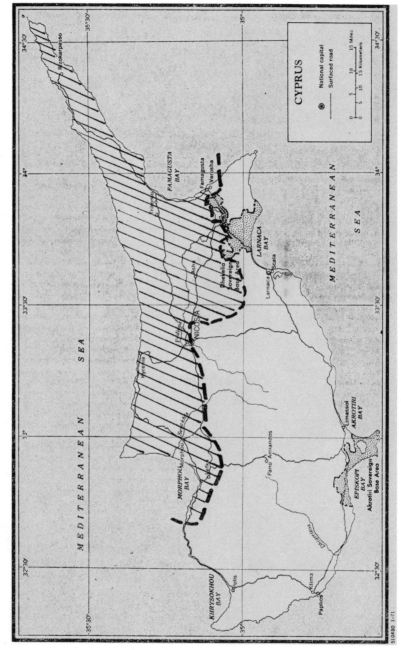

CYPRUS

⊕ National capital
— Surfaced road

0   5   10   15 Miles
0 5 10 15 Kilometers

510480 1–71

HUMANITARIAN PROBLEMS IN CYPRUS—PART II

TUESDAY, DECEMBER 17, 1974

UNITED STATES SENATE,
SUBCOMMITTEE ON REFUGEES AND ESCAPEES,
OF THE COMMITTEE ON THE JUDICIARY,
Washington, D.C.

The subcommittee met, pursuant to notice, at 9:35 a.m., in room 4232, Dirksen Senate Office Building, Senator Edward M. Kennedy [chairman] presiding.

Present: Senators Kennedy [presiding], Fong and Mathias.

Staff present: Dale deHaan, counsel; Jerry Tinker, staff consultant; Marc Ginsberg, staff assistant; and Joanna Reagan, chief clerk.

OPENING STATEMENT

Senator KENNEDY. The subcommittee will come to order.

The subcommittee has closely followed developments on Cyprus, since the outbreak of violence some 5 months ago. Earlier hearings were held in August and September—and an extensive report of a factfinding mission to the area was released just a few weeks ago. Our primary concern has been the humanitarian crisis produced by the Turkish invasion—and what our Nation is doing to help bring peace and relief to the people of Cyprus.

Regrettably, in these past 5 months little has changed on Cyprus. The Turkish occupation of at least 40 percent of the island continues. The economy deteriorates every day. And over 200,000 people, both Turkish and Greek, remain refugees—driven from their lands and homes only a few miles away. For 5 months they have lived in fields, under trees, along the roadsides, in tents, in schools and churches—wherever they could find shelter and help. And today they shiver—idly in the winter cold—still waiting the opportunity to return to their livelihoods and homes, and to their families and friends.

The tragedy on Cyprus remains the same, but so do the issues in American policy toward ending the crisis. Our Government still persists in viewing the Turkish action on the island as simply a new reality to cope with. We still fail to condemn the invasion and occupation of an independent state. We still fail to acknowledge that the human tragedy on Cyprus was brought about with the illegal use of American supplied weapons. We still relegate to the sidelines a central issue for Cyprus—the return of refugees to their homes. And, as in so many other recent world problems with heavy American involvement, the administration is still asking for a little more time on Cyprus, in order to bring about its repeated assurances of early negotiations to achieve a political settlement.

(1)

And so, as the human suffering and political tragedy of Cyprus drags on, American policy continues its tacit support for consolidating Turkey's control over northern Cyprus. And in the absence of any new directions or initiatives in our policy, we see our diplomats avoiding testimony before the committees of Congress. We see them withholding information on the issues at stake—and searching around for new explanations for the continuing refugee problem, and the lack of progress in bringing peace to the people of Cyprus.

I believe Congress has acted responsibly in strongly asserting its concern over the Turkish invasion and occupation of Cyprus—and over the deadlock in negotiations that has prevented the return of refugees to their homes. In October, Congress acted to give the President time to break this deadlock, and to secure some progress in negotiations. The President now says he needs more time. And Congress is now working its will, and will vote on this crucial issue within the next few days.

But time is running out—and the condition of the refugees is getting no better.

American goals toward Cyprus are as clear today as they were 2 months ago when this subcommittee last met.

First, our Government must unequivocally affirm American support for the restoration of the full independence, sovereignty, and territorial integrity of Cyprus. No other goal will satisfy the demands of justice, or really bring peace and relief to the people of that tortured island.

Second, we must show a more active concern over the rehabilitation needs of the refugees. Moreover, the fate of these people is central to the Cyprus issue, and to any negotiations over the future of the island. We must finally put the problem of Cypriot refugees at the top of our agenda for Cyprus.

And third, given our close political and defense ties with Turkey, and the administration's repeated assurances of productive relations with Ankara, we must express more urgently the need for a Turkish gesture of goodwill—involving the return of refugees to their homes—to break the impasse in negotiations. This would not only serve the interests of the Greek Cypriot refugees, but also those of the Turkish Cypriot community, which is also suffering the ill effects of an occupation army.

The purpose of today's hearing is to up date congressional and public understanding of conditions on Cyprus, and of America's ability to assist further in fulfilling the hopes and aspirations of the Cypriot people.

This subcommittee over the period of years has been extremely interested and concerned about humanitarian problems as they have existed in all parts of the world. Its early interest focused on the enormous problems of refugees in Southeast Asia, and it continued with the problems of Biafra, and Bangladesh—the 10 million refugees there, more than 3 million of whom died. We have also focused our attention on the problems of the Sahel and the devastating problems of food and hunger that exist in that part of the world. And we have attempted to play a constructive role in dealing with the problems of hunger that exist in Ethiopia—long before that was even generally understood or made known to the American people.

We tried to work with the administration in a constructive way, both across the table in the course of these hearings and in our continued contact with the administration, both Democrats and Republicans, because we recognize that humanitarian concerns have no partisanship and no party banner.

We on this committee have recently focused on what I think is a desperate plight of hundreds of thousands of Cypriot refugees—they number approximately 280,000—living in some of the most desperate conditions on that island. The committee staff report has described the conditions under which they live, separated from their families in many instances, from their homes and employment, and have had to depend upon the response of the international community to help meet their basic needs.

This has been as a result of actions which have been taken by Turkey, which run completely contrary to not only agreements that have been made with the United States in the use of various military equipment, but I believe which violate international law in their military aggression on Cyprus. Their present occupation of Cyprus and, more, their failure and unwillingness to really respond to the legitimate rights of the people who live on that island by their continued occupation, has resulted in tragedy. People have been suffering, old women, old men, children as well, have had their lives interrupted in the most cruel and unreasonable way.

We recognize—I do, and I am sure other members of this subcommittee do—that in order to restore their lives and sense of well-being, it is going to take a political settlement I have expressed before my own view on the nature of that which will be dependent upon the withdrawal of foreign forces and the return to their homes of refugees. We recognize that this really is the basis for any long term solution to the problems of refugees. We as individuals of this subcommittee are going to pursue this goal in the way which we feel it can best be done. I have expressed my views on that particular issue.

The question which brings us here this morning is the humanitarian issue—the humanitarian problems of the people of Cyprus. We recognize again that it is carefully intertwined with the overall political problem, but nonetheless, we want to make sure that we as a country and individuals are responding to the humanitarian needs.

WELCOME TO WITNESS

So we are fortunate this morning to have a distinguished church leader for our leadoff witness.

Before recognizing him, I will recognize our ranking member, Senator Fong, who has been an extremely active member of this subcommittee, and ask him if he would like to make a statement.

Senator FONG. Mr. Chairman, I want to thank you for calling this meeting. I think it is a very appropriate time for us to have another meeting on the question of Cyprus.

I am very happy to welcome His Eminence.

Senator KENNEDY. Senator Mathias.

Senator MATHIAS. Thank you, Mr. Chairman.

I also want to join in welcoming the Archbishop this morning, His Eminence, so he can give us from a human point of view some of the facts that will be helpful to this committee and will be helpful in illuminating this problem for the whole American public, because we have to keep in mind the problems on Cyprus, human problems, problems capable of solution, but problems which will not be resolved unless there is a full understanding by the American public of just the depth and nature of the problem, and I think that is what this morning's hearing will do.

I will only say to His Eminence that we appreciate his presence here, and say that I hope that it will be helpful and worthwhile to the cause that we all want to serve.

Senator Kennedy, as the chairman of this subcommittee, has led the committee into studies of various human problems, and he has said in Southeast Asia and Bangladesh and other areas, and I think the attention that has been brought to the problems of refugees as a result of his leadership and the committee's work have been helpful in those instances. I have confidence and hope and pray that the same will be true in this case.

Thank you for being here.

Senator KENNEDY. Your Eminence, you have, as you can understand, a warm welcome extended to you. You follow other religious leaders who have appeared not only before this subcommittee and before the parent committee, the Judiciary Committee, and other committees, who bring to our Nation's policy a deep seated sense of moral concern to these issues. Too infrequently, perhaps, our legislative efforts are not identified with those moral concerns and those moral needs. But, as you understand as a church leader, this is really the basis for all government and for all society.

We welcome you here and we value very highly the message you bring to this committee and to the Senate this morning. We thank you very much for arranging your program to join us.

STATEMENT OF ARCHBISHOP IAKOVOS, PRIMATE OF THE GREEK ORTHODOX CHURCH IN THE AMERICAS

Archbishop IAKOVOS. Allow me, Mr. Chairman, to express to you directly and personally my most profound gratitude, which I also address to your distinguished colleagues, Senator Fong and Senator Mathias, for having concerned yourselves with the plight of the almost 300,000 refugees and displaced persons in Cyprus, including the Greek and Turkish Cypriots.

I am fully aware, and as a matter of fact, very proud of the humanitarian record of our people in the United States; in presenting myself to you. I feel dutybound to verify what my fellow men and colleagues in Cyprus are suffering these days as a result of Turkey's invasion in July.

I do not have to go into the circumstances which caused this uprooting of innocent people, for the circumstances are very well known, not only to the American public, but to the world as well.

The end result of that invasion, which in my judgment was totally unjustified, caused the uprooting and misery of thousands of people who are now seeking refuge under trees, under tents, and always under the eyes of God in whom they have placed both their faith and their trust.

THE ABSENCE OF HOPE ON CYPRUS

What concerns me more than anything else is not the conditions under which they live, but the absence of hope from their minds and from their hearts that someday they will be helped to rediscover their homes and establish themselves where most of them were born and where they have lived all these years.

For 4 months already these thousands of Cypriots are waiting for a ray of encouragement, why the sky hangs very heavily over their heads. There is a long night of fear and uncertainty, and they would very much like to see a ray of hope. This is what I am soliciting today on their behalf.

The graveness of the situation does not lie simply in the fact of their pride of their basic livelihood, but in the fact that there are very few people in the world who understand their true situation, the tragic conditions which surrond their lives for the past four months.

Many governments, starting with our own here in the States as well as in Western Europe and including the Government of Greece, are doing their best in order to provide them with the necessary nourishment and basic food stuff so they may prolong, so to speak, their endurance until the day comes when they will be helped to go back to their own homes.

FAILURE TO SUPPORT HUMAN RIGHTS

I feel certainly very unhappy when I think of our age, an age during which we have come to recognize human rights, civil rights, equal opportunities, equality among races, and yet it seems that we cannot be effective in our attempts to establish such an equality among men throughout the world.

Ours has been a Nation which has played always a leading role in humanitarian activities. I feel that if we fail the Cypriots in their plight today we may fail all of the people who are suffering because of similar reasons which have caused the creation of so many refugee camps in the Middle East area as well as in Hong Kong.

HELP REFUGEES RETURN HOME

The United States has been always helpful, has been always stretching a helping hand to all suffering, but I think what we need to do for the Cypriots is not simply to help them in their present need, but also in their other expectations so they may be able to go back to their own homes.

The American Red Cross as well as the International Red Cross and many other organizations, the Greek American community in the United States and Canada and South America have done their utmost in order to be of asssitance to their brothers, both because we share their suffering and because we feel it is our moral responsibility to assist them in their painful anticipation of a better day.

I understand that you, my respected and honored friend, Senator Kennedy, have presented to your committee an amendment to the pending foreign aid bill, an amendment providing foreign aid up to $100 million in order that Cypriot refugees, both Greeks and Turks, may be helped and may be rehabilitated.

It is true that all American people, including the Greek Americans, are deeply indebted to you and to your distinguished colleagues. I know, not because I have been in Cyprus, but because I have been in constant correspondence with people in Cyprus, that their only hope is that we in the United States, as a matter of fact, the United States may take the initiative in their behalf and bring about a much desired peace which will help them to reacquire their dignity and their self-respect.

I don't need to come into details describing their needs, because a special study group sent to Cyrpus has reported already to you in detail some months ago. I don't need to say that the winter, although brief in Cyprus, becomes very cold at times and very dangerous, especially when people live in continued suffering and misery.

I know that we Americans have been always concerned with people who have been victimized as a result of war, violence, or injustice, and I am more than convinced that we will do our utmost in order, once again, to be helpful to those who need to be helped, who need to be encouraged, who need to be saved.

I don't mean to give you the impression that I may be sermonizing, but in the name of Him who came as a man, to put an end to servitude, in the name of Him who came as a poor boy so that He may bring an end to poverty, in the name of Him who was forced to leave His home town and go into Egypt as a refugee so that He may put an end to human injustice and to inhumane actions, permit me to place my appeal before you so that you take under serious consideration and personal concern the plight of our Cypriot brethren and not allow the issue to be buried under political or diplomatic considerations.

I am most grateful for your inviting me to give this kind of testimony or statement in behalf of my Cypriot coreligionists and allow me to repeat that my hope and my trust is in God and in you.

Senator KENNEDY. Thank you very much, Your Eminence, for a very moving comment and statement, and one which we value very, very highly.

CHURCH RELIEF EFFORTS

I was wondering if you might share with us the efforts that you have been making personally, and that the Church has been making, to provide some relief for the human suffering in Cyprus. Tell us a bit about that.

Archbishop IAKOVOS. My efforts go back to the month of August, beginning of August, when I invited Greek-American community organizations to come for a special meeting in New York, at which time we decided to address an appeal to our fellow communicants throughout the States so that they may help those who have suffered as a result of the war on Cyprus. Individual organizations and communities have responded most generously in offering blood, medicines, blankets, cots, foodstuff, clothing, money, and I must inform you that I am informed by my 50 regional chairmen that our church communities have generously responded to my appeal. I thank God for them and I am very proud of them. They have directly sent to Cyprus thousands of tons of material aid, and through the Archdiocese have offered as much, as a $1 million in cash. Already $500,000 has been given to Archbishop Makarios and his representatives and another $500,000 will be presented to the Ambassador of Cyprus at the end of this week.

My fellow communicants in South America were also instrumental in sending 150 tons of sugar and coffee and other foodstuff to Cyprus, while the Canadian community has been more than active in helping the refugees in Cyprus.

I must add as a footnote that all we did was in response to the dictates of our conscience and heart. The Church ladies, the youth societies, are doing their utmost in order to provide help for a number of children, orphaned children in Cyprus. We already have adopted in excess of 600 children and we shall continue to do so.

On the other hand, the American institutions both here and in Greece, the college, the American farm school in Salonika, and the Athens College have offered scholarships to young Cypriot students, and we shall never cease doing what we feel is our moral and religious responsibility toward them.

Senator KENNEDY. Well, it appears that the community and the Church have really led the effort in trying to reflect what I think is one of the finest characteristics of the American people, and that is their sense of generosity for those in need. Under your leadership, your Church has, I think, made an extraordinarily important contribution to the relief of the suffering of the refugees.

ATTITUDE OF REFUGEES

I would like to ask you if you would develop for us a bit the attitude of the refugees themselves. You commented, and I thought very movingly, about the real lack of hope that exists, and I think this was something which is terribly important. Besides their physical adversity which they are facing in terms of the winter and in terms of living in tents, I would also be interested in how they look toward the future and what their view about their future lives might be. I think this is terribly important.

Archbishop IAKOVOS. I have working for the Archdiocese in New York two ladies who came from Cyprus. They are rather young. Another secretary of mine left New York for Cyprus some months ago. She went to Cyprus to stay, and all three of them describe with very, very discouraging color the future of the refugees in Cyprus. I cannot comment in detail, because as I said earlier, I think your committee is rather well informed of the existing conditions in Cyprus.

I also receive, almost daily, letters from young people of both sexes who would like to continue their studies in Cyprus or Greece and need help. Since this is impossible under the present circumstances in Cyprus they ask me to provide scholarships for them. They tell me that it seems impossible for them, even to live, unless something is done, and done within a reasonably short time. They also tell me that people in Cyprus have lost faith. They are presently left in a completely chaotic situation. They are demoralized. People who found it necessary to go back to the Turkish zones find their homes either demolished or in complete ruins, and on their way back to their tents are being mugged and tortured by Turkish peasants and soldiers.

I don't like to give you the impression that I color politically my sentiments or the description I am trying to give you, but I feel that there is no man who can describe justifiably the extent of the tragic conditions under which these people live without dramatizing the degree of suffering.

Senator KENNEDY. Senator Fong?

RESETTLEMENT OF REFUGEES?

Senator FONG. Your Eminence, is there any resettlement going on at the present time?

Archbishop IAKOVOS. As far as I know, your Honor, I don't think so. I have no information of any kind of a settlement.

On the other hand, I know that the Cypriot Government does not like that word settlement. They prefer the term rehabilitation.

Senator FONG. I said resettlement of the people, not settlement; resettlement of the people back into their homes, is that going on?

Archbishop IAKOVOS. I don't think so.

NEW REFUGEES?

Senator FONG. Is the number of refugees growing at the present time?

Archbishop IAKOVOS. New refugees are being made, especially under present conditions, because people who remain back in villages, now with the winter around the corner, prefer to leave their homes and join their compatriots so they may suffer together and thus alleviate their own actual suffering.

Senator FONG. Do you believe many are still leaving their homes at the present time?

Archbishop IAKOVOS. Yes.

Senator FONG. You don't believe that many are returning to their homes?

Archbishop IAKOVOS. As I commented a few minutes ago, very few have tried to go back home, and they were prevented or sent back to their refugee camp by the Turkish authorities.

BRITISH RELIEF EFFORTS

Senator FONG. Do you know of any effort that has been made by England, for example, to ameliorate some to these conditions?

Archbishop IAKOVOS. I think England has done its best in order to alleviate the suffering and also to give some protection to the Turkish refugees who have fled their homes; thousands of Turkish refugees are hosted, so to speak, and protected by the English forces in certain areas, especially at the Dhekelia Base.

TURKISH REFUGEES

Senator FONG. What do you estimate to be the number of Turkish refugees?

Archbishop IAKOVOS. From figures in my possession it is 34,000 refugees or persons who have fled.

Senator FONG. Approximately how many Greek Cypriot refugees are there?

Archbishop IAKOVOS. In excess of 240,000 people.

Altogether displaced persons are reaching the figure of 284,000, including Turks and Greeks.

9

SUFFICIENT FOOD FOR REFUGEES?

Senator Fong. Has the effort of the United States been such that everyone has been able to receive some food?

Archbishop Iakovos. All the people are receiving at least one substantial, decent meal a day. But I know very little about what our own Government has done in that respect. I know Sweden and West Germany and England are doing their part while Greece is spending between $5 and $6 million a month just for food for the refugees, both Turkish and Greek refugees.

Senator Fong. Do you envision this is going to be a long term refugee situation?

Archbishop Iakovos. I am afraid that if we cannot separate the two issues, the political settlement of differences between Greece and Turkey the plight of refugees in Cyprus or accept the Turkish position that the refugee problem will be part of the expected discussion between Turkey and Greece, we may be presented with some more tragic situations.

REFUGEE PROBLEM IS A POLITICAL PROBLEM

Senator Fong. You don't think the refugee problem can be solved until the political problem is solved?

Archbishop Iakovos. As a layman in political affairs I can only say that the two issues should be separated before the whole issue of Cyprus is politically resolved. But it seems that this is difficult because, from several discussions I have had here in the United States with people in authority, I formed the impression that the problem of refugees is one of the most important subjects to be discussed on the table of negotiations.

Senator Fong. You fear that the problem is that we are wrapped up in political negotiations?

Archbishop Iakovos. I am very much afraid so.

Senator Fong. Under those circumstances, you believe it will not be resolved until the political issues are worked out?

Archbishop Iakovos. I have that impression, and I am terribly upset with the idea.

Senator Fong. Thank you.

Senator Kennedy. Senator Mathias.

REFUGEES ON BRITISH BASES

Senator Mathias. Your Eminence, can you tell us the situation with regard to those refugees who were living within the British bases? Are there still numbers of people there?

Archbishop Iakovos. My information about the Turkish Cypriots who have sought refuge in British bases comes from England, from official or semiofficial reports as well as from the World Council of Churches. As you have probably read, the Turkish authorities demanded these refugees to be freed, so to speak, by the British, and be transported to the northern part of Cyprus which they like to Turkishize complete.y.

Senator Mathias. In other words, this would be an effort at a forced resettlement project?

Archbishop Iakovos. Exactly.

Senator MATHIAS. Rather than an effort at maintaining a sub-sistence level of life while the political situation is going on?

Archbishop IAKOVOS. I had discussions with Archbishop Makarios the very same day that he left the United States, and he told me that what he thought was important was not simply to recognize full citizenship to Turkish Cypriots, but to form cantons and to those which are inhabited by a majority of Turks, be given complete antonomy. Those on the other hand which are inhabited by a clear majority of Greek Cypriots be given equal autonomy and be incorporated, together with the Turkish cantons, into a federal government. He doesn't like the idea of dichotomy, which seems to be the demand of Turkish Cypriots or the Turkish Government.

Senator MATHIAS. So, in fact, these Turkish refugees who are living in the British bases are resettled, it would have the effect of increasing segregation rather than decreasing it?

Archbishop IAKOVOS. Yes. I called such a resettlement unjust because it will make things more difficult for a final settlement of differences between Turkey and Greece.

EXTENT OF DESTRUCTION

Senator MATHIAS. Do you have any more information as to the number of houses that have been destroyed and the number of people that were actually without homes either because they were destroyed or driven from the areas in which they lived?

Archbishop IAKOVOS. According to reports received from the Government of Cyprus, at least 30 percent of the houses and the establishments, generally speaking, in the areas occupied by the Turks have been destroyed.

Senator MATHIAS. So that those people are now effectively homeless?

Archbishop IAKOVOS. They are in fact homeless and even those who have fled and sought refuge in churches were chased out of them after having been brutally tortured—punished—let me use a less impressive word—by Turkish authorities.

Senator MATHIAS. Merely punished for being Greeks?

Archbishop IAKOVOS. Yes. The fact that old men and children and women of all ages have been tortured in the churches, where they had sought refuge, or the fact that organs of public order, the police, have been slain—all attest to the statement that their only crime was that of being Greek. But this is beyond the realm of, I think, our present discussion.

POLITICAL SOLUTION NECESSARY

Senator MATHIAS. Of course, the Senator from Hawaii has brought out the political aspect as the very key and prime requisite, but do you have any suggestions to the committee as to the type of aid which you feel is most urgent?

Archbishop IAKOVOS. As I stated earlier, I think the most important kind of aid we can give them is that they sustain in their hearts a reasonable amount of hope that they will be rehabilitated in their own homes. I don't call the aid, in the form of food or clothing or tents, as the most important one. It is up to us to give them something more substantial, something more precious, and that is hope.

I like to repeat that word: "Hope." Because committees which have been sent by the Cyprus Government to the States, and which they came to see me, asked me to round up the efforts, so to speak, so that this hope for Cypriots in despair may be given precedence here in the United States, and especially among people in the Government. The American public should be informed that their Cypriot brothers are not begging for food, but for justice and dignity.

Senator MATHIAS. Thank you.

SILENCE OVER HUMAN RIGHTS VIOLATIONS

Senator KENNEDY. Your Eminence, from my point of view, one of the very deep and genuine concerns that I have had about Cyprus, and on human rights issues, generally, has been the failure of those who have information, or knowledge, or understanding about the violation of human rights to raise their voices about these issues. I am just wondering from your position as a church leader what sort of sense of morality exists under these circumstances?

One of the quotes that President Kennedy used to use was Dante's that, in times of moral crisis those who remain silent, there was going to be a special place in hell reserved for them.

I am just wondering, in listening to you this morning, what your views are. There is certainly no other American who has felt this as deeply as you have, someone who has such a deep concern, and yet in listening to your voice it is powerful for not only what it says, but it is powerful for the restraint as well.

Of course, you haven't been restrained in responding to the humanitarian needs in your efforts in trying to provide some relief to people.

But, as a church leader, what do you tell your parishioners about this dilemma of silence on moral issues?

Archbishop IAKOVOS. I am glad, Senator Kennedy, you mentioned the name of President Kennedy because I was afraid for a moment that I would be considered as paying compliments to the Kennedy name, but I had in mind telling you that it was President Kennedy who raised the issue of morality as a very important issue, and I feel that these last years of our history have given full justification to the great principle established by President Kennedy that we should be capable of even capturing again the morality and the purity of the American mind and the American soul in all we do and all we say.

The last 3 years told us and told the world all over again that morality is much more powerful than any kind of material power or political preeminence. I tell these things to myself because I don't like to give you the impression that I came here to teach morality. I am not the teacher of morality. I prefer to be a doer of moral things.

TARNISHED AMERICAN IMAGE

I have the fear, however, and because of this I will allow my feelings to dictate my response to a certain question by Senator Mathias. I have a feeling that our whole attitude toward Cyprus and toward our Cypriot brethren has not been in the best tradition of American morality. I don't think for instance that by sending through the Red

Cross or through the United Nations special funds, $2 to $4 million to Cyprus, we can be proud of ourselves for having done what we ought to do, and I don't think by discussing the problems of Cyprus extensively in the press or over TV or among high officials that we can say that we have done our part.

I think this Nation has given to the world an image which was unknown before the end of the last war, an image of a Nation concerned, a Nation guided by moral principles, a Nation which could believe in a code of ethics in international politics. I am terribly sad, as a matter of fact, very unhappy whenever I see with my own eyes that we are losing gradually that respect which was centered on the moral tenets of the American Nation and of the American politics.

Therefore, if I am allowed to add one more thing before I conclude what I have already stated, I would say that it is up to us to recapture that fiber which would make us a much stronger Nation in the sense that we can regain once again the confidence and the trust of the rest of the world.

CYPRUS RELIEF: MORE THAN BREAD ALONE

Senator MATHIAS. This very literally, if I interpret what Your Eminence says, is a case where bread alone does not suffice. We have to do what is necessary from a humanitarian standpoint as far as human suffering—but bread alone could prolong this problem if we simply decide, as we have seen in other parts of the world, that we will support the refugees indefinitely without coming to grips with the problem that has made them refugees. We will prolong the difficulties that have been brought upon the people of Cyprus.

Archbishop IAKOVOS. Thank you for expanding my thoughts.

Senator MATHIAS. I hope I have done it accurately.

COMMENDATION OF WITNESS

Senator KENNEDY. I want to thank you, Your Eminence, very much, for your extremely helpful comments. They have been of great value to me, and I know all of us on this committee appreciate your sharing your thoughts and your concerns with us.

We will look forward to working with you in the future, in meeting needs that I think you have challenged us to meet over the coming days and over the long run.

I want to thank you very much.

Archbishop IAKOVOS. I thank you and I hope God gives you the strength to do your best.

Senator KENNEDY. Your Eminence, you are welcome to stay if you care to, or whatever your program is. We will go on until the full Judiciary Committee calls us to a scheduled meeting. Whatever your program is.

We had planned to have the Administration as No. 2, but we have some out-of-town witnesses. So I would like to give them a chance to speak because I don't know how long we will be able to continue.

I will ask that Mr. Tsaffaras, who is from my State of Massachusetts, if you will come and introduce Mr. Chirgotis.

Mr. TSAFFARAS. May I at this time present to you the supreme president of the Order of AHEPA, American Hellenic Educational Progressive Association, Mr. William Chirgotis.

The other members are not here, Mr. Chairman, but I think we will cover the subject quite extensively.

Senator KENNEDY. We extend a warm welcome to you, Mr. Chirgotis.

We will start out by noting that you contributed to what I think is an excellent report in reviewing the situation in Cyprus. As one who has followed refugee problems not only in Cyprus but also other parts of the world, I want to commend you and your organization for the work you have done. Your report is just first rate, and it will be of great value and help to us. I am going to include it as a part of the record.

As you know, we had a team in Cyprus in October, and we follow very closely the events and the happenings on that island. So we look forward to hearing from you this morning.

STATEMENT OF WILLIAM G. CHIRGOTIS, SUPREME PRESIDENT, ORDER OF AHEPA AND WILLIAM P. TSAFFARAS, COCHAIRMAN AHEPA JUSTICE FOR CYPRUS COMMITTEE

Mr. CHIRGOTIS. Thank you, Mr. Chairman.

Mr. Chairman and members of the committee, I would like to thank you for the opportunity of appearing before you to give a very brief report of our factfinding mission to Cyprus.

I do not appear before you today with a prepared statement. However, I have brought with me several copies of our monthly publication, which includes a 37-page factfinding report as was witnessed by the seven members of our delegation that went to Cyprus on October 1, 2, and 3, 1974.

I would like to refer to a speech that I made in Chicago just the other day in which I gave them my views of our factfinding analysis. These are some of the things that we actually saw and not things that we read in local newspapers.

CYPRUS: MASSIVE HUMAN SUFFERING

In my entire life, I have never imagined or seen suffering like our mission of mercy delegation saw on this Mediterranean island. We saw many small children going to a class which seated 25 youngsters and there were 90 in the class. We saw families living in bamboo huts, living under trees without the facilities of tents or blankets. We saw a 96-year-old Cypriot who begged us to return him to his home so that he might die in peace. We also saw a young boy about 14 or 15 years old who handed us a piece of shrapnel and said take this back to America, he said, with our regrets. He also told us in the brief conversation that we had with this young man that his father and mother were both killed by fire bombs during the Turkish invasion.

VISIT TO REFUGEE AREAS

We went to four of the refugee camps, and in one camp there was approximately 11,000 displaced persons. In the second camp I believe there was 8,000 or 9,000. The one plea of pleas seemed to be return us to our homes. It appeared at that time that food was in short supply. Most of them hadn't had a hot meal for days, and they were living on spaghetti and rice.

We saw the delivery of many of the supplies that the order of AHEPA had just delivered, and to date we have shipped overseas about 500,000 pounds of supplies, and because the supplies are coming in faster than we can airlift them overseas, we hope that within the next few weeks we will send by ship another million pounds of supplies.

HOPE IS IN SHORT SUPPLY

The actual physical conditions that we saw there were expressions of uncertainty almost on every face. As I mentioned a few moments ago, the one plea of all pleas was please return us to our homes. Of course, the feeling of hope seemed to be in very short supply.

The Order of AHEPA is a nonpolitical organization, a fraternal organization, but we are very much concerned about what has happened in Cyprus and we are doing whatever we can to help our Cypriot brothers.

We very often think of the many sacrifices that our American forefathers went through for the preservation of liberty in this country, and because of the application of these cherished principles may I say that this country has earned first place in the hearts of the people of all free nations, and I personally believe that the violation—that any violation of these principles would certainly endanger the moral foundations of this Nation, perhaps of the entire civilized world. This is my own personal opinion.

Our trip to Cyprus was made possible, may I say, through the courtesy of the State Department; as you well know, gentlemen, there is no transportation between Athens and Cyprus. The only transportation is by means of ship, and that takes about 36 hours to get to the island of Cyprus. So through the courtesy of the State Department they made available to us an Air Force plane which made our trip to Cyprus possible.

REFUGEES ON BRITISH BASE

We landed at a British airbase and we were very happy to see that at one of these camps it was supervised by the British, and they were making every effort to see that the refugees and displaced persons were extended the courtesies, help, and assistance that was possible.

HELPING CYPRUS

In one of these camps water was in very short supply. They were bringing the water in by means of tanks, and many of the people that we saw there in Cyprus hadn't bathed for days.

The situation is indescribable. I have been told recently that the only great effort that is being done to assist our unfortunate brothers in Cyprus is that the Greek Government is sharing the load, and at the present time they are constructing semipermanent homes there to house the refugees through the winter season. They are spending millions of dollars, and it is necessary, I believe, that some effort be made to assist these people.

I don't know what else, Mr. Chairman, I could add to this brief report. As I said, I have come here today without a prepared statement. These are just my extemporaneous remains. I have brought several copies of our report here which I would like to leave with you which has a complete factfinding report of the mission to Cyprus.

Senator KENNEDY. Thank you very much.

We will include that, the relevant parts in the record,[1] and the whole report in the file of the committee.

Mr. CHIRGOTIS. Mr. Tsaffaras is with me today, our past president of the organization, and perhaps he may have some comments.

Mr. TSAFFARAS. Thank you, Mr. Chairman, members of this committee.

Let me state that as a member of AHEPA factfinding mission to Cyprus I welcome the opportunity to appear before you and to submit for your consideration the reasons for financial assistance to the people of Cyprus.

I could spend several months relating my experiences and describing the various events during our visit to the island of Cyprus. All the events and the pain, suffering, and misfortune of these 200,000-plus refugees are well described in your excellent report "Crisis on Cyprus, 1974," prepared for your subcommittee, and also this "AHEPA Cyprus Mission of Mercy," published in the AHEPAN magazine, the official publication of the Order of AHEPA.

ECONOMIC DISASTER FOR CYPRUS

Aside from the very important human suffering, let us look at the economic disaster of Cyprus. Although it is difficult to estimate accurately the damage incurred in the area controlled by the Turkish invasion forces; some estimates have been made, however, on the consequences of the invasion on the economy. It is estimated that the country of Cyprus is losing about $5 million a day in production; a major part of the labor force is unemployed or seriously underemployed compared with a state of full employment before the invasion.

It is estimated that over 40,000 households have been broken up and forcibly expelled from their homes, leaving behind all of their property. These properties are estimated to be in the order of over $150 million. Goods left in warehouses, shops, and factories under Turkish control amount to many millions of dollars.

Destruction to cultivated lands, pinewood forests by the bombing of some 100 square miles cannot be expressed in pecuniary terms. It will take many years to restore these resources.

Tourist activity which brought into the country more than $75 million annually is lost, and this loss is expected to continue for a number of years.

Major losses have been suffered in livestock, agricultural products, mineral resources, and many other sectors of the economy. A conservative estimate of the economy that is a total loss is well over $1 billion during these past 5 months.

REFUGEE SITUATION

With your kind indulgence may I say a word or two about the refugee problem. As we walked through these refugee camps the one thing that stands in my mind were the words expressed by the old and the young when we asked what help we could offer. This one expression was, "help us to go back to our homes."

[1] For the text of the AHEPA report, see app. 1.

These people are a proud people. They do not seek charity. They seek justice, and they look to the United States for assistance to that end. They want the opportunity to rebuild their economic position. This financial assistance that we are seeking today will be a beginning, a new beginning, for these 230,000 refugees, a new hope that someone cares.

With this statement, Mr. Chairman, I would like to bring to mind the traumatic experiences that these refugees are experiencing, and it is most difficult to visualize this experience.

I well remember, and if I may, through an experience of my own, as of yesterday, December 16, some 30 years ago, I was in Germany at the Battle of the Bulge and we were captured as prisoners of war and we witnessed this traumatic experience, this hope, this nightmare that one goes through in wondering what the next day will bring. This is the exact thing that these refugees are experiencing today. They look to you. They look right into your eyes and say, "when will this nightmare be over?"

I think it is incumbent upon us in the United States to provide whatever financial assistance we can to help bring Cyprus back on its feet. They want to work. They want to build. They want to build their own economy as best as they can. They don't want charity; they want to get back to work and build their economy.

Thank you very much, Mr. Chairman.

ROLE OF AHEPA

Senator KENNEDY. Thank you very much, Mr. Tsaffaras, for a helpful comment, as always.

Let me ask you what the Order of AHEPA is doing and what it plans to do over the long term. I would be interested in that.

Mr. CHIRGOTIS. While we were in Cyprus we took a camera crew with us and we took photographs of the existing conditions in Cyprus. Several weeks ago I took the film to Universal Studios in California and we had TV personality Telly Savalis narrate this film for us, and the final print should be available in the next few days. We are making about 50 copies of this film and it is our intention to use it to raise funds for the people of Cyprus.

Senator KENNEDY. You are planning to continue your program of help and assistance?

Mr. CHIRGOTIS. Definitely.

Senator KENNEDY. That is based upon your sense of the need that exists there, gathered from your factfinding group that visited in October?

Mr. CHIRGOTIS. 234,000 refugees, Mr. Chairman, is a lot of people.

Senator KENNEDY. But as I understand, you have ongoing and continuing plans to reach out to your membership and also to other citizens in this country as well, who have the sense of concern about the plight of these people, and you are going to be raising funds for Cyprus?

Mr. CHIRGOTIS. Yes.

WHAT SHOULD THE UNITED STATES DO?

Senator KENNEDY. Do you have some ideas or suggestions about what the United States can be doing to supplement your efforts?

As I understand, Cyprus is a rather unique situation where, because of the fact of trained and skilled people that exist in Cyprus, it hasn't been necessary to set up a whole new relief infrastructure. It has been done through groups and churches and the government quite effectively. I wonder if you would like to comment on how the relief effort is going.

But we know that the extent of U.S. assistance has been approximately $10 million. When you look at the fact that you have raised, and the archbishop has raised, a very substantial amount of resources just through your own efforts, I am interested in what you think we ought to be urging our government to be prepared to undertake, both in the short term and probably in the long term, for Cyprus.

Do you think that funds could be wisely spent now if additional funds were made available by the U.S. Government to provide some relief from the suffering of people there? Are you satisfied that would be the case and it would be justifiable? You obviously believe it, because you are going to your members to raise additional resources. What I am trying to do is to build a case so we can go to the Department of State and say we have a case here—there are additional needs—and let's provide some assistance.

ASSISTANCE FOR CYPRUS

Mr. CHIRGOTIS. Mr. Chairman, there are probably several things that can be done. While we were on Cyprus it seemed that the most important thing was that these people wanted was to return to their homes as soon as possible. As you well know, Turkey at the present time occupies about 40 percent of the island, and the most fertile area of Cyprus as well.

The displaced persons in the southern part of the island is very nonproductive. The one thing that should be looked into very seriously, I think, is the problem of restoring the economy of the country. These people are very desperate in these camps for lack of something to do, and if some method could be found or established whereby the economy of the country can be restored to get these people back on their feet, I think the longer they remain in the situation the more depressed they are going to get.

The Turks at the present time occupy Famagusta, which is one of the main seaports. We have been told if it were possible for the Turkish Army to leave Famagusta, one-third of these people could be accommodated in the homes and the hotels and the buildings that are there, and I think this is one thing that could be looked into as a temporary situation to relieve the requirements and necessities of one-third of the refugees, about 70,000 or 80,000.

But the most important thing, I think, is to see these people get self-determination.

Senator KENNEDY. Senator Fong?

MILITARY SITUATION STABILIZED?

Senator FONG. Is the military situation stabilized now?

Mr. CHIRGOTIS. It appears to be, sir.

Senator FONG. Is it a question of having the political situation resolved before many of these things can be accomplished?

Mr. CHIRGOTIS. It appears that way.

Mr. TSAFFARAS. If I may make a comment on that one. We were over there and visited with Mr. Denktash, the leader of the Turkish group, and we asked if it would be possible to retreat some of these troops from the city of Famagusta, and he indicated to us that nothing would be done until the political problem is resolved and this is where it is stalemated and this is where it is very important, so we seek some form of adjustment so some of these people can go back to their homes.

RETURN OF REFUGEES TO FAMAGUSTA

Senator FONG. What suggestions have you along that line?

Mr. TSAFFARAS. We think we would like to have this country, through our State Department, convince the Turkish people there, and the country of Turkey, to pull some of the troops back and let some of these refugees return to their homes.

Senator FONG. You think if they gave up Famagusta——

Mr. TSAFFARAS. Famagusta, 50,000 refugees from that one city, and they indicated they could accommodate another 30,000 if they were allowed to go back to their homes.

Senator FONG. As a member of this committee I will try to ascertain if that can be done.

Mr. CHIRGOTIS. That might be a temporary starting point, anyway.

Senator KENNEDY. Senator Mathias?

Senator MATHIAS. I think it has been very helpful to have your testimony this morning, particularly as it comes firsthand as a result of a field investigation.

I would join with Senator Fong in his suggestion to the chairman that we do make that recommendation to the State Department.

I would only add further, and I am sure the chairman would be agreeable to this, that you feel you have an open line to this committee, and as you get additional information, that you think will be helpful to us, that you will feel free to supply it to us on a continuing basis; in that way, we can keep in touch with the Cyprus situation and with the immediate and crucial problems that affect the refugees.

Mr. CHIRGOTIS. Thank you for your concern, Senator.

Senator MATHIAS. I would ask the chairman that we arrange to have the staff prepare to accept any communications of any kind that you may wish to give us.

LETTER TO DEPARTMENT OF STATE

Senator KENNEDY. We have been summoned, which I knew we would be, to attend a full committee meeting, so we will have to adjourn.

But I would like to mention just before we do, that one of the recommendations that the subcommittee study mission made was the need for a Turkish gesture of good will, that would involve, perhaps, the return of the refugees to Famagusta and breaking of the deadlock over Nicosia Airport—that they would serve as a meaningful step to negotiations.

We have sent the recommendations of this report down to the Department of State on October 25, and we still haven't received a response, which is a little perplexing.

What I would like to suggest is that, as members of the committee, and we have our own views about the political situation, as I think you have gathered here—but I think what we ought to do is to take our humanitarian recommendations and the ones you have suggested and see if we can't press these again to the Department on the basis of our hearing this morning, and see if we can't keep after this issue. Shall we do that?

Senator FONG. We will get a special communication to the State Department.[1]

Mr. CHIRGOTIS. It will be very helpful.

Senator KENNEDY. We will have to stand in recess now.

I will say to Mr. Eagleton, we will try and resume in a short while for your testimony. We have it here. But perhaps what we could do is have that submitted for the record, and then maybe we can submit a series of detailed questions for the Department. We also want an answer to the recommendations sent in our October 25 letter. We want it soon, and we are going to address the letter to the Secretary about these humanitarian concerns and we hope that you will press when you return to the Department our very deep sense of concern about efforts that are being made for Cyprus.

We will submit your statement for the record, Mr. Eagleton, and permit you to make any response on earlier comments that have been made.

[The above referred to statements follow:]

DECEMBER 17, 1974.

STATEMENT BY WILLIAM EAGLETON, JR., BEFORE SENATE SUBCOMMITTEE ON REFUGEES ON EMERGENCY RELIEF EFFORTS ON CYPRUS

The plight of the refugees on Cyprus remains serious, and is a continuing reminder of the need for early progress on a settlement that will enable the people of Cyprus to live together in peace and security. Without minimizing in any way the hardships and suffering of the refugees on the island, it can nevertheless be said that the emergency relief program has been reasonably successful to date in providing the refugees with their immediate needs in food, shelter and medicine.

The international community responded to the UNHCR appeal for $22 million for September–December relief efforts with contributions in cash and kind totalling $23.1 million. The United Nations High Commission for Refugees (UNHCR) has acted as the coordinator for these and most other contributions and has been responsible for arranging the purchase and shipment of food and relief items. The International Red Cross (ICRC), the first major international organization to provide relief on Cyprus following the July events, has concerned itself with POWs, treatment of detainees, protection of civilians, missing persons, and humanitarian matters such as providing food, shelter and medical assistance to displaced persons and returnees. (The U.S. contribution to the ICRC has been $3.37 million.) UNFICYP (UN Force on Cyprus) has also supported relief activities, delivering on behalf of the UNHCR food and relief goods to the Turkish Cypriot community in the south and to the Greek community in the north, assisting the ICRC and UNHCR in the evacuation of the sick, pregnant, aged, and stranded civilians in both sectors, and providing medical evacuation services. (The U.S. contribution to UNFICYP thus far this fiscal year has been $4.8 million.)

The bulk of the operational aspects of the relief work, however, has been carried out by local authorities. The Government of Cyprus has established an Office of Special Services for Refugees, which has provided assistance to Greeks and (through UNFICYP) to Turks in the south, overseen the construction of permanent camp facilities, and collected statistics on refugees in order to formulate an effective refugee relief program. According to statistics released by the Government of Cyprus, Greek Cypriots displaced to the south since July number 180,716

[1] For the text of the letter of the subcommittee to Secretary of State Henry Kissinger, and his reply, see app. II.

of which 41,260 are completely self-supporting at this time and 139,456 are considered needy and are now receiving food and/or money for subsistence. In addition the UNHCR and the ICRC are providing food aid for about 18,000 Turkish Cypriots in the north.

The Cyprus Government reports that of the displaced persons (a) 102,572 are satisfactorily housed, (b) 2,269 are living in public buildings, (c) 55,888 are living in permanent structures but in overcrowded conditions, (d) 7,558 are living in garages and unfinished structures, and (e) 12,429 are in tents. There are believed to be few, if any, refugees still living in the open. The housing situation seems to be stabilizing, and thus the emphasis of the Government's relief efforts, which in the early days was on protection and housing, is shifting to food assistance.

FUTURE RELIEF REQUIREMENTS

The relief program for Cyprus in 1975 is still being developed by the Government of Cyprus in collaboration with the UN, the ICRC, and other organizations concerned with Cyprus relief. As noted above, the Government of Cyprus has shifted its emphasis to food assistance, and it has approached the UNHCR for financial assistance to help cover the majority of these expenses. Most of the funds provided under the UNHCR's $22 million appeal have been expended and thus additional contributions will be necessary. We understand that the UNHCR is considering the implementation of a Food for Work Program through the World Food Program (WFP). The WFP would have the responsibility for purchasing food, shipping it to Cyprus on the UNHCR account, and arranging for the shipment of food pledged on the UNHCR by the EEC and other in-kind donors.

The WFP is now working on a plan to channel all food and humanitarian assistance through a series of food for work projects. The WFP has worked out preliminary understandings with authorities on both sides on compensation for participants in the food for work programs. Details of proposed projects involving reforestation, irrigation, agricultural development, road construction, etc., are now being worked out. Preliminary WFP planning is based on an estimated 210,000 participants for a four-month trail period beginning in January 1975. The cost of such a program to the UNHCR would be about $8 million.

U.S. RELIEF ASSISTANCE

The United States has contributed $10.5 million to the Cyprus emergency relief effort through the ICRC and the UNHCR. We began by contributing $3.2 million in cash and relief supplies (tents, food, medical supplies) including a $725,000 cash grant to the ICRC. In September, in response to a UNHCR appeal for $22 million for relief efforts through December, we agreed to provide one-third of this amount ($7.3 million). Since August a US disaster relief specialist has been assigned to Nicosia to coordinate US assistance with UN agencies and the Cyprus Government and to help evaluate continuing relief needs.

As for the US role in 1975, specific funding requirements are not yet fully known and we are not yet in a position to state with certainty the exact amount that the US should be prepared to contribute. However, based on current spending patterns, AID believes that additional US assistance of from $8–10 million will be needed during the first six months of 1975. We appreciate and support action by Congress to provide funding for Cyprus relief efforts in 1975 and wish to continue to work with the Subcommittee on Refugees to ensure that the US carries its full share in meeting the humanitarian needs of the people of Cyprus.

Senator KENNEDY. I regret we have to adjourn, but I think, realistically, we will be in the Judiciary Committee for some period of time. Unless you have objection, that is the way we will proceed.

We will stand in recess.

[Whereupon, at 10:55 a.m., the subcommittee was recessed, subject to the call of the Chair.]

APPENDIX

APPENDIX I

Humanitarian Mission to Cyprus: A Special Report

(By William G. Chirgotis, Supreme President, AHEPA)

November 1974

My fellow AHEPANS and Greek Americans: We have just returned from an eight day fact finding mission to Cyprus—and what we witnessed during this short but productive period was something we never expected to find in the 20th century.

Seeing is believing—and we saw 234,000 refugees living in tents, others under trees, on the beaches, in the city streets. We saw doctors examining children in tents which would make M.A.S.H.'s medical tents look like modern hospital facilities. We witnessed children slowly dying due to a lack of medicine and proper facilities to stop diarrhea and dehydration. We saw a baby left on a blanket unattended, the father captured by the Turks, the mother frantically seeking to find her other two infant children—

These were only a few of the initial tragic sights we saw.

The six man team was headed by the Supreme President of the Order of AHEPA William G. Chirgotis and included John Plumides, Chairman of the AHEPA International Justice for Cyprus Committee; Past Supreme President William Tsaffaras; Past Supreme President Peter Bell; Cyprus Committee Coordinator, George Douris—who said as Boston Supreme Convention Chairman, "We shall go to Cyprus in six weeks," and we did—and James S. Scofield, Past Supreme Governor of the Order of AHEPA and Past Supreme President of the Sons of Pericles. Aides to the committee, Archie Mavromatis and Peter Sideris, also attended with the mission.

To these Brothers I am grateful. They proved their devotion for AHEPA and above all their love for all Hellenes. We were told before we left that we were going into a war zone—we know now they were not joking. We visited both the Greek Cypriot and Turkish Cypriot sections. We passed through a fourblock "no-man's land" zone of empty houses and buildings where not even a bird would dare fly or a rabbit run without being shot at by Greek Cypriot or Turkish guns.

It was common to hear the quiet of the night broken by machine gun tattering; and the beautiful mornings of Cyprus shattered by rifle fire. We heard bombs in the distance and prayed for the safety of the Cypriots and only ten minutes after we met Acting President Glafkos Clerides, an attempt was made on his life.

We met with Prime Minister Constantine Caramanlis of Greece, Foreign Minister of Greece George Mavros, United States Ambassador Jack B. Kubisch, Vice Premier George Rallis, Ambassador George Petrounakos of Hellenism Abroad, Turkish Vice President Rauf Denktash, Acting President Clerides, United States Ambassador to Cyprus William R. Crawford, and of course, a man who we can't thank enough, an AHEPAN of 20 years standing—the third man in the American Embassy, Zachary P. Geaneas. This man did everything possible to make our trip comfortable and safe. We also thank the two pilots of the small U.S. Air Force Dakota airplane that flew your AHEPA delegation to Cyprus and back, and to the British for their hospitality and for quickly expediting the AHEPA delegation in Cyprus and for providing whatever security that might have been needed.

To the press, radio and television in Greece, in Cyprus, and in our own country for fairly reporting the facts of our mission and helping get our message across to the public. To all the concerned individuals who helped in making our "Fact Finding Mission" possible, we say a collective thanks.

We thank the eleven publishers and editors of the Athens newspapers and news media who accepted the invitation of the Order of AHEPA to a luncheon at the Athens Hilton Hotel in which we explained our position and our efforts to help correct the unfortunate course of the foreign policy of the United States Government towards Cyprus—and they did make our story known!

To the people of Greece, including the 15,000 who demonstrated past our hotel rooms at the Athens Hilton as they proceeded towards the American Embassy with anti-American government slogans, we are grateful for making us more aware of the problems facing mother Hellas, and we in turn made them understand that the American people are solidly behind the cause of Cyprus as proved by the tremendous favorable vote of the United States Congress. To the Senate and the Congress of the United States, for their action on the Turkish Military Aid cut-off, we are grateful.

As Supreme President, I was proud to lead this non-partisan AHEPA delegation of dedicated Brothers, all with their own strong opinions; men of different political parties in AHEPA: but Brothers united in one cause—to help the people of Cyprus, in their hour of need, to correct the tragic mistake of the foreign policy of our country towards Cyprus. I am grateful to each and everyone for dedicating eight days of their lives, with very little rest and sleep, and in some instances, with very little food, to accomplish what I believe was so very much for humanity as the following report will show.

It all began with our first meeting on August 23, 1974 during the Boston Supreme Convention with Secretary of State Kissinger. The delegation very strongly told the Secretary of State of our disappointment in regard to the policy of the United States towards Cyprus.

At the second meeting with Dr. Kissinger on September 19th, once again the Supreme President of the Order of AHEPA told Dr. Kissinger that we were bitterly disappointed that the State Department apparently tolerated Turkish military aggression by continuing its economic and military aid to a country which was in violation of all its NATO commitments, and the United States Foreign Assistance Act of 1961.

We saw unexploded bombs that Greek Cypriots recovered and we witnessed American-made arms, American uniforms, American jeeps and other American military equipment on Cyprus in the hands of the Turkish invaders, which indeed is a clear violation of the U.S. Foreign Assistance Act of 1961 which denies the use of such arms for aggressive purposes against a sovereign nation.

When we told Dr. Kissinger we are going to Cyprus, he offered to assist our mission of mercy by facilitating our air transportation from Greece to Cyprus and for this, we say thanks.

Prior to our departure on Thursday, September 26th, Brother George Douris met privately with Archbishop Makarios and explained AHEPA's mission to Cyprus and received the blessings of His Beatitude. On Friday, September 27th, the AHEPA was host to Archbishop Makarios, President of the Republic of Cyprus, and Mr. George Mavros, Foreign Minister of the Republic of Greece, at a cocktail reception held at the Plaza Hotel in New York City.

Both these leaders encouraged our "Fact Finding Mission of Mercy" and asked us to strongly urge acting Cypriot President Glafkos Clerides to stand strong and not to be swayed by internal strife.

Following the reception, Mr. Douris, AHEPA International Justice for Cyprus Committee Chairman John Plumides and counsel to the Committee and Former Under Secretary to the U.S. Treasury, Eugene Rossides, met in Plaza Suite 1141 for more than an hour with Foreign Minister Mavros, and Professor Basil Vlavianos, Past President of Hermes Chapter, and discussed Mr. Mavros' appearance on Tuesday, October 1, before the Senate Foreign relations committee.

The AHEPA delegation advised Mr. Mavros to take a strong stand in condemning Turkish aggression, as well as expressing shock and indignation that the United States would allow the Turkish invaders in Cyprus to use guns, bullets, bombs, tanks, and American invading launches to accomplish their mission of invading and conquering a sovereign nation.

Mr. Mavros informed the committee going to Cyprus, that they should urge the Acting President, Mr. Clerides, to hold out, not to negotiate under duress with the Turks and that AHEPA will do everything possible for the 234,000 refugees.

What follows is a chronological report of the fact finding mission from the moment we boarded TWA flight #880 (Olympic Airways was on strike) which left Kennedy Airport at 6:45 p.m., Sunday September 29th, for Athens Greece.

Fraternally yours,

WILLIAM G. CHIRGOTIS, *Supreme President.*

At 10:00 a.m. Athens time Monday, September 30th, the mission arrived at Athens Airport. It was met at the airport by Greek Government officials, headed by Ambassador George Petrounakos and by Brother Zachary P. Geaneas of the American Embassy. After a brief stop at the Athens Hilton Hotel we met with

United States Ambassador Jack B. Kubisch, who himself was a recent arrival in Athens. Following the brief meeting with the Ambassador we were briefed by Embassy officials on the current situations in Greece and Cyprus. Following this meeting we had lunch with Ambassador Kubisch and the Embassy staff, the first social occasion to be hosted by Ambassador Kubisch and his charming wife since their arrival in Athens.

On Tuesday, October 1st, we had our initial press conference with newspaper, radio and television representatives. At 10:30 a.m. we met with Minister of Public Welfare, Athanasios Tsaldaris, who outlined to us the relief needs of the Greek Cypriot refugees.

Minister Tsaldaris indicated that the immediate need in Cyprus is for blankets, tents and camp beds and for money to buy needed relief supplies. He said 100,000 blankets must be supplied immediately and that there is a need for a total of 600,000 blankets. He also said that there are 5,200 students who now are attending schools in Greece and that $5 million a year will be needed for their education.

At 11:45 a.m. we met briefly with Prime Minister Constantine Caramanlis of Greece, the first of two meetings held with him during the week.

At 1:00 p.m. we met with the Ambassador of Cyprus to Greece, Nicos Kranidiotis, who briefed us with regard to Cyprus relief needs and made final arrangements for our visit to Cyprus. He informed us that all of the relief goods from the United States had already been sent by boat to Cyprus. We checked and found out that this was true, but much more had arrived that day and was still in a warehouse awaiting shipment to Cyprus.

The AHEPA mission brought 10,000 pounds of AHEPA relief supplies for our Cypriot Brothers.

At 2:00 p.m. we were guests of Ambassador Petrounakos at a luncheon held at the King George Hotel where we also discussed the situation in Greece and Cyprus and the relief needs in Cyprus. Later that evening we witnessed a massive, yet disciplined and peaceful demonstration, of students at the American Embassy which was against American Government Foreign Policy and of great emotional intensity. It created tremendous traffic jams and chaos in the streets immediately surrounding our hotel; some 15,000 students participated. This rally made us even more determined in our efforts to explain to Greece and Cyprus what AHEPA has done to correct the tragic mistakes of United States Foreign Policy and that we were disturbed by the anti-American government feeling. We wanted them to know the American public overwhelmingly supported Greece and Cyprus.

On Wednesday, October 2nd, at 9:30 a.m. we departed from Athens Airport aboard a U.S. Air Force C47 Dakota airplane. We landed at 1:30 p.m. at the British Sovereign Base of Akrotir in Cyprus. We were met by Phoebus Zachariades, District Officer of Limassol; Kyprianos Kyprianou, Foreign Office, Acting Chief of Protocol and Jay R. Grahame, of the American Embassy in Nicosia, We were briefed about Cyprus by the U.S. Embassy staff. Immediately thereafter, at 4:30 p.m., we met the Acting President of Cyprus, Mr. Glafkos Clerides, in the first of two meetings which we had with him.

Mr. Clerides, who impressed us very much with his decisive and forthright manner and grasp of the problems of Cyprus, told us that he deeded assurances from Archbishop Makarios that he could negotiate with his Turkish counterpart and make the necessary decisions needed to implement these negotiations. He indicated that without these assurances he would be forced to resign. We asked that in the interests of world peace and the future of a sovereign Cyprus that he stay on as Acting President.

Thereafter, we met with Ambassador William R. Crawford, U.S. Ambassador to Cyprus, and discussed aspects of United States Foreign Policy as promulgated by the State Department in regard to Cyprus and the Mediterranean. Ambassador Crawford assured us that the United States has a deep interest in achieving justice in Cyprus. We informed him of our meeting with Secretary of State Kissinger and of our basic disagreement with the policies thus far followed by the State Department.

Ambassador Crawford said that he would attempt to arrange a special meeting for us with Vice President Rauf Denktash, who represents the Turkish Cypriots. Later that evening at the Skorpios restaurant in Nicosia we were dinner guests of Panikos Sivitanides, Minister of Labor and Social Insurance.

At dinner, we discussed in a most strenuous manner our views of State Department actions in regard to Cyprus with U.S. Embassy officials who were present. They were quite taken aback with the intensity of our emotions and the extent of our knowledge regarding the Cyprus crisis. We also exchanged views with the Cypriot officials present and were advised as to the relief needs of the refugees of

Cyprus. Brother Tsaffaras, Scofield and Bell had heated discussions with the American Embassy staff members pertaining to their seemingly pro-Turkish positions.

On Thursday, October 3rd, we departed from Nicosia for Larnaca, the city to which most of the Greek Cypriot refugees have fled. There we met with the Mayor of Larnaca, Dr. H. J. Francis and the Mayor of Famagusta Andreas Pouyouros and other officials of the City and the District of Larnaca. We were accompanied by K. Kyprianou, Acting Chief of Protocol; George Iacovou, Director of Special Services for the care and rehabilitation of displaced persons; Savas Antoniou, Police Commissioner; Jay R. Grahame of the American Embassy and Bruno Kosheloff, U.S. Aid Relief Officer.

We began a tour of Displaced Persons Camps with the above and with other officials and with District Officer of Famagusta Mr. Paralikis; District Officer of Larnaca, Mr. Vryonides; Mayor of Larnaca Dr. H. J. Francis and Police Superintendant Zindellis.

The first camp we visited was Ormedia with a population of 10,000 Greek Cypriot refugees. During the first few days at this camp there were 20,000 refugees who have since been relocated to other camps. We met with Dr. Vasos Vasilopoulos of the Ministry of Public Health for the Republic of Cyprus. The good Doctor told the AHEPANS that he was grateful for the medical supplies sent by AHEPA during its Supreme Convention in Boston. Furthermore, he disputed reports as "unfounded" that there were any Cypriot women who had their breasts cut off or boys emasculated. He said if there were any such cases behind Turkish lines it was never brought to the attention of his Ministry. The Doctor said that they had several cases of victims who needed artificial limbs and that East German doctors had volunteered medical facilities for such purposes.

Dr. Vasilopoulos further added that because of the Turkish invasion and the crisis that followed there were many young men and women, as well as the elderly, in desperate need of open heart surgery. He said: "If you can bring these victims to the United States to have open heart surgery, you would be doing our nation a great service." He added; "the world community has been of tremendous service during the crisis and what is now needed is additional medical aid."

Dr. Vasilopoulos also told us that there are thirty young Greek Cypriot victims being treated in the Athens Hospitals for extremely serious napalm burns as a result of the illegal Turkish fire bombing of Cyprus by Turkish American-made warplanes.

At the first camp, the AHEPANS were greeted by thousands who applauded and the following speech was given in Greek by a spokesman of the camp.

As the delegation was walking down the camp area, one young boy, not more than 14, handed the delegation a piece of shrapnel and said:

"Here is a piece of American made shrapnel. Take it back to America—with our regrets". We did not know how to answer this young man. His mother and father were both killed by bombs during the Turkish invasion.

Many young children, both male and female, had necklaces . . . with the compliments of the American Government. The necklace had a pendant which was a bullet manufactured in America, paid for by American taxpayers' money, and picked up by these youngsters while Turkish invaders were advancing unchecked through their country.

In one tent, Elaine Mischel, who lived in Famagusta, was three months pregnant and had lost her husband. She was young—too young to understand—but she knew she was carrying a baby who would never have or know the love of a father. She had no fresh meat for 55 days. She and 60 others lived in a tent, a summer tent, a tent used by American soldiers during World War II. Other refugees came from other parts of Cyprus; some knew each other, while others had not met until the Turkish invasion. But they were "blood brothers and sisters" in tragedy and therefore shared what little they had with each other. All asked for one thing;

"Help us return to our homes."

In another tent, eight families (fifty persons) were living together sleeping on the bare ground with only hay separating them from the coldness of the earth. A small charcoal heater to cook on. Mostly pastas, canned meats, canned vegetables. No fresh tomatoes, no lettuce, although northern Cyprus, now held by Turkey, is so rich in both. No fresh fruit to eat, although Cyprus exported much fresh fruit to Greece and other parts of the world prior to the Turkish invasion.

These were proud middle class people. Many self-employed—Many with cars—most of them well dressed. But they left everything behind for survival. They ran from the invaders, seeking a place in Cyprus where they would be safe from the fire bombs, from the bullets, from the tanks, from the American equipped Turkish soldiers in American made uniforms advancing on their homes, their property, their business—looting while constantly pressing forward, constantly disregarding all United Nations resolutions demanding they halt their advance.

Supreme President Chirgotis and Brother Plumides spoke to the tearful refugees, many crying openly; young children tugging on our shirt sleeves seeking help. A 95 year old Cypriot man, Georgious Anastasi from Spatarikou asked Chirgotis: "I am old. I will be 96 in November. Please help me return to my home so I can die in peace."

Chirgotis choked up because his father is just a few years older. This man was sleeping on a hard bed, if you can call plywood a bed. He had one blanket with the insignia "United States Army". He had no cigarettes. Mr. Mavromatis gave him a package of Marlboros.

In the next camp of Xilotimbou, 12,000 refugees were existing. Mary Iacovidou, a camp spokesman and refugee from Famagusta, and Demetrios Stylianou, Civil Defense Director, also from Famagusta, told the Fact Finding Mission that all these people want one thing—to go home.

They told us that for 52 days these refugees had been living in the camp, under trees, like animals; surviving on spaghetti and rice and losing steadily their hope and will to live. At this point, Supreme President Chirgotis and Cyprus Committee Chairman, Plumides, walked up to a 4-by-6 foot bamboo triangular hut covered with a thin plastic sheet with bare dirt as a floor. Mr. Chirgotis and Mr. Plumides went into the structure. Both willowy men could barely fit in.

Chirgotis called out; "Who lives here?" Nikos Ioannou stepped out of the crowd and said; "This is my makeshift home".

"Do you live here alone?" Chirgotis asked. "No", said the proud Cypriot, "I exist here with my wife and four children, whose ages range from 6 to 16."

"My God!" Chirgotis said, "I can barely fit in here alone, how can a family exist here?"

"We will show you,". Ioannou said and his wife and children went into the bamboo hut, shoulder to shoulder—body to body. Sardines in a can have more room than they did. They slept propped up and suffered from backaches while trying to get what little rest they could.

At the next camp, located inside a British military installation, some 10,000 refugees were located. We found conditions here slightly better than at the other camps we had visited.

At least at this camp they were getting two "hot" meals a day and medical assistance was available. Medical assistance was administered under an old tent, which makes M.A.S.H.'s movie and television mythical hospital look like a modern General Hospital medical facility, instead of what it really is. We saw a doctor, just five months out of medical school in England, working under primitive and strained conditions. His work kept him busy from early dawn to the late hours of the night. We saw this doctor perform modern day medical miracles with insufficient lighting, no anesthetics, with no sharp medical instruments, and with a lack of modern medical supplies. But yet the services he rendered to his people were the best under adverse conditions. He would not complain!

He and "two angels of mercy" dressed in white, both young, both Cypriot, both nurses, went about their work. Eating when they could, what everybody else at camp ate. Rice and spaghetti, without fresh meat. At this camp, we saw the first of many AHEPA supplies, such as clothing, canned foods, and blankets, filling some of their basic needs. Maria Panatopoulos told the AHEPA Fact Finding Committee that clothes were coming in from Greece, Great Britain, Australia, and only recently, supplies were arriving from the United States.

She also told us that emergency medical supplies had come in large quantities during the later part of August. She said in recent weeks clothes and canned food had arrived in Cyprus from the United States. She said there were enough clothes for now, but their most pressing need at the moment was for drugs. There had been many cases of diarrhea and therefore a great need for proper medication. Also, because of the coming cold weather, antibiotics were needed.

At this camp, we saw 1914 cooking facilities. Primitive outdoor boilers looking like the old fashioned pot bellied stoves, but as far as the Cypriots were concerned, they were doing the job. They were supplying two hot meals per day.

At still another camp, we saw a "Demotikon" school now bursting at the seams with children attempting diligently to learn their ABC's under the worst possible conditions. The teachers were doing the best they could. Instead of 25 pupils per class there were 90. Giorgos, Yiannis and Maria told Mr. Scofield of their pain; and how they were living, and Maria's glasses slipped low on her nose and Jim smiled, lifting the glasses back to their proper place and saying: "This happens to me all the time too."

Maria was a thin girl, no more than 6 years old—much too young to understand war, but already much too old not to understand the suffering that she and her family were being put through.

Other children were crying because they feared all strangers. One of the teachers said to them: "Don't cry. These are American friends", and then he quickly corrected himself, adding, "These are Greek American brothers and not the Government officials of the United States". At this point, we could not help but wonder what effect the tragic episodes of the last few months would have on the minds and growth of our future Greek Cypriot generation.

This camp was well organized politically and it was evident to this committee that the left-wing element of Cyprus was doing their job, because many young and old were spouting the left-wing line

We spent a little extra time here, and explained to them that the overwhelming majority of Americans support the cause of the Greek Cypriot people.

The principal of the school told us that before the Turkish invasion there were 250 pupils in the school, now more than 2,000 between the ages of 6 to 12 were attending in three shifts, and going to classes running from 7:00 a.m. in the morning to 11:00 p.m. at night.

Here, Past Supreme President Peter Bell, made an outstanding speech in Greek, calling for the unity of all Cypriot people. The Worcester attorney was at his finest when he said, "Only if you are united—only if you speak with one voice—only if you act as one, can we overcome the odds against us. In unity there is strength. The Greek Americans are united in their strength to help you. Hellenes everywhere are united in joining you in this struggle. We will continue to be united and if we are united we shall be victorious," Bell concluded.

This the refugees understood. They applauded. They thanked the AHEPANS.

In the fourth camp at Ahna Forest, we met with British Major John Long who told us of the conditions in the refugee camp, what the British were doing and what was yet needed to be done. We met Mr. Pieris Afxentiou, the father of the EOKA hero known as Afxentiou. The old man, already feeling the loss of a son, begged the AHEPANS to use their influence to get all of the refugees back in their homes. He asked for nothing for himself. You could see he was held in great esteem. His son put his life on the line for what he believed was right for the people of Cyprus. He was now putting his reputation on the line for what he believed was justice for his people. The Justice for Cyprus mission understood.

These are the figures of displaced Greek-Cypriot persons settled in the Southern portion of Cyprus.

Displaced persons situation south: Greek Cypriot

Displaced and registered	194, 000
Self supporting	33, 000
Receiving Government assistance	161, 000

Housing:

In adequate housing	44, 000
In adequate tents	7, 000
In public buildings	22, 000
In homes of relatives	93, 000
In semi finished structures	13, 000
Living in open air	15, 000
Total	194, 000

South: Turk Cypriot:

In British Sovereign Base Area of Episkopi	8, 500
Living in isolation in the South; not all of whom are necessarily displaced	26, 000
North: Turk Cypriot: In homeless or needy situation	8, 500
North: Greek Cypriot: Living in isolation	20, 000
Total persons displaced on island since July (approximate)	257, 000

NOTE.—All figures are approximate in that movement of persons from one category to another is not infrequent.

On our way back to Larnaca, Brothers Plumides and Douris met with Colonel Constantine Zargavaras, Regional Commander of the 4th Battalion of the National guard of Cyprus at Famagusta.

He was a proud officer. A professional soldier. Born and raised in Lama, Greece, he had arrived in Cyprus only two days before the Turkish invasion began.

"We fought and fought," he told us. "We used sling shots while the Turkish had modern armament. Our men had guns from World War I, their men had modern military equipment of the atomic age. Our men had no airplanes, their men had the fastest jets. Our men had little tanks, their men had the most modern tanks America produces. Our men were poorly uniformed, their men dressed like the Green Berets of Viet Nam fame. Our men had Cypriot mortars made during World War II, their men had American mortars perfected by Americans during the Viet Nam war.

"We fought back the first invasion force. Then we fought back the second invasion force in hand-to-hand combat. The bodies of Turkish soldiers floated in the sea off Famagusta. Then the tanks came, and the American jets, flown by Turkish pilots, flew low over our lines. Like David fighting Goliath—we fought. We used our rifles and machine guns and knocked down 24 Turkish planes. Then they flew higher . . . much higher. Our bullets could not reach them. Their rockets were not as effective, because of the new higher altitude.

"More tanks came in and 10,000 more Turkish soldiers hit the beach. We fought gallantly but we had nothing to save Famagusta. We were outgunned and out-manned. I gave the order to fall back to Larnaca. We dug in. My men used their hands digging away at the hard dirt to make trenches to surround and protect the city. They were determined to lose their lives so that no Turkish soldiers would pass. We went into the Turkish villages and were surprised to find modern army equipment from the United States of America in Turkish homes. We used these guns, and these military supplies against the Turkish invaders.

Colonel Zargavaras was a soldier who did not know the meaning of defeat. He fought gallantly against overwhelming odds. He was a hero.

Later, he showed us the military equipment he had and then showed us the captured military equipment of the Turks. What a difference. It was amazing that he did as well as he did against overwhelming odds.

The Colonel said to us that notwithstanding the resolutions of the U.N. Security Council and the repeated agreements on cease-fire, Turkey continued its invasion until August 17th, 1974, and now occupied 40% of the Republic of Cyprus.

They invaded, 40,000 strong, they had 300 tanks, 1,000 motor transports, and were supported by warships and military aircraft which bombed Cyprus for five whole days, a small country without an Air Force or heavy weapons. The good Colonel told us that in its air attacks, the Turkish air force did not spare hotels, tourist establishments, civilian populations, hospitals, the Red Cross building or the Armenian School.

We were told repeatedly that the Turkish soldiers "raped and killed" civilians and systematically looted homes, shops, stores and factories.

After visiting the camps we were invited for lunch by the Mayor of Larnaca, Dr. H. J. Frances at the Four Lanterns Hotel in Larnaca.

After leaving Larnaca, we proceeded back to Nicosia to one of the most frightening moments of the trip.

Slowly our American Embassy vehicles moved onto the road that led from the Greek zone in Nicosia towards the Turkish held sector of Nicosia. Greek Cypriot soldiers challenged us at the checkpoints. Satisfied with who we were, they let us pass. They looked suspiciously at us as we were slowly leaving the Greek Cypriot quarters towards "no-man's land" between the Greek Cypriot sector and the Turkish sector. It was only four blocks. There were buildings but nobody lived there. Our car moved so slowly—ever so slowly—as we passed by the damaged Ledra Palace Hotel, the site where the Turkish Cypriot and Greek Cypriot leaders meet and exchange prisoners. There were United Nations vehicles all over the hotel grounds. It is where the U.N. has its headquarters. The old but beautiful hotel was pockmarked by machine gun bullets, rifle bullets and rockets. One of its upper floors was in shambles. Off to the right was a small building with a sign on top, "Avis-Rent-A-Car"—but there were no cars for rent.

The silence was deafening and frightening. Not even a rabbit would dare dash through "no-man's land without permission. Not a bird was flying. All of a sudden we were stopped once again. This time by Turkish Cypriot police. Satisfied as to our identity, they permitted us to proceed. Then like a modern miracle, there was life again. Turkish Cypriot children were playing; Turkish Cypriot mothers were pushing their baby carriages; Turkish Cypriot shops were operating.

Life in the Turkish Cypriot quarters continued seemingly undisturbed. Our car went through a small park and then we saw our "first" Turkish soldier dressed in a Green Beret uniform similar to the American Army. It was shocking. All of a sudden, a Turkish policeman signaled our vehicles into a parking area. A guard welcomed us and escorted us into the offices of Rauf Denktash, the Turkish Cypriot Vice President.

The meeting with Mr. Rauf Denktash resulted in a lively and informative exchange of different points of view. Mr. Denktash indicated that "everything is negotiable except the security of the Turkish Cypriot minority". He stated that he felt that he could negotiate with Acting President Clerides only if Clerides had full authority to negotiate on behalf of the Greek Cypriots.

He was intelligent, and spoke English fluently. Educated in London, he has a Law Degree. Also at the meeting were Mr. Orek, Minister of Defense; Minister of Labour, Rehabilitation and Social Affairs; I. Kotak, Member of the Social Welfare Services, TCA and H. C. Tilki, Secretary General Social Welfare Services.

We held a frank and open discussion. Denktash told us about the pains of the Cypriot Turkish community. We quickly countered with facts about the sufferings of the Greek Cypriot refugees. We spoke about alleged atrocities against the Greek Cypriots and he spoke about guerrilla warfare and killing of Turkish Cypriots. The Turkish Cypriot Vice President said, "We don't want to be small Turkish drops in a Big Greek Ocean." Denktash meant that he didn't want Turkish enclaves in the entire Island of Cyprus but wanted his people located in one area of the island.

Denktash told our Mission of Mercy Committee that a Government Constitution is not made by wizards—but created by political animals. He said that the 1960 constitution of Cyprus was a partnership between the Greek Cypriot majority and the Turkish Cypriot minority and it could have worked.

Denktash told us repeatedly that he wanted security for the Turkish Cypriot minority and that once this is obtained the Turkish army shall withdraw. He said that the Turkish Cypriots did not want the Turkish Army there any more than the Greek Cypriots did. "We want a safety valve and we want that valve protected at all times," he said. "We can't have Turkish ships in the Greek sea because the call of Enosis will create waves which would sink the Turkish ships. We don't want partition. We don't want a Greco Turkish war. We never thought the day would come that a Junta would be in power in Greece and press the button of "Enosis" which led to this conflict. We never thought that the Junta would have a plan known as the "three hour lightning plan" to cut up the Turkish quarter and destroy our people.

Denktash proposed a "bi-regional federation" consisting of Greek Cypriot and Turkish Cypriot "states".

We listened to his commentary and then we countered with our own. We told him of the Greek Cypriot refugees and the conditions under which they were living. We told him that if he was sincere, he would immediately order the withdrawal of all Turkish soldiers from Famagusta and allow the 80,000 Greek Cypriot refugees to return to their homes and to the modern hotels where they can be housed under a modern roof instead of being left outdoors to the elements of nature. We told him that this would be the first step in achieving a peaceful coexistence which would lead to the security of both the Greek and Turkish Cypriots. We told him we were dismayed over the reports that the Turkish Army was looting Greek Cypriot homes, raping Greek Cypriot women, destroying Greek Cypriot property, and stealing Greek Cypriot livestock, which he, of course, denied. We showed him documents relative to the above which were hard to disprove. We told Denktash that we felt there could be no peaceful solution until the Greek Cypriot refugees were allowed to return to their own homes. We told him there were 5,000 Greek Cypriots killed, many of them merchants, doctors, lawyers, architects and teachers. We told him of a report brought to our attention by the Maronites that a Maronite Church in the Kyrenia District was loaded with refrigerators, television sets, and other household equipment looted from Greek Cypriot homes by the Turkish Army which were awaiting shipment to Turkey.

The Maronites said that this church was sealed by the Turkish soldiers and only opened when the Maronite Bishop threatened to go to the U.N. officials. He said he was shocked with what he saw. Denktash's parting words were:

"Everything is negotiable except the security of the Turkish Cypriot minority."

Prior to a press conference at the Cyprus Hilton Hotel in Nicosia we met with leaders of the Armenian Cypriot community. They told us of their immediate relief needs which included the repair of an Armenian school. They stated that their immediate need was primarily for money.

The following were present at the meeting: Reverend Sasken Sandronnin, Dr. Antranig Ashdjian, Mr. Arania Mahdessian, Member of the Armenian Administrative Council; Miss Keghdsin Guebenlian, Mr. Berdge Tibbian, Mr. Sempad Devletian, Advocate, Mr. Asadour Bedian, Principal of the Melkonian Institute. They told us that the Armenian Orthodox Church in Famagusta was destroyed, that their church in Nicosia was fire bombed, that the upper floors of the Armenian school was destroyed and many olive and carib trees, the only form of income for the monastery and Armenian churches of Cyprus, were destroyed. These consisted of approximately 5,000 acres.

At the news conference we described the terrible conditions we witnessed in the refugee camps and stated that we would press for more relief from International Agencies and from the United States Government and also stated that we would continue our campaign to gain Justice for Cyprus by crystallizing the situation in the United States Senate and Congress and by convincing the American public of the rightness of the Greek Cypriot cause.

Supreme President Chirgotis, Bell, Plumides and Tsaffaras spoke out at the News Conference which was covered by the international and Cypriot press, radio and television.

Later, we again met with Ambassador Crawford and his staff and repeated our strong thoughts relative to what must be done to achieve justice in Cyprus and to assure its future as a free and independent sovereign nation.

We told Ambassador Crawford, in very strong words, that we felt the young men of his staff should not show any pro-Turkish sympathies, which we felt was so. We further told the Ambassador, who was a schoolmate of Congressman John Brademas of Indiana, that we felt his staff should be more sympathetic to the Greek Cypriot cause and if not openly favoring it, to at least understand it. We further told him we would express this concern through Secretary of State Henry Kissinger. Of course, we told him we were grateful for his hospitality and for the assistance given to us in Cyprus, particularly by Jay R. Grahame and Bruno Kosheloff. Other members of the Embassy that we met included Frederick Z. Brown, James A. Williams, David D. Grimland and Daniel Mudrinich.

On our way to the airport, for our departure from Cyprus, we again met with Acting President Clerides for nearly one hour. We relayed our observations to him and reassured him of our now even more intensified support for the cause of Cyprus. We wished him success now that he had received assurances of "unqualified support" from Archbishop Makarios.

We were extremely impressed by Acting President Clerides, educated in London, and a lawyer by profession. He showed himself to be a man of witty intelligence, articulation and concern over the plight of his people.

He thanked the AHEPANS and the Greek-Americans in general, for their concern and the help they have given the people of Cyprus; "We know how much you all felt for us during this tragic time; we also know that our Greek Brothers throughout the world are united in their concern about the fate of Cyprus. This is the most difficult time in the short but volatile history of Cyprus. It's our struggle for survival. It's an unparalleled struggle for us," he said.

"Our problems are not with the Turkish Cypriots but with the Turkish nation, Cyprus was invaded by a Turkish Army, a Turkish Navy, and a Turkish Air Corps. Some 40% of our Island, the most productive part of the Island, is occupied by the Turkish invaders. More than 200,000 refugees, nearly half of our entire population, are refugees. The rest of the island has financial problems, unemployment problems, productivity problems, etc. Cypriot Greeks had a high standard of living—now we are penniless.

"Livestock, in Turkish areas that were not looted, are dying because of a lack of food and care. Crops are unattended, tourist money and investments are not coming in and the best hotels are now in the areas controlled by the Turkish soldiers.

"I am in complete agreement with what AHEPA is doing to create pressure in Behalf of Greek Cypriots."

Acting President Clerides indicated he has been in constant contact with Archbishop Makarios, Dr. Henry Kissinger and Prime Minister Caramanlis, as well as other international, political and governmental leaders.

Acting President Clerides told us that if Dr. Kissinger wants peace and tranquility on the Island then he has to do something about it. He stood firm in saying that we will sign no agreement and that we will not be part of any talks or discussions that do not guarantee that the Greek Cypriot refugees return to their homes."

"This could very well be the seed of new troubles, new problems, new fighting which could very well destroy the peace and tranquility of the entire Mediterranean area. If the American people realize this truth then they will know that there will never be such an agreement—no Greek Cypriot will ever put his signature on a document that doesn't guarantee the refugees a return to their homes."

Clerides went on to say, "The United States must restore its image on Cyprus. Here the Greek Cypriot people believe that the United States is responsible for their problems." He also said that the Greek Cypriots feel:

"The United States did nothing to stop the invasion of the Turkish Army.

"The Geneva Conference did nothing to stop the Turkish Army from continuing their invasion."

Clerides said that, now that Dr. Kissinger is getting involved we must give him breathing space so that we can see what active role and what solutions he can come up with. He must give us a sign first. He has to do something constructive. He must move in the right direction and then the Secretary of State can visit Cyprus and be welcomed by the Greek Cypriot people, something not possible now.

"Repatriation is the key to the problem. When Dr. Kissinger speaks of a unitary state—two independent states in Cyprus—one Greek Cypriot and one Turkish Cypriot, does he really mean a federal state?" Clerides asked.

Clerides told us that the Turkish Cypriots are already issuing visas, birth certificates and designating certain areas of Cyprus as Turkish districts.

Clerides told us he was concerned about reports about extensive Turkish looting of Greek Cypriot property in Turkish occupied areas, adding, "Anything that can be taken has been taken."

He said, "the Turkish Government is already moving towards setting up a Turkish state in Cyprus," and stated the following:

They are building a heavy concrete fortification line a little behind the area they are now occupying.

They have set up a tenth Turkish District with letters being mailed in from all over the world marked as Kipris, Mersin 10, Turkey.

They have set up a Turkish Post Office.

The Turkish Government has issued an order to all companies, both Cypriot and foreign that they are not now recognized as doing business in Cyprus unless they sign up with the Turkish Government in the Turkish held zone.

The Turks are issuing passports and visas.

The Turks are using an old air field and have established a commercial airline between Cyprus and Turkey.

The Turks are issuing their own birth certificates.

The Turks are issuing their own death certificates.

The Turks have set up their own Port Authority.

The Turks have taken over Greek Businesses and have turned them over to the Turkish Cypriot businessmen.

The Turks have set up their own Police Department.

Clerides said that as Acting President he has been negotiating with the Cypriot Turkish leaders with "very little power" and this was a hindrance initially, but now that the complete support of the President of the Republic, Archbishop Makarios, and the Greek Government had been received, "I can negotiate with new strength."

"I know all the negatives and now I have the positives on my side as well. He said "the unaligned nations like Algeria, India, Mali and Yugoslavia among others, support our position. International support is mounting daily, but since the Turkish do not respect the United Nations we don't see any other hope but to negotiate here on Cyprus. We have established a trust in each other, Denktash and myself."

It was obvious to us that his worried look of the day before was gone. The concern that he was a leader with no power was eliminated. Archbishop Makarios had spoken . . . loud and clear.

President Clerides then departed under armed protection and only minutes later Cypriot Police exchanged gun fire with a suspicious vehicle that obviously harbored persons who were attempting to intercept his motorcade in an attempt on his life. We were shocked by this action, and were indeed happy that the assassination attempt did not succeed.

The machine gun chatter could be heard over the quiet of Nicosia. It happened only yards away from where we had dinner the night before. Our car was similar to that of Acting President Clerides. We were scheduled to move out minutes earlier than the Acting President but we were detained because the film we were to take back to the United States with us—to be made into a special documentary "AHEPA in Cyprus"—had not, as yet arrived. We were concerned. We were worried, but we were glad that the attempt on Clerides' life was unsuccessful. We feel that he is the only man who is on the scene, who can negotiate the return of the refugees to their homes. He must be assisted. He must be successful He needs everyone's help. AHEPA pledges that support.

Before departing Cyprus we stopped at Limassol to pick up an aide to our committee, Mr. Mavromatis, the son of a Cypriot who begged for a few minutes to visit his paternal grandparents. He saw his 76 year old grandmother and other members of the family. It was the first time in 17 years that he had seen them. You can imagine the joy of these Cypriots who again embraced their American born grandchild. The tears flowed freely and Mr. Mavromatis' joy was that his family was safe and alive. Only moments earlier, machine gun fire erupted a few yards away from where we were scheduled to pick up Mr. Mavromatis. After we left, bombs exploded near the same area, which destroyed several houses and automobiles. No one knows who committed this crime—but it was committed. This is what the stark reality of life in Cyprus is today.

It is difficult at this juncture to determine the financial loss to the people of Cyprus but it is in the millions of dollars; it is also difficult to predict the future financial chaos to the Cyprus economy as a result of the Turkish invasion, but it will be considerable. It is even more difficult to estimate accurately the damage incurred in the areas controlled by the Turkish invading forces in terms of residential buildings, hotels, factories, etc. but the Cypriot Government is now trying to do so.

Since the invasion, the entire economy of this once well to do nation has been completely disrupted. It is estimated that the country is losing about 6 million dollars in production each day. So far more than $300,000,000 of production has been lost because the economy has ground to a halt. Virtually 80% of the labor force is unemployed and the refugees have little or no money to keep the economy moving. The Cypriot Government is now preparing to give each refugee stipends of several Cypriot pounds per day which is equivalent to about $5 in American money, so they can move the economy forward once again. That is why they need money. That is why they urge Greek-Americans to send money for refugee relief and we urge that cash donations should be remitted immediately to the Order of AHEPA and make checks payable to:

THE FUND FOR THE RELIEF OF DISPLACED PERSONS

This fund is under civilian administration. We met and discussed this freely with George Iacovou, Director of Special Service for the Care and Rehabilitation of Displaced Persons, 7 Byron Avenue, Nicosia, Cyprus, and the AHEPA Mission is satisfied that these monies will be used exclusively to help the displaced refugees. To date the following help has been given by the United States Government to Cyprus.

Needs and/or commodities delivered, on the way, or pledged, as of Sept. 22, 1974

(A) Ambassador's fund	$25,000
(B) Cash grant to ICRC	725,000
(C) Items purchased for or consigned to ICRC:	
Tents: 5,700 units, 5,600 family tents, 5 persons, 100 large 80-ft marquis-type	793,290
Blankets: 70,591 units, 10,000 light-weight cotton, 60,591 wool blankets	300,623
Cots: 9,998 units	101,625
Water cans: 10,000 plastic units	10,500
Red Cross markers: 79 units	4,000
400 gal water trailers: 4 units	8,000
Body bags: 200 units	4,120
Tent repair kits: 3 units	218
Cost above items	1,222,366
Transportation cost above items	1,244,395
Total cost associated with above items	2,466,761
(D) Use pledged contribution via UNECR:	
Obligated for 5,600 tent flies with transportation	400,000
Cash grant authorized	1,000,000
Unfunded balance: (May be cash or goods)	1,600,000
Total contribution via UNECR	3,000,000
Grand total USG assistance to Cyprus to date	6,216,761

At 12:30 A.M. Friday, October 4, we departed Akrotiri for Athens aboard our United States Air Force plane, arriving in Athens at 4:35 A.M.

At 9:30 A.M. Friday, after only a brief rest, we met with more than 20 reporters and writers, radio and television commentators of the Greek Press and outlined the story of our tour of Cyprus indicating the tragic conditions of the refugees and stressing the need for Greek Cypriot unity. In addition there was television and radio coverage of the news conferences.

Just before noon, we met with Foreign Minister George Mavros who told the AHEPA delegation: "Your work in the Cyprus crisis is marvelous. Your work is remarkable. Your contribution is enormous. We are indebted to you for serving both the interests of Greece and the United States of America. We salute you."

At a second meeting with Prime Minister Caramanlis the AHEPA delegation told him of what we saw in Cyprus and of our meetings with Acting President Clerides, Turkish Cypriot Vice President Denktash and the plight of the refugees and assured him that AHEPA, as always, is ready and willing to take the responsibility to correct the foreign policy of the United States towards Cyprus.

The Prime Minister, who again showed his concern that the Greeks in America be united so that they may better help the cause of Cyprus and Greece, reiterated that he has full confidence in the leadership of the Order of AHEPA and in its goals and aims.

Plumides added that a united Greek force in the United States, as exists now over the Cyprus crisis, can accomplish wonders. He said that every Greek-American organization, from the smallest to the largest, has played a major role in aiding the people of Cyprus and in helping change the direction of the Foreign policy of the United States.

The mission was host of a luncheon for publishers and editors of the Greek Press. This well attended event featured full and free discussion of the Cyprus situation and the important role played by the Order of Ahepa in the United States. These leading opinion makers were informed, many for the first time, as to the significance of Ahepa on the American political and social scene, of its strength, and of its successful efforts to correct American foreign policy on Cyprus. It appeared that the media leaders of Greece were quite impressed by the past and present endeavors of the Order of Ahepa and left more knowledgeable and very enthusiastic as to its worth and its achievements.

At this point the delegation divided, with Messrs. Plumides, Scofield and Douris remaining at the luncheon with the publishers and editors of the Greek newspapers, radio and TV stations. Supreme President Chirgotis, after making an initial appearance with the publishers and editors, left to go to a luncheon at the Grand Bretagne Hotel with Vice Premier George Rallis and Past Supreme Presidents Tsaffaras and Bell. Several high Greek Government officials were present and all again thanked Ahepa for the leadership provided in the Cyprus crisis.

The delegation was interviewed on Greek National radio and television. The Associated Press, United Press International and Reuters News Agency sent out international dispatches on Ahepa's mission to Cyprus and its findings. Also, the film of Ahepa visiting the refugee camps was shown Saturday, October 5, on Greek National Television.

On Sunday, October 6th, we departed Athens airport at 10:30 A.M. Athens time; changed planes in Rome, and arrived at J.F.K. Airport in New York City at 4:40 P.M. New York Time, grateful that we were once again on American soil.

Our conclusions are:

1. The tragic mistakes of our United States foreign policy toward Cyprus must be corrected if the United States is to retain its prestige and strength in the Mediterranean and among the people of both Greece and Cyprus—and to possess moral integrity in the eyes of the World.

2. The people of Cyprus are rapidly moving toward unity in the face of the adversity of the current Cyprus crisis.

3. All the Greek Cypriot refugees must be returned to their homes and lands immediately.

4. The Turkish armed forces which illegally invaded Cyprus using American arms and equipment must be withdrawn from the sovereign nation of Cyprus immediately.

5. The relief program in Cyprus is being administered efficiently and well despite difficult circumstances; but that the great need for relief must now be in the form of cash to buy blankets, camp beds and tents and to provide pocket money for the refugees—thus allowing them to purchase the necessities of life

and to thereby help move the economy forward. (The need for 100,000 blankets is immediate).

6. The rights of both the Greek Cypriot majority and the Turkish Cypriot minority be respected in any peace settlement and in the future governmental structure of the Republic of Cyprus.

7. The Order of Ahepa should continue its relief efforts for Cyprus and its public relations campaign to convince the United States government and the American people that justice must be served in Cyprus; it should continue to battle for legislation to immediately halt the illegal military aid from the United States to aggressor Turkey; it should press efforts to obtain millions of dollars in emergency relief funds from the United States government for the Cypriot refugees.

This report has been prepared by Ahepa's Mercy Mission to Cyprus to inform the Ahepans, the Greek-Americans, and the American public on the true picture of what exists now in Cyprus. The report is a true picture—as the members of the mission saw it. The findings are ours. The quotes are as they were told to us. It is Ahepa's attempt to bring to you the true story of the tragic situation on Cyprus—and this we believe we fulfilled.

We again urge that cash donations be made to help the people of Cyprus. For the present, there is no longer a need for clothing or food, but a desperate need for money. We urge that your contributions be made through Ahepa to: "*The fund for the Relief of Displaced Persons.*"

APPENDIX II

I. SUBCOMMITTEE ON REFUGEES' CORRESPONDENCE WITH SECRETARY HENRY A. KISSINGER

DECEMBER 19, 1974.

Hon. HENRY A. KISSINGER,
Department of State,
Washington, D.C.

DEAR MR. SECRETARY: As you know, since the outbreak of violence last July, the Subcommittee on Refugees has closely followed developments on Cyprus. Our primary concern has been the refugee and related humanitarian problems resulting from Turkish military operations, and the kinds of efforts our country is making to help bring peace and relief to the people of Cyprus.

In addition to a series of three public hearings on this issue of concern to Congress and the American people, members of the Subcommittee have exchanged views with officials in the Department of State, and a special Study Mission, representing the Subcommittee, traveled in the field during August and September. A report of their findings and recommendations was submitted to the Department of State for comment on October 25th.

We share the view of many Americans that the plight and fate of the refugees is central to the Cyprus issue, and to any meaningful negotiations over the future of the island. We further believe that a viable solution to the Cyprus problem, much less peace on the island, will not be readily accomplished unless and until a significant number of Greek Cypriot refugees are permitted to return safely to their lands and homes in areas currently occupied by Turkish forces. We believe, therefore, that the United States must finally use its vast influence and good offices with Turkey to persuade the Ankara Government of the need for an immediate "gesture of goodwill", which includes a meaningful withdrawal of occupation forces and the return of refugees to their homes. In purely human terms, such a "gesture of goodwill"—involving the orderly return of refugees to the Famagusta and, perhaps, the Morphou areas of the island—would significantly ease the tragic plight and humanitarian needs of many refugee families. Such a development would also offer an immediate opportunity to break the deadlock over the resumption of negotiations among the parties involved, and serve as a meaningful first step toward a negotiated settlement of the Cyprus problem and the restoration of the island's full independence, sovereignty and territorial integrity.

As members of the Refugee Subcommittee, we would like to recommend that an immediate withdrawal of Turkish forces from the areas cited, and the orderly return of refugees to their homes and lands in these areas, be a clearly understood and primary objective in current American diplomacy over Cyprus. We share the strong conviction that such development would accomplish important humanitarian and diplomatic ends, which will contribute positively toward a resolution of the Cyprus problem and the renewal of peace and stability in the Eastern Mediterranean.

We would also like to express our concern over the absence of any visible progress in efforts to open the Nicosia airport, which has been closed since July. Most observers agree that the opening of this airport, under United Nations auspices, would, among other things, greatly facilitate international relief operations in behalf of the Cypriot refugees and others in distress, both Turkish and Greek. We are extremely hopeful that the problem of the Nicosia airport is high on the diplomatic agenda, and that the United States will lend a greater measure of diplomatic support to the opening of this important facility under appropriate international auspices until the island's future is determined.

Finally, we commend the Administration for its important humanitarian contributions to international emergency relief efforts in behalf of the refugees and other Cypriots in need. We are hopeful that our Government is prepared to

(37)

continue this tangible expression of America's traditional generosity and compassion overseas, and that efforts to meet growing rehabilitation and reconstruction needs on Cyprus will also receive our Nation's active concern and support.

We would appreciate very much your early consideration and comment on these areas of public policy and concern.

Many thanks for your consideration, and we look forward to hearing from you soon.

Best wishes.

Sincerely,

EDWARD M. KENNEDY,
Chairman, Subcommittee on Refugees.
PHILIP A. HART,
HIRAM L. FONG,
CHARLES McC. MATHIAS, Jr.

II. SECRETARY KISSINGER'S LETTER TO SENATOR KENNEDY AND THE SUBCOMMITTEE ON REFUGEES

JANUARY 6, 1975.

Hon. EDWARD M. KENNEDY,
Chairman, Subcommittee on Refugees,
U.S. Senate,

DEAR TED: Thank you for your letter of December 19 and for your views and those of Senators Fong, Mathias, and Hart on the Cyprus problem and the role the United States should play in it. Happily, it appears that we share many views on this question. In particular, we share your deep concern for the plight of the refugees and believe that resolution of this tragic human problem is central to the Cyprus issue and to any meaningful negotiations on a political settlement. Likewise, we believe that the question of Turkish troop withdrawals will be part of any settlement and that arrangements must be worked out among the parties involved which will preserve Cyprus' sovereignty, independence, and territorial integrity and enable the people of Cyprus to live together in peace and security.

Our primary objective, from the outset of the crisis, has been to bring about negotiations between the parties concerned which would address these urgent questions. We have worked closely with all the parties to this end, encouraged flexibility and moderation, and supported various United Nations resolutions urging the parties to make early progress on the refugee and troop withdrawal issues.

Fourtunately, some progress has been made in recent weeks toward getting substantive negotiations underway. I had good talks in Brussels on December 11-13 with the Greek and Turkish Foreign Ministers which led in turn to the resumption of discussions between the representatives of the two communities on Cyprus on December 19. They are now working to resolve one final point so that political negotiations can begin. In light of these developments, I believe we have progressed beyond the point where gestures are needed as a means of getting negotiations launched. However, a conciliatory approach by all parties and the creation of a favorable atmosphere remain as important as ever to successful negotiations. We will therefore continue to encourage all parties to make whatever contributions they can to improve the atmosphere and to proceed as rapidly as possible toward a negotiated settlement. At the same time, while we can take and advocate positions on some issues in the negotiations, it is important that we keep the process moving without ourselves getting in the middle prematurely with suggested solutions.

I can assure you that both from a humanitarian and practical point of view, we agree on the importance of the reopening of Nicosia Airport. My talks led to agreement that this will be a priority agenda item once negotiations get underway, and there are good prospects that interim arrangements for operating the airport can be worked out and agreed upon without too much difficulty.

In closing, I would welcome and appreciate your cooperation and support for our efforts to facilitate a negotiated settlement to this troublescme and deeply rooted historical problem. Let me also thank you and your committee for your support of United States contributions to the Cyprus refugee relief effort. These contributions have been, as you aptly put it, a "tangible expression of America's traditional generosity and compassion overseas", and we fully intend to express our continuing concern for the refugees in Cyprus through further contributions, as necessary and appropriate, to the relief effort.

Warm regards,

HENRY A. KISSINGER.

III. EARLIER EXCHANGE OF CORRESPONDENCE ON CYPRUS

OCTOBER 25, 1974.

Hon. HENRY A. KISSINGER,
Secretary of State,
Department of State, Washington, D.C.

DEAR MR. SECRETARY: As you know, there is continuing and, I feel, growing Congressional and public concern over the course of American policy towards recent developments on Cyprus. Of special concern to many Americans are the refugee and related humanitarian problems resulting from Turkish military operations on the island.

In this connection, the Subcommittee on Refugees has conducted two days of hearings with Assistant Secretary for European Affairs Arthur A. Hartman, and a three member Study Mission, representing the Subcommittee recently travelled to the island to survey humanitarian needs. I have also introduced a foreign aid amendment, prepared in cooperation with officials in the Executive Branch, which, among other things, would authorize humanitarian assistance to Cyprus.

With the full cooperation of the Department, the Subcommittee's Study Mission travelled to Cyprus and the Eastern Mediterranean in late August and early September, and recently they filed a report of their findings and recommendations. The report has been informally made available to officials in the Executive Branch, and some conversations have followed between members of the Department's Cyprus Task Force and the Study Mission. The findings and recommendations focus on humanitarian issues, but they also include material on the broader aspects of United States policy towards Cyprus. A copy of the recommendations is enclosed, and I would appreciate very much getting the Department's detailed comments on the Study Mission's views and suggestions.* I would also appreciate the Department's comment and views on the enclosed series of questions based on the hearings with Assistant Secretary Hartman and additional inquiry of the Subcommittee.

In light of the urgent humanitarian problems on Cyprus, and the intense congressional and public interest in developments on the island, I am extremely hopeful, Mr. Secretary, that the Subcommittee can anticipate a response to the enclosed inquiries within the next ten days. Many thanks for your consideration, and I look forward to hearing from you soon.

Sincerely,

EDWARD M. KENNEDY,
Chairman, Subcommittee on Refugees.

NOVEMBER 22, 1974.

DEAR SENATOR KENNEDY: Knowing that you would be anxious to have a reply before he returns from his current trip to the Far East, Secretary Kissinger has asked that I answer the questions contained in your letter of October 25 concerning current US views and policies regarding Cyprus. We had hoped to get a response off to you sooner. However, I hope you will understand that the fluidity of the situation, the comprehensive nature of your questions, and our desire to give as full a response as possible prevented us from doing so.

The Secretary would like you to know that he fully shares your concern over Cyprus—both as a humanitarian and political problem. The Secretary would also like you to know that he is urgently concerned that Congress and the Administration work together and that he stands ready to cooperate as fully as possible with you and your colleagues.

Should you have any further questions, we would be happy to answer them informally with your staff, or more formally through testimony before your Subcommittee on Refugees.

Cordially,

LINWOOD HOLTON,
Assistant Secretary for Congressional Relations.

Enclosure: Detailed Responses to Questions on Cyprus.

QUESTIONS AND ANSWERS ON U.S. POLICY TOWARD CYPRUS FROM CORRESPONDENCE BETWEEN SENATOR EDWARD M. KENNEDY AND THE DEPARTMENT OF STATE

(1) Generally define the objectives and content of current United States policy toward Cyprus.

---

*Formal comment on the Study Mission's list of 8 recommendations has not been received from the Department of State.

Answer. "The United States has four principal objectives in Cyprus: a) to support the independence, sovereignty, and territorial integrity of Cyprus; b) to relieve the human suffering on the Island caused by the tragic outbreak of fighting this summer; c) to achieve a negotiated settlement which will enable all Cypriots to live in peace and security; and d) to remove Cyprus as an irritant in Greek-Turkish relations, and as a source of instability in the Eastern Mediterranean.

"Thousands of Cypriots have been displaced from their homes, and this means that we view movement on the Cyprus issue as much from a humanitarian as from a political standpoint. To meet urgent humanitarian needs, the United States has contributed over \$10.5 million to the international relief effort (including \$7.3 million toward the UNHCR's \$22 million appeal), has actively supported the UNHCR appeal by urging other countries to respond generously, and has sent disaster relief specialists to the field to coordinate U.S. assistance, assess relief needs on a continuing basis, and advise how we can most usefully be of assistance in the coming months.

"Throughout the present crisis we have urged moderation and restraint on the parties, worked to foster a climate for negotiations, and actively supported the intercommunal talks between Acting President Clerides and Vice President Denktash. These talks have achieved agreement on a number of important humanitarian issues and have established an essential framework for broadened discussions on a political settlement. We have also explored in detail with the parties directly involved ways in which these broader discussions might be facilitated.

"The negotiating process has, to be sure, moved more slowly than we had hoped. Nevertheless, our efforts to advance this process continue. The elections in Greece which have given Prime Minister Caramanlis a substantial majority and the designation of yet-to-be-confirmed new government in Ankara give promise of moving the parties involved on Cyprus to early negotiations."

(2) Apart from the Cypriot inter-communal talks between Acting President Clerides and Vice President Denktash, generally define the current status of negotiations over Cyprus. (a) Does the United States anticipate a resumption of the Geneva talks? Are alternative formats, involving other governments or NATO or the United Nations, possible or desirable?

Answer. "(a) Our current efforts are aimed at facilitating broadened discussions within the framework of the Clerides-Denktash talks. We anticipate that at some stage Greece and Turkey will participate more directly in the discussions, and this could of course involve a Geneva-type framework. At this time, however, we have no fixed ideas on the type of framework that would be more appropriate, other than our general view that a smaller forum involving only the parties directly involved is likely to be more productive than a larger forum."

(b) In his October 14 message to Congress, the President stated that "the United States is making every effort to play a useful role in assisting the parties to a resolution of the Cyprus dispute." Define and characterize these efforts and the kind of "useful role" the United States is or anticipates undertaking to encourage and facilitate "a resolution of the Cyprus dispute."

Answer. "(b) We believe we have played a useful supporting role in the effort to move the negotiating process forward. The Secretary has met with the Foreign Ministers of Greece, Turkey, and Cyprus, and with Archbishop Makarios on several occasions in an effort to develop a dialogue, identify areas of possible agreement, and sustain momentum toward negotiations."

(c) In his September 26 testimony before the Refugee Subcommittee, Assistant Secretary Hartman repeatedly spoke of American efforts to find and suggest "common ground", between the parties to the Cyprus dispute, in order to facilitate a resumption of negotiations. What should Congress and the American people understand by "common ground"? What, in the Department's view, are the ingredients of this "common ground" in light of the Turkish occupation and what is the appropriate basis for negotiations?

Answer. "(c) The 'common ground' to which Assistant Secretary Hartman referred in his September 26 testimony before the Refugee Subcommittee is an expandable concept. In the early stages of the crisis, the only 'common ground' was the belief of all parties that the sovereignty, independence, and territorial integrity of Cyprus should be maintained and that the crisis should be resolved through negotiations. Now the common ground includes agreement by Greece, Turkey, and Cyprus on the November 1 UN Resolution which outlines some of the essential subjects that will have to be addressed in any future negotiated agreement."

(d) Earlier, at a news conference on August 19, Secretary Kissinger spoke of the need for Turkey "to display flexibility and a concern for Greek sensitivities ... " What should Congress and the American people understand by the need for Turkey "to display flexibility and a concern for Greek sensitivities"? Does this include a "gesture of goodwill" which is often mentioned in public debate over Cyprus, and which Assistant Secretary Hartman spoke of in his September 26 testimony before the Refugee Subcommittee? And, in practical terms, what kinds of action by Turkey, in the Department's view, would constitute a meaningful "gesture of goodwill"? And what are the possibilities for such a gesture being made before the end of the year? In the Department's view, does such a gesture require the return of a substantial number of refugees to their homes?

Answer. "(d) The Secretary's August 19 statement about the need for Turkey to display flexibility and a concern for Greek sensitivities was meant to include possible steps designed to advance the negotiating process. These steps might be made in areas such as refugee return, troop withdrawals, pullback from present lines, and the reopening of Nicosia Airport. The parties themselves must decide what steps or gestures are necessary and meaningful. In this regard, what we meant here were first steps, indicating an intention to negotiate rather than final positions to be taken in the negotiations. Given the uncertainties in the governmental situation in Turkey, it is difficult to estimate when some kind of initial steps or gestures will be made."

(e) Also on August 19, Secretary Kissinger said that "we will use our influence in any negotiation to take into full account Greek honor and national dignity." In his October 14 message to Congress, the President also refers to "the honor and dignity of Greece" as a factor in our diplomacy toward the Cyprus problem. What actions or developments, in the Department's view, would "take into full account Greek honor and national dignity"—in terms of a resumption of negotiations, the negotiating process, or a final settlement.

Answer. "(e) Only the Greek Government can decide what would satisfy Greek honor and dignity vis-a-vis Cyprus. We would imagine, however, that further indications of Turkey's good faith and progress toward negotiations, are essential prerequisites."

(f) What are the Department's views on what Assistant Secretary Hartman calls "the guarantee for the eventual outcome", or settlement, of the Cyprus problem?

Answer. "f) We believe that some system of guarantees, like those written into the 1956–60 negotiations will probably be required but we have no fixed views on what guarantees will be necessary or who the guarantor powers will or should be."

(g) What are the Department's views on various proposals for the neutralization and demilitarization of Cyprus?

Answer. "g) The nature and size of the armed forces in the Republic of Cyprus are matters to be decided by the parties themselves."

(3) Assess the status of Turkish military forces on Cyprus in terms of their numbers, kinds of units, equipment, maintenance costs, resupply, et cetera.

Answer. "We are in the process of improving our information about the size and status of Turkish military forces on Cyprus. Our best current information is that there are 35–37,000 Turkish troops on the Island."

(4) What is the Department's assessment of reports that Ankara has introduced civilian administrators, laborers, and others from the mainland into the occupied areas of Cyprus?

Answer. "Some civilian administrators, laborers, and others have been sent to Cyprus from the mainland. Our understanding is that most of these people have been assigned to the Island on a temporary basis, and have come without their families."

(5) Assess the stability of the ceasefire line, and the frequency and source of ceasefire violations.

Answer. "The cease-fire line has been stable since mid-August. There have been only a few brief, isolated, and militarily insignificant incidents. According to the UN Forces in Cyprus, which investigate each incident as part of their peace-keeping duties, both sides have at various times provoked minor infractions."

(6) Comment on recent reports that Turkey has systematically and extensively mined the ceasefire line on Cyprus, and has constructed heavy fortifications or other barriers on or behind this line.

Answer. "The Department does not have precise information regarding the extent to which Turkey has fortified its line of control in the northern region of Cyprus. Construction of some defensive fortifications has been reported, however."

(7) In the context of explaining American policy towards Cyprus, officials in the Executive Branch have spoken of the need "to protect American interests" in Turkey. Define these interests and their significance to our immediate and longer term national interest and security in the Eastern Mediterranean area.

Answer. "The United States and Turkey share a common interest in preventing Soviet aggression and expansion southward into the Mediterranean. We are both NATO allies, and by participating in this common endeavor, we share basic foreign policy and defense goals. Through this mutuality of interest, we have built common defense installations, are granted overflight rights and port facilities. It is also in the U.S. interest to have a friendly ally control access to the Black Sea. We welcome continued Turkish membership in CENTO, and Turkish assistance in our common efforts to combat international narcotics trafficking."

(8) In this regard, define the number, nature and, purposes of American military/intelligence and related installations in Turkey. What is the number of American personnel maintaining and operating these installations? And how many of these are involved in intelligence operations?

Answer. "Turkey and the US maintain one large, two medium, and several smaller common defense installations in Turkey. There are between seven and eight thousand American military personnel working at these installations. Further questions about the number of US personnel assigned to monitoring or intelligency duties should be addressed to the Director of Central Intelligence."

(9) Define the kinds, categories and levels of economic and military assistance given or projected to the government of Turkey for fiscal years 1973 through 1975.

Answer. "The following table shows military and economic assistance to Turkey for FY 1973 through FY 1975:

[In millions of dollars]

	1973	1974	1 1975
Economic assistance:			
Development loans	9.0	0	0
Technical assistance	2.8	1.8	1.1
Public Law 480 school lunch	6.1	2.8	2.1
Opium agreement	5.0	0	0
Total economic	22.9	4.6	3.2
Military:			
Credit sales	20.0	75.0	90.0
Grant	58.5	63.7	80.0
Excess equipment	43.9	37.3	35.0
Supply operations	10.6	11.4	13.0
Total military	133.0	187.4	218.0

1 Fiscal year 1975 military assistance/sales figures are requested amounts and should not be compared with 1973 and 1974 figures which are actual amounts disbursed.

(10) On a monthly basis since January 1974, define the volume and kinds of American military shipments to Turkey, and those scheduled or projected for delivery through the end of the current fiscal year.

Answer. "[Department of State estimates put Military Assistance Program deliveries for CY 1974 at $46,175,000 through September. Foreign Military Sales deliveries total $43,409,000 during the same period. The combined total is $89,584,000.]"

(11) Comment on reports that American military equipment is being or has been, transferred, or sold to Turkey through third parties, such as Iran.

Answer. "Except for unconfirmed reports that some quantity of US-manufactured small arms and ammunition have been sent to Turkey by Libya, the Department is unaware of any military equipment of US origin having been sold or otherwise transferred to Turkey by third countries. The Federal Republic of Germany had until mid-1974 a military assistance and sales program. Similarly, we understand that the Turkish and Italian Governments have recently concluded a commercial sales agreement providing for Turkish purchase of Italian-made aircraft of US design. This transaction was arranged by the Governments of Turkey and Italy, and the US Government was informed in advance about the arrangement."

(12) Given the Turkish invasion of Cyprus, what is the Department's final conclusion on the legality of continuing military assistance to Turkey, under the provisions of the Foreign Assistance Act of 1961, as amended?

Answer. "Turkey has maintained that its actions were justified as measures consistent with the UN Charter under the 1960 Treaty of Guaranty to which the Government of Turkey, the United Kingdom, Greece and Cyprus are parties. It was clear that Turkey felt its actions were justified and necessary in light of the events which had transpired on Cyprus prior to the Turkish intervention. After carefully weighing the legal and foreign policy considerations, the Administration decided that it was impossible publicly to express a legal conclusion on the issue of Turkey's eligibility for further assistance and sales without undermining our foreign policy objective of persuading Turkey and Greece to enter into direct negotiations for a solution of the Cyprus problem."

(13) In his September 26 testimony before the Refugee Subcommittee, Assistant Secretary Hartman said:

And when I saw the Deputy [United Nations] High Commissioner [for Refugees], I said to him, I do not think it is realistic at all for you to be talking only about this period from September 1 through December 31, because when you are talking to these governments, you cannot just come around to them sometime in December and say, look, we have a new requirement now for 1975. While, none of us want to give the impression that we think this is a problem that is not going to be solved by negotiation, I think it is only wise and prudent . . . to hope for the best and plan for the worst.

Elaborate on this statement in terms of the Department's views, as of now, on the time frame for contingency planning, the costs involved in providing relief assistance to the refugees, and the level of support the United States is prepared to give to the UNHCR program. Also, in what other ways is the United States prepared to support rehabilitation and recovery efforts on Cyprus?

Answer. "We understand that the UNHCR's current $22 million appeal has been met, and that some of this money will be available for relief efforts in 1975. Additional assistance, however, will definitely be necessary for at least 6-12 months and perhaps longer. Accordingly, we are keeping a disaster relief specialist in Cyprus to advise us of relief requirements on a continuing basis and AID is asking Congress in its budget request for an additional $10 million for the Cyprus relief effort."

APPENDIX III:

SELECTED PRESS REPORTS AND COMMENTARIES ON THE SITUATION IN CYPRUS

[From the New York Times, Jan. 24, 1975]

CYPRUS TALKS STALL ON AIRPORT QUESTION

ETHNIC GREEKS AND TURKS FAIL TO AGREE ON HOW TO REOPEN FACILITY

(By Steven V. Roberts)

Nicosia, Cyprus, Jan. 23—After two working sessions, the talks on the political future of Cyprus appear to be off to a rocky start.

When the talks resume tomorrow, Greek and Turkish Cypriotes will again consider the international airport at Nicosia, which has been closed since the Turkish invasion last July. The proposals made thus far by the two negotiators—Glafkos Clerides for the Greek Cypriotes and Rauf Denktash for the Turkish Cypriotes—seen quite far apart.

This has been dispiriting to diplomats here, who hoped that rapid progress on the airport question might give some * * * feelings of trust between the two sides.

The Americans are particularly disappointed, since continued military aid to Turkey, which they do not want to terminate is linked to progress on a settlement of Cyprus.

In the face of Administration protests, Congress voted last month to cut off aid to Ankara on Feb. 5 unless substantial progress was made in Cyprus. Yesterday, a Defense Department statement that it intends to sell Turkey $230-million in arms to modernize her tank forces reopened the controversy in Washington.

Because Cyprus is an island, the airport is vital to an economy already shattered by the fighting last summer and Turkish occupation of 40 per cent of the country. Exports such as textiles and fresh produce are strangled. Tourist and business travel is down to a trickle.

Both sides are hoping to open small landing strips of their own next month, but they will only dent the problem.

Before Christmas, United States and United Nations diplomats helped draft a proposal that would provide for United Nations supervision of the airport, with Greek and Turkish Cypriotes working under them. The formula for hiring employes was deliberately left vague, to avoid political questions.

ANKARA VETOES IDEA

Mr. Denktash's response was initially favorable, but when he passed the proposal to Ankara, it was rejected. Well-informed diplomats here generally agree that the Turkish Cypriote leader has little authority. Mr. Denktash concedes that on security matters—such as the airport—Turkey calls the tune in Cyprus.

The Turkish counterproposal, presented last Monday, plunges directly into political questions. It would eliminate the United Nations' role, and have the two communities run the airport on a 50–50 basis. Even though they comprise only 18 per cent of the population, the Turkish Cypriotes will insist on an equal share of power in all major areas, Mr. Denktash said in an interview.

The Turks feel that the United Nations would act on behalf of the Government of Cyprus which is largely Greek Cypriot. Turkey refuses to recognize the Government as it existed before the war.

Turkish leaders say that the United Nations, which has a peace-keeping force in Cyprus, has generally favored the Greek side, and therefore the Turks want to minimize the organization's role here.

The Turks have suggested that each community maintain its own customs facilities at the airport, with a joint facility for foreigners. The Greek side does not like this idea.

Turkish Cypriots want the guaranteeing power—Turkey, Greece and Britain—to provide security at the airport. According to Mr. Denktash the mainland Turkish Army must have a right to a contingent at the airport because of its considerable military value.

"We are not willing to take steps that prejudice our political stand," Mr. Denktash said.

Mr. Clerides finds the Turkish attitude "ominous" and many diplomatic analysts agree with him. If anything, one Western envoy said, the Turkish line has stiffened in recent weeks and the talks are actually moving backward.

[From the Washington Post, Jan. 21, 1975]

TURKEY IS ADAMANT ON TWO-ZONE CYPRUS; OIL CLAIM PRESSED

(By Sam Cohen)

Istanbul—The present Turkish government led by caretaker Premier Sadi Irmak does not seem prepared to make any of the concessions on Cyprus that the Greek Cypriots require. It also appears determined to go ahead very soon with its plan to start oil exploration in the Aegean sea, regardless of Greek reaction.

These points were made clear in an interview with Foreign Minister Melih Esenbel, who emphasized that the new realities in Cyprus and in the Aegean have to be taken into consideration if a solution is to be found.

"I am hopeful about the intercommunal talks which have started in Cyprus," Esenbel said, "but these will be difficult talks and will take time. Considering the pressure of the realities, I am optimistic about the prospects."

Esenbel said that Turkey and the Turkish Cypriots will insist on a two-zone federation in Cyprus, with a central government having limited powers. He rejected a cantonal system and said that a federation based on geographical separation was now the only realistic solution.

"There are only 17,000 Turkish Cypriots now left in the southern part of the island," he said. "Since the exodus of those Turks continues, and since the question of the Turkish Cypriots in the British bases has been solved, a new reality, a de facto situation, has arisen. When the question of the borders and the status of the federation will be discussed at a later stage, the Greeks will understand that there is no possibility of turning the clock back."

The minister said that once the economic and other practical matters are solved in the intercommunal talks, the basic political issues will be discussed. At that stage the talks will be enlarged to a five-sided conference, including Britain, Greece, Turkey and the two communities in Cyprus, he said.

Esenbel expressed the hope that the two communal leaders, Rauf Denktash and Glafkos Clerides, will agree soon on the reopening of the Nicosia airport, based on "an equal participation to its administration. . . . There can be no question of handing over the administration or control of the airport to any foreign organization," he said.

But he said that the Turks cannot accept any participation of the Greek Cypriots in the port administration at Famagusta. "Famagusta is going to remain the major port in the future federated Turkish area in the Cyprus state," he said. "Of course the Greek side will be able to use this port, but a Greek Cypriot participation in the port authority is out of the question. The decision on this is definite."

Esenbel said that the recent British proposal to allow the 10,000 Greek Cypriot refugees in the British bases to return to Famagusta was a political question. "The British have expressed a desire, but I do not think that such a gesture can be made at this time," he said. "The question of resettling Greek Cypriots in the city of Famagusta relates to the issue of the transfer of population, and this can only be discussed at a later stage, within the framework of the status of the federation."

Esenbel pointed out that the question of the borders of the Turkish-held area will be discussed only when the Greek side accepts the two-zone federal system. "Once this is accepted, Turkey will agree to discuss modifications of the recent borders. I must repeat that the borders are negotiable, but first the bi-zonal system must be accepted," he said.

According to Esenbel, the question of the withdrawal of the Turkish forces on Cyprus is also linked to the progress in the political negotiations. "We do not want to keep these forces on the island forever. I believe a phased reduction of the forces is possible. But first the status of the Cyprus state that will guarantee the security of the Turkish Cypriots must emerge."

Esenbel declared that Turkey considers the treaty recognizing Britain. Greece and Turkey as guarantor powers as still valid, and added that the Turks will insist on its continuation, without enlarging it as suggested by Archbishop Makarios.

If the intercommunal talks fail, Esenbel said, "the present de facto situation will continue and the Turkish sector will be consolidated. Therefore the questions now discussed will become facts."

Asked whether Turkey intends to send a surveyship to the Aegean sea for seismic research for future oil exploration, Esenbel said, "Our government is determined to follow a dynamic policy on this matter. Turkey cannot make any concession on this question, which is of vital importance for her. It is desirable to establish a cooperation between Greece and Turkey on this field, again based on existing realities. But if there are people who expect us to sacrifice our national interests in the Aegean, they will be terribly mistaken."

Esenbel emphasized that Greek concessions on Cyprus could not be traded for Turkish concessions on its rights to Turkey's continental shelf in the Aegean. "Those are two separate problems, and we would never consider a package deal for solving them," he said.

Regarding recent Greek warnings that Turkey's move to explore for oil in what Athens considers its continental shelves could lead to clashes, Esenbel said, "Our intention is definite and clear. We will go ahead with our plans in the Aegean. Those who do not like it should think twice, in view of the realities, before attempting to make this an issue of tension between the two countries."

[From Time Magazine, Jan. 13, 1975]

CYPRUS—BITTER LEMONS IN A LOST PARADISE

Before last summer's short but savage war between invading Turks and the outgunned Greek Cypriot National Guard, Cyprus was an oasis of sunny prosperity in the turbulent eastern Mediterranean. Nearly six months after the end of the fighting. Cyprus today is a wrecked dream—its airports still closed, its economy shattered, one-third of its people refugees in their own land. Greek Cypriot Leader Glafkos Clerides and his Turkish counterpart, Rauf Denktas, had hoped to resume their interrupted peace talks during Christmas week but were unable to agree on a basis for further negotiations. TIME Correspondent Erik Amfitheatrof recently visited the troubled island. His report:

With no settlement of their six-month agony in sight, Cypriots are living through the bleakest, most bitter winter in memory. Though there have been losses and atrocities on both sides, the Greek Cypriots, who make up 80% of the island's population, have suffered the most. Terrified by reports of mass shootings and rapes by Turkish troops advancing in the north last July, some 200,000 Greek Cypriots fled toward the British base area of Dhekelia on Cyprus' southern coast. The more fortunate were able to squeeze into the homes of relatives, but nearly 20,000 are spending the winter in canvas tents pitched in the fields and orchards.

The temperature is near freezing after sundown. On rainy days, the muddy lanes of the refugee camps turn into streams and water seeps into the tents. On cold nights, hundreds wander like ghosts into nearby towns to bed down in cafes or hotel lobbies.

The situation of some 10,000 Turkish Cypriot refugees in the southern, Greek-controlled part of the island is no better; they, too, are living under canvas this winter. In two desolate camps at the British base in Akrotiri, many are suffering from bronchial and rheumatic conditions, and there are cases of tuberculosis. But they at least have the consolation of knowing that a few dozen miles to the north of their camps, there is Turkish armor with the capability of overrunning the entire island.

For many of the refugees, the ordeal is made more difficult by memories of the paradise that has been lost. Before last summer's upheaval, the island, which is carpeted with citrus groves and vineyards, exported lemons, oranges, grapes and wines to Europe. It produced automotive parts for Middle Eastern countries, and its beaches lured 250,000 tourists a year. By the early 1970s, Cyprus was one of the eastern Mediterranean's most prosperous nations, with a per capita income of $1,460, and there was virtually no unemployment. Even the long-festering animosity between Greek and Turkish Cypriots was sweetened by the good life, and an eventual healing seemed possible.

SILENT LEADER

Prospects for a political settlement that might revive the island's economy now appear remote. Archbishop Makarios, the prelate-President of Cyprus, returned from his enforced exile last month, but so far he has accomplished little and said even less. He has consulted with leaders of all the Greek Cypriot political parties about forming a new government, but has yet to give any indication of the composition of his future Cabinet. Meanwhile, negotiations between both sides remain stalemated over the issue of a mass population transfer. On a visit to Cyprus last week, former Turkish Premier Bülent Ecevit insisted that the geographic and administrative separation of ethnic communities be formalized through the establishment of a federal state. But the Greek Cypriots oppose any agreement that would prevent them from returning to their homes; to bolster their bargaining position, they have refused to allow Turkish Cypriots in the Greek-controlled south to move north. For the moment Makarios is silent. But he knows well that unless he remains adamant on this issue, he cannot hold the support of the Greek Cypriot community.

———

[From the New York Times, Saturday, Jan. 18, 1975]

DEATH OF A CYPRIOT MARS OPENING OF POLITICAL TALKS

(By Steven V. Roberts)

Nicosia, Cyprus, Jan. 17—Political talks began today on the future of Cyprus, but a violent protest that resulted in the death of an 18-year-old Greek Cypriot showed that the issues dividing the communities of this island remained intricate and explosive.

After months of uncertainty, Greek Cypriots and Turkish Cypriots finally got down to specific issues in a morning meeting at the battle-damaged Ledra Palace Hotel. They discussed the status of the international airport, a vital link in the country's economy that has been closed since the Turkish Army's invasion last July.

Meanwhile, hundreds of Greek Cypriots marched on the British base at Episkopi. They were protesting London's decision to allow Turkey to move about 10,000 Turkish Cypriot refugees who fled to the base for safety during the war.

According to United Nations sources, the marchers attacked a small United Nations convoy that was approaching the base, broke the windows of the lead vehicle, and tried to set it afire. In the ensuing confusion, one of the other vehicles tried to come to the rescue of the first one and accidentally struck one of the marchers.

VICTIM WAS A REFUGEE

The youth, Panikos Dimitriou, died while being taken to the base hospital. A native of Agios Memnon, a village near Famagusta, he had been forced from his home during the fighting and was living as a refugee in Limassol.

The demonstrators also threw rocks and bricks at British troops, injuring 14. They were eventually dispersed with tear gas and water hoses. More demonstrations are expected tomorrow when the first plane load of ethnic Turkish refugees is expected to leave the base.

London has been hoping that the Turks would make a reciprocal gesture and allow some ethnic Greek refugees to return to their homes. This morning Rauf Denktash, the Turkish Cypriot leader, said the British move might "open a new road" towards peace, but he did not elaborate.

The political talks are being held between Mr. Denktash and Glafkos Clerides, the ethnic Greek representative who is speaker of the Cypriot Assembly. The two met during the autumn months to discuss humanitarian issues. They agreed to enter substantive negotiations after Secretary of State Kissinger met in Brussels last month with the Foreign Ministers of Greece and Turkey.

The initial session last Tuesday was spent on preliminaries. The first substantive question of the agenda, the airport, demonstrates the complexity of the Cyprus problem.

Now occupied by United Nations troops, the airport is surrounded by Turkish and Greek soldiers. According to diplomatic sources, the Turks have proposed that any administration be divided equally between the two ethnic groups—a reflection of the Turkish assertion that they are equal partners in the Cypriot state. The Greeks say that any division should follow the population distribution— four Greeks for every Turk.

The Turks also want separate customs facilities, the diplomats say, because they do not recognize the central Government of Cyprus as it now exists. The Greeks reply that the Government is still valid and functioning.

The United States has proposed that the United Nations administer the airport on a provisional basis, and that all political questions be postponed. But even though the airport is important to the economy of both communities, the feelings run so deep that the negotiators failed to make much headway today, according to a United Nations spokeman.

In their communiqué, the negotiators mentioned that preparatory work was being done by a separate group on the powers of a central government in a federal state. They also formed a subcommittee to deal with humanitarian matters.

The British decision to release the Turkish Cypriots has infuriated many ethnic Greeks, since London had been insisting for months that the refugees were a political question that had to be settled by talks between the two communities.

Then, the Greeks complain the British yielded to Turkish pressure just at the moment when the talks were beginning.

The Greek anger is heightened by an expectation that the Turkish Cypriots will be kept in mainland Turkey only a few weeks. Then Ankara likely will transfer them to northern Cyprus, where Turkish troops are in control. Once there, they will be given homes and businesses abandoned by Greek Cypriots.

The British move thus supports the Turkish plan of dividing Cyprus into two zones.

[From the New York Times, Dec. 21, 1974]

TURKISH CRISIS OF RULE PERSISTS AND CRIPPLES THE CYPRUS TALKS

(By Steven V. Roberts)

ANKARA, TURKEY, Dec. 18.—The Government crisis in Turkey is now three months old, and there are few prospects for improvement.

Since Premier Bulent Ecevit resigned on Sept. 18, the country has been run by caretaker administrations. Meanwhile, various politicians have tried, and failed, to form a stable government.

Mr. Ecevit won wide popularity here for his decision to invade Cyprus last summer following a coup against Archbishop Makarios. But he failed to gain approval for quick elections after his resignation, and now the next feasible date is late spring.

The continuing instability here has hampered efforts to begin peace negotiations on Cyprus, where Turkish troops still control almost 40 percent of the territory. As one Western diplomat put it: "Turkey picked a bad time to have her Government unravel."

The current caretaker government, led by Prof. Sadi Irmak, a 70-year-old Senator, now seems ready to begin preliminary talks. Turkish leaders insist that Cyprus is a "national issue," and that they all agree on a common policy.

Diplomatic analysts note, however, that Professor Irmak would have far less power and flexibility than an elected leader, and they wonder whether he will be able to make the compromises necessary to reach a settlement with the Greeks.

DIFFICULTIES IN OTHER AREAS

The Government crisis has crippled Turkey's ability to deal decisively with such economic problems as inflation and food shortages. Signs of discontent are appearing among the trade unions.

In addition, recent outbreaks of violence between extreme rightist and leftist student groups have sent a chill through the country. Similar clashes led to the civil unrest that plagued Turkey from 1969 to 1971. Calm returned only after the army forced the elected Government to resign, and squashed the dissidents with extra legal methods.

The military has traditionally played a major political role here, but in the last year or two a new generation of commanders has come to power. They are not as eager as their predecessors to intervene in governmental affairs, and so far there is no indication here that they are preparing to make a move.

Following the military takeover of 1971, Turkey was ruled for two years by an army backed, nonpolitical government. Then, in a rather remarkable display of confidence, the military permitted parliamentary elections last year.

Turkey uses a system of proportional representation, and with eight parties competing for votes, no one emerged with a clear mandate. Confusion reigned for three months. Then Mr. Ecevit, the leader of the Republican People's party, who are social democrats, formed a shaky coalition with the National Salvation party, a right-wing group of Moslem fundamentalists.

MANEUVER BY ECEVIT

The alliance never worked well, and after his triumph in Cyprus, Mr. Ecevit saw the chance to improve his position and resigned. But the other parties, fearful that he would sweep to a sizable victory, refused to vote for early elections and the current crisis ensued.

Mr. Ecevit stayed on as a caretaker Premier. Secretary of State Kissinger scheduled a visit here last month, and Mr. Ecevit was preparing to make several conciliatory gestures to help get Cyprus talks started. But at the last minute, the National Salvation party objected, the Kissinger visit was canceled, and the gestures were never made. Mr. Ecevit then resigned even his caretaker assignment, and the Irmak Government replaced him.

At the moment, the five conservative parties are trying to form a coalition government under Suleyman Demirel, who served as Premier from 1965 to 1971. The parties are torn by bitter personal rivalries, however, and diplomats do not expect the effort to succeed.

"This is the last attempt I am making," Mr. Demirel said in an interview. "We will either have a government or go to elections."

The prospect haunting this capital city is that once elections are held, the results may still be inconclusive. As Mr. Ecevit put it, "If the Government crisis is prolonged indefinitely, no one knows what will happen."

[From The Times (London), Dec. 6, 1974]

EOKA READY TO ACCEPT MAKARIOS RETURN TO RESTRICTED CHURCH ROLE

(From Paul Martin)

NICOSIA, Dec. 5.—The Eoka guerrilla movement has declared that it will accept the return of Archbishop Makarios if he gives up the presidency and restricts himself to church affairs. The Eoka declaration came as thousands of Greek Cypriots began to arrive in the capital to hear the archbishop speak on his return from the exile forced upon him by the July coup.

There is a growing air of excitement among the archbishop's supporters as the hour of his return approaches. Originally he was to have flown in from Athens on Friday. However, at the last minute, it was announced by his supporters that "technical reasons" had caused a delay of 24 hours.

The Eoka movement, which remains bitterly opposed to the archbishop, made its stand clear in a 10-point manifesto circulated in Nicosia overnight. Although it takes a strong line against the archbishop it is the first time it has agreed to his return.

Calling for national unity among Greek Cypriots, the manifesto sets out the conditions under which the Eoka movement would accept his return. It accused the archbishop of deliberately ignoring advice from "friends and foes" about the possible adverse consequences of his decision.

"Makarios has declared that on his return he will succeed in securing a return of Greek Cypriot refugees to their homes", the manifesto said. He also declared that he would lead the struggle to end the Turkish occupation. We believe that both are illusions. However, we shall not block his way in order to prove once more that he conscientiously deceives his people."

The manifesto declared that the task facing the Greek Cypriot people allowed "room for everybody to take part in the national struggle". However, it added: "It is necessary for him to realize that his presence in the political arena will result in division and conflict." This rendered his "speedy withdrawal from politics" a necessity.

It went on to reiterate the Eoka stand that any attempt to reestablish the Makarios order, ousted by the coup, would result in continued conflict in the Greek Cypriot community, "If Makarios does not heed this then his return will constitute an epilogue to the Cyprus tragedy."

Opening the way for the Archbishop's return as head of the Cyprus church, the manifesto said: If he comes to give a solution to the ecclesiastical problem in accordance with the church heirarchy, then we shall contribute. The solution of the church problem is a basic ingredient for national unity among the Greek Cypriots. It is a question of great urgency."

The manifesto then went on to warn the Archbishop that even if he does restrict himself to the church, he must heed the factions inside the church who opposed him. "If Makarios does not take a responsible line he will find us a strong and unyielding opponent."

The Eoka movement, the manifesto added, did not try to prevent Archbishop Makarios's return by using force. "However the national centre must know that if Makarios is to repeat the recent past, Cyprus will inevitably be led to a bloody civil strife."

MARIO MODIANO WRITES FROM ATHENS

One of the vital facts that emerged from the archbishop's talks in Athens, is that so far as post-junta Greece is concerned no lasting settlement on Cyprus is possible without the approval and cooperation of President Makarios.

The Greek Government, therefore, did not discourage him from returning to Cyprus despite Turkish hints of a third military operation to capture the entire island, on the ground that the remaining Turkish Cypriots in the south might be endangered by a renewal of violence within the Greek community.

"Greek diplomatic sources" denied today, vigorously though anonymously, assertions by the Turkish Defence Minister that Greece was despatching troops to Cyprus. "This is grossly inaccurate", the sources said. "Greece has not sent a single man to Cyprus in recent months other than reliefs for outgoing servicemen."

Next week's scheduled meetings in Brussels, for instance, between Dr Henry Kissinger, the American Secretary of State, and the Foreign Minister of Greece and Turkey, may set the pace for substantial intercommunal negotiations on the future of the island.

———

[From the New York Times, Dec. 23, 1974]

TURKEY RULES OUT CYPRUS NEGOTIATIONS WITH MAKARIOS

(By Steven V. Roberts)

Ankara, Turkey, Dec. 18—Turkish officials say they are ready to begin serious negotiations over Cyprus, but they have set down two conditions that could hinder progress toward a settlement.

They do not want Archbishop Makarios, the President of Cyprus, to control the negotiating position of the Greek side. They know it is unrealistic to expect the Archbishop to resign, but they hope he will delegate full negotiating authority to Giafkos Clerides, the President of the House of Representatives.

The Turks also want the Greeks to acknowledge the principle that any settlement must be based on a "geographical federation." By that, they mean that Cyprus should be divided into two zones, linked by a federal government but administered separately.

One zone would be controlled by the ethnic Turks, who make up 18 per cent of the population, and the other by the ethnic Greeks, who account for 80 per cent.

52

AN EXPRESSION OF OPTIMISM

Turkish officials have expressed guarded optimism following the recent meetings in Brussels between Secretary of State Kissinger and the Greek and Turkish Foreign Ministers. As a member of the Turkish delegation put it, "We found out that Greece is willing to have negotiations—and vice versa."

The Turks urged Mr. Kissinger and the Greek delegation to put pressure on the Archbishop to withdraw from the negotiating process. President Makarios has been making conciliatory statements lately, but analysts have long considered him masterful at ambiguity.

If all goes according to the plan sketched out in Brussels, the next step would be for Mr. Clerides and Rauf Denktash, the Turkish Cypriote leader, to start preliminary discussions on political subjects.

The two men, who are old friends, have already been discussing humanitarian issues raised by the Turkish invasion of the island last July. There was wide agreement in Brussels that these talks should now become "much more meaningful," according to a Turkish official. However, he added, any final settlement would have to be negotiated between Athens and Ankara.

The Turks are pleased that Greece now has a strong leader, Constantine Caramanlis, who established good relations with Ankara during his previous tenure as Premier. They realize that only a strong government can make the compromises necessary to reach an agreement, and they worry about the weakness of their Premier, Prof. Sadi Irmak.

All Turkish leaders seem to share a common policy toward Cyprus, however, and they agree that it would be "difficult but not impossible" for the Irmak Government to pursue a settlement. These leaders say that the climate for a settlement improved when Congress agreed to delay cutting off United States military aid to Turkey, since they do not want to make concessions that would look like "knuckling under" to Washington.

FULL AUTHORITY SOUGHT

In Turkish eyes, the big question mark is Archbishop Makarios. The Turks simply do not trust him and prefer to deal with Mr. Clerides, who was acting President for several months after the Archbishop fled Cyprus last July, following a coup organized by the military, junta that was then ruling Greece.

That coup led to the Turkish invasion, which in turn provoked the collapse of the Greek junta.

Mr. Clerides has said publicly that the Greek side must accept the principle of geographical federation, a view that is shared privately by the Government in Athens.

The Greek side prefers an arrangement that would give the ethnic Turks control over several areas throughout the island, rather than one large zone. They feel that this would minimize shifts in population and the possibility that the island might be partitioned.

The Turks insist on a "bizonal" federation, which they say would make it easier for them to provide security for Turkish Cypriotes, and to develop a viable economy that is not too reliant on the Greeks.

[From the New York Times, Nov. 30, 1974]

MAKARIOS OFFERS TURKS AN "OLIVE BRANCH"

(By Steven V. Roberts)

Athens, Nov. 29—Archbishop Makarios, the proposed President of Cyprus, said here today that he would offer an "olive branch" to Turkey in negotiations over the island's future. But the conditions he outlined indicate that a settlement is still far away.

The Archbishop came to Athens for talks with Premier Constantine Caramanlis of Greece and Glafkos Clerides, who has been President of Cyprus since last summer. It was the Archbishop's first visit here since July, when he was ousted in a coup d'etat organized by the military junta then ruling Greece.

That coup provoked the invasion of Cyprus by Turkish troops, who still occupy almost 40 per cent of the island. The invasion then led to the collapse of the junta here, which ceded power to a civilian government four days later.

The Archbishop spoke from a hotel balcony to tens of thousands of supporters massed in Constitution Square. Red flags bearing the hammer and sickle flared in the cool sunshine and many of the crowd's signs and slogans carried anti-American themes.

"We are prepared to give the Turkish Cypriotes the right of self-government," the Archbishop asserted. "But we will not consent to the forcible movement of the population or the creation of conditions which will lead to the possible partition of the island."

OPEN TO FEDERATION PLAN

As he stated in London last week, Archbishop Makarios is ready to discuss a "multi-regional federation" for Cyprus. Under this plan, Turkish Cypriots would have administrative control over their own communities scattered throughout the island.

This puts Archbishop Makarios in sharp conflict with the Turkish side, which favors division of Cyrpus into two separate districts, and the massive shift of population. One district would be controlled by the ethnic Turks and the other by ethnic Greeks.

The Archbishop is also at odds with Mr. Clerides, who insists that the only "realistic" solution would be separate geographical areas linked by a federal government. Like the Archbishop, Mr. Clerides opposes the "forcible movement" of populations. But Mr. Clerides would accept voluntary exchanges that would give the ethnic Turks a majority in their own sector, even though they comprise only 18 percent of the population.

Mr. Clerides has conducted preliminary discussions with Rauf Denktash, the Turkish Cypriote leader. But he is said to be worried that, with the archbishop in the background, he does not have adequate authority to pursue serious negotiations or conclude an agreement.

WHAT CLERIDES SEEKS

For this reason, Mr. Clerides has placed great emphasis on the meetings here this weekend. He wants the Archbishop to commit himself to a clear negotiating position. But as one well-informed diplomat here said: "That kind of commitment is exactly what Clerides is not going to get from Makarios. What Makarios is really ready to accept, no one knows. Not even Makarios."

The main interest of the Caramanlis Government is to avoid spending its hard-earned political capital. In this vein, the Premier has insisted that Cyprus should be a "national issue," outside partisan politics, and that Athens would accept any solution that is agreeable to the Cypriotes.

Mr. Caramanlis wants to get rid of the Cyprus problem, but he prefers no solution to a humiliating one. As one astute Western diplomat put it: "I don't believe the Greeks care very much about the substance of the solution. What they care about is their national honor vis-a-vis Turkey."

The Archbishop reiterated today his determination to return to Cyprus next week. Mr. Clerides has warned that the Archbishop's presence could cause bloodshed within the Greek community, and the Turkish side has insisted that the prelate would impair prospects for peace by returning.

This view is shared by many diplomats, here and in Nicosia, who wish the controversial Archbishop would stay in exile. But these diplomats also concede that Archbishop Makarios remains extremely popular in Cyprus, and that most Greek Cypriotes would reject any solution that lacks his endorsement.

[From the Wall Street Journal, Dec. 13, 1974]

KISSINGER SEEKS TO PROMOTE CYPRUS PEACE BUT WITH LITTLE DISCERNIBLE
SUCCESS SO FAR

(By Richard J. Levine)

Brussels—Under growing congressional pressure to produce progress, Henry Kissinger has spent much of his time here seeking ways to promote peace on Cyprus—with little discernible success so far.

Officially, the Secretary of State came to this wet and windy capital to attend a routine meeting of North Atlantic Treaty Organization foreign ministers.

But while here he has expended considerable effort on the Cyprus problem in a series of private talks with the foreign ministers of Greece and Turkey, the two nations most deeply involved in the affairs of the divided island nation in the eastern Mediterranean.

Mr. Kissinger, who sandwiched this trip between Washington talks on the Mideast and this weekend's coming U.S.-French summit conference in Martinique arrived in Brussels with modest expectations about what could be accomplished in the Cyprus situation. His talks were labeled "exploratory," and that is what they have been.

Mr. Kissinger is convinced that the congressional cutoff of American military aid to Turkey, which went into effect Tuesday, and the presence of a caretaker government in Ankara make major diplomatic progress difficult at this time.

Perhaps even more important in the long run, however, is the return of Archbishop Makarios to Cyprus as president after being ousted in a coup last July. President Makarios is the major unknown in the Cyprus equation, and his return to power complicates enormously the diplomatic problems confronting Mr. Kissinger, U.S. officials say.

UNDERMINE DIPLOMATIC EFFORTS

Until the archbishop spells out clearly his formula for solution of the Cyprus problem, Mr. Kissinger is unlikely and unwilling to make any bold moves, regardless of congressional pressure.

Indeed, much of Mr. Kissinger's effort here seemed designed to forestall the House vote Wednesday to cut off military aid to Turkey until "substantial progress" has been made toward a Cyprus peace settlement. Mr. Kissinger had hoped that the House would go along with an earlier Senate move to postpone the aid ban until mid-February. Toward this end, he has argued that the congressional action would undermine American diplomatic efforts to get the Turks to make necessary concessions on Cyprus.

As a result of its invasion of the island last July 30 to protect the Turkish Cypriot community following the coup that deposed President Makarios, Turkey currently controls some 40 percent of Cyprus' territory. U.S. officials say that a few months ago Turkey was willing to make concessions that would have enabled negotiations to start.

But this initiative was thwarted by early congressional votes to cut off aid to Turkey. If Turkey had made concessions in the face of congressional action, U.S. officials say, it would have been put in the politically unacceptable position of bowing to pressure from Washington.

Turkish Foreign Minister Milih Esenbel makes the same point. After meeting with Mr. Kissinger, he told reporters: "Turkey and the U.S. decided on a course of action in October on Cyprus. But unfortunately the action taken by the U.S. Congress since then hampered the progress we could make."

Despite the imponderables in the Cyprus situation, U.S. officials are convinced that Glafkos Clerides, former acting president of Cyprus and currently President Makarios' designated negotiator, and Vice President Rauf Denktash, the leader of the Turkish Cypriot community, could work out a solution to the Cyprus problem in two months—if left to their own devices and backed by Athens and Ankara. While U.S. experts believe the Greek and Turkish governments would go along, it seems clear that President Makarios doesn't intend to allow Mr. Clerides much latitude.

WHAT FORM IS UNCERTAIN

With some 40,000 to 45,000 Turkish troops in control of a large part of Cyprus, and solution is likely to involve division of the nation into two communities under some kind of federation arrangement. But exactly what form such a federation might take it uncertain, and President Makarios has indicated he will resist any solution that leads to a distinct partition of the island.

Since Turkish Cypriots comprise only 18 percent of the island's population, Turkey is said to be willing to surrender some of the territory it seized in last summer's fighting. But while Turkey is willing to accept less than the 40 percent of the island it holds, experts say it wants more than 80 percent. Moreover, time would appear to be on Turkey's side. With each passing day, the de facto separation of the island makes the eventual legal partition more likely.

55

Meantime, Cyprus has become still another test of strength between the powerful, prestigious Mr. Kissinger and a Congress increasingly intent on playing a
more forceful role in foreign policy. In Mr. Kissinger's view Cyprus has become a
major tragedy, not only because of the tremendous suffering among the Greek and
Turkish communities on Cyprus, but also because of the adverse effects on
American national security interests.

For at a time when Mideast tensions run high, U.S. officials argue, Washington
can ill afford to antagonize a major NATO ally in the eastern Mediterranean.

[From Manchester Guardian Weekly, Dec. 14, 1974]

TURKS READY FOR CYPRUS DEADLOCK

(By Eric Silver, Nicosia, December 10)

Turkish Cypriot leaders are working on contingency plans for breaking off
negotiations with the Greek community and refusing to admit the United Nations
peacekeeping force to the "Autonomous Turkish Region Cyprus."

They are waiting not only for Archbishop Makarios to clarify his bargaining
strategy, but also for a new Cyprus resolution which is due to come to a vote by
the weekend in the Security Council. The Turks believe that the United Nations
formula will have an important influence on the Archbishop's decision.

Makarios repeated at a press conference here today that he believed a solution
was possible, though it should not give "excessive privileges to one side at the ex-
pense of the other." He hoped that the intercommunal talks would resume in about
10 days. He would be giving the Greek negotiator, Mr. Clerides, detailed guide-
lines within a few days.

The Archbishop did not, however, approach the Turkish requirement which
is that he accepts the present geographical position, with the Turkish Army
occupying 40 percent of the island, as the basis for further negotiation. He said, as
he did on his return from exile on Saturday, that a settlement must not entail the
"removal or exchange of population."

If he holds to this position, the Turks (and possibly Clerides) will find it hard to
continue talking. The Turkish negotiator, Mr. Denktash, is also making it a
sticking point that Makarios must stop calling himself President and accept that
he is only leader of the Greek community.

At his press conference, the Archbishop refused to comply. "I would not like to
negotiate," he said, "as representative of the Greek Cypriot community. I am the
President of the republic, which includes Greek and Turkish Cypriots."

Makarios suggested that Clerides would be a more appropriate negotiator. The
former Acting President would take part as the representative of the Greek
Cypriots. Makarios said he did not expect the new talks to last as long as the
intercommunal negotiations that preceded the July coup. Since these dragged on
for eight years without achieving a solution, the remark drew a rueful smile later
from Denktash.

The Archbishop dismissed as "entirely unfounded" reports of a rift between
himself and Clerides. Relations he insisted, were "very harmonious" and Clerides
had done a "commendable" job during his absence.

It is no secret, however, that contact between the two Greek leaders is as cold
as a winter night. Makarios did not mention his stand-in when he addressed
100,000 Greek Cypriots who welcomed him home on Saturday. Clerides was kept
waiting until this afternoon for his first working session with the Archbishop.

Makarios, as always, will not tolerate another figure of comparable stature in
the Greek community. He is trying to put Clerides back in his place. After his
achievements of the past four months, in which he weaned the volatile Greeks to
the ugly realities of the Turkish occupation, Clerides is less disposed to accept a
subordinate role. He has earned respect and authority.

The chill will become a crisis if it affects policy—if it means that Makarios
cannot stomach the kind of concessions Clerides knows are unavoidable, or if it
means that Clerides, who has a unique rapport with Denktash, resigns as the
Greek negotiator.

Then Cyprus will be back in the world of fait accompli, enforced partition, and
guerrilla warfare.

56

[From The New York Times, Friday, Jan. 17, 1975]

CYPRUS SPLIT SEEMS CLOSER AS TURKS PLAN TO EVACUATE REFUGEES

(By Steven V. Roberts)

Episcopi, Cyprus, Jan. 16—The division of Cyprus into two districts came a bit closer today as about 10,000 Turkish Cypriot refugees prepared to leave the southern part of the island for Turkey and probably eventual resettlement in areas in Northern Cyprus now controlled by Turkish troops.

Britain announced yesterday that she would allow Turkish Cypriot refugees to leave the British base here, where they have been living since last July, to go to the Turkish mainland.

Today, base officials carried out a census, asking all refugees whether they wanted to leave the base or stay. The next step is uncertain, but it is likely that Turkish aircraft will fly the Cypriots to Turkey. Later they are expected to be transferred to northern Cyprus.

Greek Cypriot leaders denounced the British decision today, saying it would further Turkish plans to partition the island and harm the possibilities for peace. Some leaders also threatened to press for the removal of the two large British bases here, key western outposts in the eastern Mediterranean.

THOUSANDS ALREADY IN NORTH

The Turkish Cypriots came to Episcopi to escape the fighting that followed the Turkish invasion of the island. It has cost the British almost $2-million to feed and house the refugees, who refused to return to their homes. Sixty Turkish-Cypriot babies have been born in the base hospital and 300 patients have been treated, according to base officials.

Ankara had been insisting that she be allowed to remove the refugees from the base, The British resisted, saying that the matter must be settled within the refugees from the base. The problem.

The British came under growing pressure from Turkey to relent. But in explaining the decision to allow the refugees to go, the British cited humanitarian motives.

Turkish Cypriots have been making their way northward by various methods since the fighting stopped. Thousands have already moved into houses and shops abandoned by the 180,000 Greek Cypriots who fled from the advancing Turkish Army.

Ziya Rizki, the leader of the ethnic Turks here at the base, sat in a crowded tent, his overcoat buttoned against the cold, and explained why almost all his people wanted to go north.

"They have no confidence in going back to their villages and living with the Greeks. They can't live with the people who have been attacking them."

The Turkish Cypriots have suffered a lot and have heard a good deal of propaganda from their own leaders. They clearly want to move somewhere they consider more secure.

They are leaving homes in the south, their jobs, the graves of their parents. "A lot of them have said, enough is enough," a British official said. "But a lot of them are sorry to go, too."

Greek Cypriots have been hoping that Turkey would respond to the British move by allowing some ethnic Greek refugees to return to the eastern port city of Famagusta. But Ankara has been silent.

TURKEY PLANS AIRLIFT

Ankara, Turkey, Jan. 16 (Reuters)—Turkey will organize a huge airlift within the next few days to evacuate thousands of Turkish-Cypriot refugees from a British base in Cyprus.

Foreign Minister Melih Esenbel told a news conference here today that a fleet of Turkish Airlines planes would shuttle the refugees to temporary accommodation—mostly under canvas—in southern Turkey. He said he hoped the operation would start this weekend and last less than two weeks.

Mr. Esenbel said that the British decision had averted damage to Anglo-Turkish relations and would create a more relaxed atmosphere for negotiations between Greek and Turkish Cypriots on the island's political future.

57

[From the Times (London), Jan. 9, 1975]

CYPRUS SETTLEMENT IN SIGHT AS GREEKS AGREE TO FEDERATION

Nicosia, Jan. 8—The Greek and Turkish Cypriot sides agreed today to resume negotiations for a settlement of the Cyprus problem, on the basis of the establishment of a federal state.

The breakthrough came during a 90-minute meeting between Mr. Glafkos Clerides, the president of the House of Representatives, and Mr. Rauf Denktash, the Turkish Cypriot leader, in the presence of Señor Weckman-Muñóz, the United Nations special representative on the island.

This was the fourth exploratory meeting between the two Cypriot leaders to find a basis for resuming their talks, since these were interrupted early in December. Their agreement ended weeks of uncertainty and gave rise to hopes that a settlement might be reached within five to six weeks, once the talks get under way.

An official announcement at the end of the meeting said the two leaders had agreed to continue their talks on humanitarian issues (arising from the Turkish invasion) and "to commence talks on the substance of the Cyprus problem."

The statement then added; "They will begin their work by discussing the function of the central Government in a federal state." This was seen as a clear indication that agreement had already been reached that the basis of the peace talks would be a federal settlement.

The substantive negotiations will get under way next Tuesday, at the Ledra Palace Hotel conference centre on the Green Line, which divides the Greek and Turkish sectors of the capital.

The talks were called off early in December by Mr. Denktash, just before Archbishop Makarios returned to the island from his five-month exile. Mr. Denktash stated at the time it would be pointless to continue until the Archbishop made his intentions clear.

Now, a month and a day after the Archbishop's return, the way is open at last for meaningful negotiations.

The Turkish demand for a federal form of government for the island's two communities was rejected as completely unacceptable by the Archbishop before the Turkish invasion.

It is obvious that the Archbishop now has recognized the grim reality brought about by the occupation of nearly 40 percent of the island by the Turkish Army and the establishment of a de facto Turkish Cypriot administration in the occupied region.

Whereas before the invasion the main Greek Cypriot preoccupation was to preserve the format of a unitary state, the return of some 200,000 Greek Cypriot refugees to their homes in the Turkish-controlled area is now the primary aim.

Observers feel that by accepting the demand for a federal settlement the Archbishop hopes that the Turks may be more willing to consider the refugee question.

It is noteworthy that the agreement for the resumption of the peace talks came on the same day that President Ford was conferring on Cyprus with Dr. Kissinger and the American ambassadors to Athens, Ankara and Nicosia.

The United States is particularly anxious to see some progress towards a settlement before February 5, the date when all American military aid to Turkey is scheduled to end, if there is no progress.

[From The Times (London), Dec. 31, 1974]

NOW THE TURKS MUST DECIDE WHAT TO DO WITH THE PART OF CYPRUS THEY WON

(By Paul Martin)

Sombre looking Turkish troops stand guard over the forlorn flotilla of pleasure boats moored round the once picturesque Kyrenia harbour. An austere bust of Ataturk stands in the main square, and Turkish flags flutter from the battlements of Kyrenia Castle. This is the front door of Turkish Cyprus.

Five months after the invasion, the Turks have imposed their desired majority in the north of Cyprus. More than 40,000 Turkish Cypriots have filtered there from the south of the island, and the remaining 20,000 in the Greek areas are arriving at the rate of about 100 a day. With only 13,000 of the former Greek population of 160,000 in this area north of the Attilla Line left, the ethnic and geographic partition of Cyprus is almost complete.

The power that 36,000 troops affords has placed the Turks in control of 40 percent of the island. In this area they have more than 80 percent of tourist accommodation, about 60 percent of agricultural export potential, more than £2,000m worth of land and buildings, and more than half of the country's earning potential. Turkish Cypriots are so eager to point out to foreign visitors: "Now all the Greeks have left is their grapes."

Nevertheless, anyone asked to draw a comparison between the two areas at this stage would come to the conclusion that the Greeks were the victors and the Turks the vanquished. Faced with 200,000 displaced persons—about a third of their numbers—on top of their economic losses, the Greeks have been quick to adapt. Refugees have been absorbed into the houses of friends and relatives, into requisitioned hotels, apartment blocks and public buildings. So that today, fewer than 13,000 are refugees living in tents.

In the north, the Turks have been slow to exploit the fruits of their victory. The bulk of the rich citrus crop has been lost and the grain producing Messaoria Plain has lain fallow so that no crop can be expected for at least a year. Though the Turks boast that they will resurrect the now dead hotel trade in the north, officially condoned looting of deserted hotels continues. And, so bad has the Turkish record been on this score, Turkish families from the south find themselves inheriting vacated Greek houses stripped bare. This has sparked off another cycle of looting.

Clearly, the problems facing the Turkish administration are great. Whereas the accommodation found for Greek refugees is temporary, the resettlement of the Turks in the north is part of a campaign to ensure permanence. Housing is allocated on the basis of what a Turkish family owned in Limassol, Larnaca, Paphos or any other of the southern towns or villages. "It is only natural that a refugee family will tell you they left behind a mansion when in fact they lived in a shack", said a member of the administration. "Hence the process of sifting is extremely important."

On top of that are the problems that partition (whether disguised in federation or not) impose. Kyrenia is the perfect example. So far the Turkish administration has flooded the town with as many as 3,500 Turkish Cypriots mostly from the Limassol area. All Greek Cypriot businesses have been taken over, and apart from the homes of the 550 Greek Cypriots who remained after the Turkish invasion, the Turks have requisitioned all the houses.

"Kyrenia is not Turkish or Greek but is foreign also," a Turkish Cypriot who shared a business with a Greek before the invasion said. "I like to look at it as a sort of Riviera. I don't know the Riviera, but I think in terms of a tourist town where all can feel at ease. We won the war. But the Kyrenia I see today is not the Kyrenia I wish to see. We must all sit down and decide what must be done for the future—otherwise all is lost."

As any visitor to the Turkish controlled north of Cyprus can see, it is with the Greek Cypriots that the skill in running hotels, restaurants and the like lies. The Turks have done their utmost to encourage the two main restaurants in Kyrenia— the Harbour and the Red Shark—to get back into full swing. However, try as the respective owners may, they lack the trained staff who are now south of the dividing line. The same goes for the hotel trade.

Whatever it is called, partition has imposed its settlement on the island. However, for the Turks more than the Greeks this solution brings difficult social problems. For instance, most of the Limassol Turks who now populate Kyrenia earned their living from the docks. Short of a twice-a-week ferry to Turkey there is no dock work in Kyrenia. Few of the immigrants have savings, and live on a meagre dole. And since there is a strong force of dock workers in Famagusta, now in Turkish hands, it is unlikely they could find jobs there.

The fact remains that in the Greek administered south there is every indication that things are returning to normal. Prices are rising and everybody watches the level of Cyprus's foreign reserves—which have remained steady around £100m.

However, the disasters which many felt would have hit the community by now have not come. The unusual spectacle of beggers on the streets near large refugee concentrations has disappeared. The danger of unemployment remains, but initial predictions of as much as 30 per cent have not been fulfilled. Furthermore, private construction and public works projects have begun to regenerate the economy.

"Give us five years", no the promise one has heard from a good many Greek Cypriots, "and Turks or no Turks we will make the north look like the devastated Cyprus.

59

[From Worldview, December 1974]

CYPRUS: THE DRIFT TO DISASTER

(Lord Caradon)

As Sir Hugh Foote, Lord Caradon was Colonial Secretary in Cyprus from 1943 to 1945 and Governor and Commander-in-Chief of Cyprus from 1957 to 1960.

Anything I write may be quickly overrun by new developments—in Cyprus, in Greece and Turkey, at the United Nations in New York and Geneva.

I started to write in a plane flying from New York to Geneva to see Prince Sadruddin, the U.N. High Commissioner for Refugees; I went on in hurried interludes during a hectic general election in England; I finished on another plane to New York.

With so many uncertainties and imminent dangers, I am tempted to write mainly about the past. And I shall speak from my own experience. Yet whatever the difficulties of forecasting, one must turn presently to the prospects for the future. To anyone deeply concerned for all the people of Cyprus, the prospects are terrifying.

I first went to Cyprus more than thirty years ago. It was then a British Colony, and I went as Colonial Secretary. I acted as Governor of Cyprus for several months as long ago as 1944, I went back to Cyprus as Governor in 1957 in the middle of the EOKA rebellion, and stayed till I sailed away in 1960 when Cyprus attained independence as a republic. As the last Governor of Cyprus I am tempted, as I say, to speak of the past.

I like to remember that when I was first in Cyprus, during the Second World War, relations between Greek Cypriots and Turkish Cypriots—roughly 80 percent to 20 percent—were peaceful, as they had been for as long as anyone could remember. They participated as officials and judges and police in the same administration, and they served in the same regiments in the war. When I went back as Governor in 1957 the violent EOKA rebellion against British rule and in favor of union with Greece had already soured relations. Communal bitterness and bloodshed, which have since reached such a pitch of fear and anger, began less than two decades ago. I take some comfort in reflecting that relations between the two communities were not long ago easy and freindly. I do not for a moment discount the terrible damage that has now been done. Maybe it is irreparable. But I persist in reminding myself that what we see now, all the hatred and all the cruelty, is comparatively recent. The future of all the people of Cyprus is one of utter misery if Greek Cypriots and Turkish Cypriots cannot recover the peace and amity which reigned in their beautiful island for a hundred years.

Before I left Cyprus in August, 1960, I signed on behalf of the British Government the complicated agreements which had been worked out over the previous year and a half. The agreements were signed that same night by the representatives of Greece and Turkey and by Archbishop Makarios and Dr. Kutchuk, the leader of the Turkish Cypriots at the time. The ceremony was conducted in a spirit of achievement and hope. The credit for the agreements went primarily to the Foreign Ministers of Greece and Turkey, Averoff and Zorlu, who at Zurich had worked out the framework of a settlement for the future. They showed admirable courage in doing so. The framework was filled in by a Constitutional Commission which sat for many months in Nicosia and to which Greek Cypriots and Turkish Cypriots and representatives of Greece and Turkey worked together in confident compromise. For more than a year I worked in the Executive Council with seven Greek Cypriot Ministers and three Turkish Cypriot Ministers, and cordial cooperation and trust prevailed.

On the initiative of Archbishop Makarios they agreed, I remember, on the the distribution of portfolios between the Ministers—a distribution which allotted the important Ministries of Agriculture and Defense to Turkish Cypriots.

It was a good start in freedom.

I have no firsthand knowledge of the subsequent tensions and frictions leading to the crises of 1964 and 1967. I shall not attempt to go over the wretched story of the breakdown of the 1960 agreements.

It is generally accepted that the constitutional plan agreed at Zurich was too set, too rigid, to work smoothly. After a few years of uneasy trial, proposals were made for changes. They were rejected and the opportunity for a new negotiation lost. So from 1964 onward the Zurich constitution was no longer in effect. Archbishop Makarios and his Greek Cypriot Ministers ruled. The Turkish Cypriots, sustained from Turkey and based in separate and isolated enclaves, no longer shared in the administration of the island.

Economically, however, the island prospered, the United Nations Force helped to keep the peace, and it is said that the long drawn-out constitutional discussions between Clerides and Denktash made some progress. It is even claimed that earlier this year there was rough agreement on the structure of a new constitutional plan giving the Turkish Cypriots a reasonable prospect of partnership and security. For several years there had been no communal bloodshed. There was some hope that, with Greek and Turkish encouragement, a peaceful and acceptable settlement would be found.

Then, suddenly, in July this year there was the coup. Early that Monday morning the National Guard, led by officers from Greece, drove their tanks into the grounds of the Presidential Palace, destroying the building with cannon fire. They believed they had killed President Makarios in the rubble. There is evidence that the attack was authorized by and planned from Athens.

It seems almost incredible that the Greek Junta, in spite of long, sustained American support in the past, could have dreamed that the coup would succeed, that the way could be opened to union of all Cyprus with Greece, that the Turkish Government would not react violently.

It is also difficult to understand, to say the least, why the American and British Governments decided to take no action in the Sec..rity Council till after the Turkish invasion had begun.

I cannot think of any single act which has caused more suffering and more prospect of continuing misery than the crazy assault that Monday morning. True, one result was the end of the Junta in Greece, and that is certainly cause for rejoicing. But every other consequence has been utterly disastrous.

The human suffering in Cyprus has only just begun. As the winter approaches it will get rapidly worse. A third of the whole population of Cyprus has been uprooted from homes and livelihood. The immediate outlook is very bad. The further future is dreadful to contemplate.

The Turks have no intention of withdrawing their army, except perhaps for a limited withdrawal in Famagusta and Morphou. Nor are they allowing the Greek Cypriot refugees to return to their homes and lands. The Greek Cypriots and the Greek Government, on the other hand, can never accept what amounts to the partition of the island, leaving so many Greek Cypriots without shelter or income. No Turkish Government and no Greek Government could survive if it gave way.

So what hope is there now for peace, for conciliation and cooperation? Precious little. If the present drift continues, the disaster will be deep and permanent. A situation not dissimilar in some respects to that in Northern Ireland or the Middle East will persist. Tensions may well lead to conflict—conflict into which larger powers, having failed to prevent or deal with the tragedy, may well be drawn. What conceivable escape can there be from drift into despair and bloodshed?

How bitter it is to reflect that only a few months ago a fruitful settlement was for the grasping. How tragically was the prospect of a lasting cooperation in peace shattered by the gunfire on that fateful Monday morning.

A partition weakly accepted is a bleak prospect. One envisions cruel transfers of population, economic ruin, and the certainty of continuing friction and conflict, with Greece and Turkey constantly on the brink of war and the great powers dragged ever nearer to the explosive dispute. Surely there must be another way.

It seems to me that hope must lie in two factors. First, the good sense of the Cypriot people themselves and their able leaders. And second, in the capacity of the international community, acting through the United Nations, to insulate the island from outside pressures and to encourage, facilitate, and guarantee a fair settlement.

I do not doubt the capacity of the Cypriot leaders. On the Greek Cypriot side there is an array of able and experienced politicians, officials, lawyers, industrialists. Glavkos Clerides, the Acting President, is specially qualified by experience and temperament to conduct the negotiations on behalf of his people. Archbishop Makarios has a prestige and skill and courage which may in the future rally his people to repair the damage and overcome the enmities of the past.

On the Turkish Cypriot side too there are experienced and able leaders, Raouf Denktash outstanding among them.

The weakness on the Greek Cypriot side arises from their factional disputes and violence amongst themselves. On the Turkish Cypriot side there is subservience to the negative reaction of Ankara. These difficulties were great enough before recent events created new suspicions and mistrusts. They are much greater now. Nevertheless, it is of the utmost consequence that Cyprus has the advantage of a people of shrewdness, adaptability, and exceptional ability. Left to themselves they would, I am sure, come to a sensible solution of their formidable problems.

There is, however, no prospect of their being enabled or allowed to work out their own salvation without urgent and decisive international action. Effective international leadership means there must be a clear reaffirmation by the United Nations Security Council of the aim to ensure an independent, sovereign Cyprus. The fundamental provision of the Zurich agreement was the elimination of both *enosis* and partition. That must be the key to settlement. Then the Security Council must call on the Cypriot leaders to work out a new constitution giving the Turkish Cypriots communal security and regional autonomy, including their rights to administer their own autonomous municipalities and local government councils.

Meanwhile it must be stipulated that all Cypriots must be allowed to return safely to their homes, with protection where necessary from the United Nations Force. A new mandate for the U.N. Force must consequently be given, and the Force considerably expanded in numbers. Finally, the United Nations must reaffirm the call for a phased withdrawal of all Greek and Turkish troops.

The United Nations Security Council passed a number of resolutions during the Turkish invasion. They did more harm than good, for they were in pursuit of events, not in control of them. They were disregarded, and the authority of the United Nations was consequently diminished.

Now, the United Nations faces a challenge more important, it seems clear, than anything the Organizaticn has had to tackle before. Cyprus is a comparatively small island, but here is an issue of which the United Nations has been seized for more than a decade, where a U.N. force still operates, where the Security Council's decisions have been flouted, where the accepted U.N. principle of the "unacceptability of acquisition of territory by war" is at stake.

Now there is an oppoturnity to save the situation: to bring relief to the refugees and let them go safely home, to revive the agriculture and industry of the island, to start a new era of trust and cooperation between the two communities; and at the same time to save the Cypriot people from further bloodshed, to prevent conflict between Greece and Turkey—and to revive faith in international justice and in the authority of the United Nations.

We may pray that the clumsy and costly blunders of bilateral diplomacy will not be repeated, that this great opportunity to make amends by international action will not be thrown away.

"That is what we mean by conscientious objection," I said, feeling I had made an important point. "These young men are recruited by a country which maintains conscription but no provision for conscientious objection and alternative service. As you know, they can only follow their conscience by becoming exiles. Many of them have deserted the army."

"Could you then support in principle a resolution on conscientious objection, since it covers cases like this?" I asked.

"No," he replied. "We could not support it in the abstract. The Portuguese soldiers should stop fighting. Portugal should stop that colonial war. That case does not refer to us. Our constitution obliges everyone to perform military service. Van Boven's resolution is too abstract."

"Under what conditions could you support a resolution on conscientious objection?" I wanted to know.

Evdokayev pondered several seconds.

"The resolution would have to define the type of war that the person objects to. War objection that could be understood, against unjust wars—like the war in Vietnam—also wars of aggression, colonial wars, against serving in occupation forces in foreign territory. The resolution would have to be more specific."

"But is it possible to be specific in a resolution that is to be applied generally?" I asked.

"It would be sufficient to specify the type of unjust wars, without naming places like Angola or Mozambique." Evdokayev focused his narrow blue eyes on me as if I were a slow-witted student. "But it must be understood that when the war is just, then everyone must obey the order to fight. A just war," he intoned, "is a war in defense of one's territory if it is invaded and for the independence of one's country."

He continued impatiently. "When we fought Hitler, everybody in the whole country fought. That is why we won—and maybe why the Netherlands did not win. What would you want us to do when the Germans came into Russia? Let them come and do what they wanted? We had to resist."

"I agree with you," I said, and he nodded with satisfaction, as though at last he had penetrated a slow mentality.

"But suppose," I went on, "a few people wanted to resist nonviolently. I myself belong to the Gandhian tradition of resisting evils, including violence, by means of nonviolence, by means that do not kill or injure another human being."

I suddenly thought back to my first intervention at the United Nations, and I continued: "Even Krupskaya and the Christian Socialists, believed in resistance that did not involve killing. Wouldn't it be possible to permit conscientious objectors to killing to fight disease or epidemics instead of people? Couldn't they serve the country that way?"

"No, we do not allow nonviolence," said Evdokayev.
"Everybody must obey the call of the country. To allow a different type of service would not be possible."

His companion interjected; "If there was another type of service, some clever people would find a way not to fight. Everybody must obey and fight together."

"But I still look at it from the other side," I insisted, though I could see that both men were restive. "I still see the plight of Franz Jägerstätter, who refused to kill Russians and Poles for Hitler, though Hitler said that everybody must fight together.

"I repeat," said Evdokayev, "a just war in the defense of the integrity, the sovereignty, and the independence of one's country is something that no one can refuse to take part in for any reason whatsoever." He considered the conversation closed.

I took a deep breath. I had to strike one more nonviolent blow for the principle of conscientious objection. "If the resolution would state that one can only be a conscientious objector to unjust wars, and every country says that every war it is fighting is just, where does that leave the conscientious objector?"

There was an uncomfortable silence, which Evdokayev did not break. His face was red, perhaps with anger, perhaps with impatience at having a peaceful air crossing interrupted by such arguments. Humanly speaking, I could hardly blame him. Yet I waited. The other Russian finally remarked: "It is a very complicated matter." And we left it at that.

I realized as I went over our exchange in my mind that Evdokayev had never once used the word "conscience" or "conscientious." War objection he could accept, as long as it was political and as long as the political stripe was that of the USSR. It was the word "conscientious," a word implying that a person has choices, free choices that may not jibe with those of his own nation, that caused the gulf across which communication could hardly be maintained. It is exactly on that word and on what it implies that the collision of worldviews is likely to continue.

I have no firsthand knowledge of the subsequent tensions and frictions leading to the crises of 1964 and 1967. I shall not attempt to go over the wretched story of the breakdown of the 1960 agreements.

It is generally accepted that the constitutional plan agreed at Zurich was too set, too rigid, to work smoothly. After a few years of uneasy trial, proposals were made for changes. They were rejected and the opportunity for a new negotiation lost. So from 1964 onward the Zurich constitution was no longer in effect. Archbishop Makarios and his Greek Cypriot Ministers ruled. The Turkish Cypriots, sustained from Turkey and based in separate and isolated enclaves, no longer shared in the administration of the island.

Economically, however, the island prospered, the United Nations Force helped to keep the peace, and it is said that the long drawn-out constitutional discussions between Clerides and Denktash made some progress. It is even claimed that earlier this year there was rough agreement on the structure of a new constitutional plan giving the Turkish Cypriots a reasonable prospect of partnership and security. For several years there had been no communal bloodshed. There was some hope that, with Greek and Turkish encouragement, a peaceful and acceptable settlement would be found.

Then, suddenly, in July this year there was the coup. Early that Monday morning the National Guard, led by officers from Greece, drove their tanks into the grounds of the Presidential Palace, destroying the building with cannon fire. They believed they had killed President Makarios in the rubble. There is evidence that the attack was authorized by and planned from Athens.

It seems almost incredible that the Greek Junta, in spite of long, sustained American support in the past, could have dreamed that the coup would succeed, that the way could be opened to union of all Cyprus with Greece, that the Turkish Government would not react violently.

It is also difficult to understand, to say the least, why the American and British Governments decided to take no action in the Security Council till after the Turkish invasion had begun.

I cannot think of any single act which has caused more suffering and more prospect of continuing misery than the crazy assault that Monday morning. True, one result was the end of the Junta in Greece, and that is certainly cause for rejoicing. But every other consequence has been utterly disastrous.

The human suffering in Cyprus has only just begun. As the winter approaches it will get rapidly worse. A third of the whole population of Cyprus has been uprooted from homes and livelihood. The immediate outlook is very bad. The further future is dreadful to contemplate.

The Turks have no intention of withdrawing their army, except perhaps for a limited withdrawal in Famagusta and Morphou. Nor are they allowing the Greek Cypriot refugees to return to their homes and lands. The Greek Cypriots and the Greek Government, on the other hand, can never accept what amounts to the partition of the island, leaving so many Greek Cypriots without shelter or income. No Turkish Government and no Greek Government could survive if it gave way.

So what hope is there now for peace, for conciliation and cooperation? Precious little. If the present drift continues, the disaster will be deep and permanent. A situation not dissimilar in some respects to that in Northern Ireland or the Middle East will persist. Tensions may well lead to conflict—conflict into which larger powers, having failed to prevent or deal with the tragedy, may well be drawn. What conceivable escape can there be from drift into despair and bloodshed?

How bitter it is to reflect that only a few months ago a fruitful settlement was for the grasping. How tragically was the prospect of a lasting cooperation in peace shattered by the gunfire on that fateful Monday morning.

A partition weakly accepted is a bleak prospect. One envisions cruel transfers of population, economic ruin, and the certainty of continuing friction and conflict, with Greece and Turkey constantly on the brink of war and the great powers dragged ever nearer to the explosive dispute. Surely there must be another way.

It seems to me that hope must lie in two factors. First, the good sense of the Cypriot people themselves and their able leaders. And seocnd, in the capacity of the international community, acting through the United Nations, to insulate the island from outside pressures and to encourage, facilitate, and guarantee a fair settlement.

I do not doubt the capacity of the Cypriot leaders. On the Greek Cypriot side there is an array of able and experienced politicians, officials, lawyers, industrialists. Glavkos Clerides, the Acting President, is specially qualified by experience and temperament to conduct the negotiations on behalf of his people. Archbishop Makarios has a prestige and skill and courage which may in the future rally his people to repair the damage and overcome the enmities of the past.

On the Turkish Cypriot side too there are experienced and able leaders, Raouf Denktash outstanding among them.

The weakness on the Greek Cypriot side arises from their factional disputes and violence amongst themselves. On the Turkish Cypriot side there is subservience to the negative reaction of Ankara. These difficulties were great enough before recent events created new suspicions and mistrusts. They are much greater now. Nevertheless, it is of the utmost consequence that Cyprus has the advantage of a people of shrewdness, adaptability, and exceptional ability. Left to themselves they would, I am sure, come to a sensible solution of their formidable problems.

There is, however, no prospect of their being enabled or allowed to work out their own salvation without urgent and decisive international action. Effective international leadership means there must be a clear reaffirmation by the United Nations Security Council of the aim to ensure an independent, sovereign Cyprus. The fundamental provision of the Zurich agreement was the elimination of both *enosis* and partition. That must be the key to settlement. Then the Security Council must call on the Cypriot leaders to work out a new constitution giving the Turkish Cypriots communal security and regional autonomy, including their rights to administer their own autonomous municipalities and local government councils.

Meanwhile it must be stipulated that all Cypriots must be allowed to return safely to their homes, with protection where necessary from the United Nations Force. A new mandate for the U.N. Force must consequently be given, and the Force considerably expanded in numbers. Finally, the United Nations must reaffirm the call for a phased withdrawal of all Greek and Turkish troops.

The United Nations Security Council passed a number of resolutions during the Turkish invasion. They did more harm than good, for they were in pursuit of events, not in control of them. They were disregarded, and the authority of the United Nations was consequently diminished.

Now the United Nations faces a challenge more important, it seems clear, than anything the Organization has had to tackle before. Cyprus is a comparatively small island, but here is an issue of which the United Nations has been seized for more than a decade, where a U.N. force still operates, where the Security Council's decisions have been flouted, where the accepted U.N. principle of the "unacceptability of acquisition of territory by war" is at stake.

Now there is an opportunity to save the situation: to bring relief to the refugees and let them go safely home, to revive the agriculture and industry of the island, to start a new era of trust and cooperation between the two communities; and at the same time to save the Cypriot people from further bloodshed, to prevent conflict between Greece and Turkey—and to revive faith in international justice and in the authority of the United Nations.

We may pray that the clumsy and costly blunders of bilateral diplomacy will not be repeated, that this great opportunity to make amends by international action will not be thrown away.

[From New Outlook, October 1974]

THE CYPRUS TRAGEDY

(By Robert Weltsch)

Robert Weltsch, prominent leader of the German Zionist movement, former editor of "Die Jüdische Rundschau" and London correspondent for "Ha'aretz", gained fame through a series of articles written after Hitler came to power and published in a special volume, "Ja-Sagen Zum Judentum".

The author draws on the Cyprus experience to reflect on the concept of bi-nationalism as a solution to national conflicts. Bi-nationalism was conceptualized by Martin Buber and supported by large sections of the Zionist movement before 1948.

In 1453 the Turks conquered the capital of the Eastern Roman Empire, Constantinople, on the banks of the Bosphorus —the straits that separate Europe from Africa. They first occupied the entire area west of the city which, being surrounded, could no longer resist. When I read the recent newspaper accounts of the Turkish Army's battle for Nicosia, I imagined the tactics to be the same—if on a smaller scale—as those used by the Turks 500 years earlier.

Byzantium was a cosmopolitan Greek city and, though Sultan Muhamad was tolerant of minority cultures and religious practices, the occupation was a source of hostility and hatred between Greek and Turk—a hatred that would reappear in various forms on the stage of history. We have just witnessed one such tragic reappearance: the recent flare-up that followed the Greek National Guard putsch which broke the 1960 Graeco-Turkish Constitution Treaty, deposed Makarios and brought devastation to this beautific island.

STRATEGIC INTERESTS

It still isn't clear what brought the Greeks in Cyprus to this act of insanity. Greek Cypriots in London believe that the C.I.A. had a hand in it, because they thought Makarios was leaning too far left, and endangering the global interests of the U.S. and NATO. If there is any truth in this version, then their calculation was an error and the results are tragic. At any rate, belief in the power of the C.I.A. and its nefarious machinations is widespread. West German playwright Hochhut's drama "Lysistrata" is one example of this; the action takes place against a backdrop of fears that the C.I.A. is planning an Aegean Sea fortress supported by the "Greek Colonels" against the Russians.

Whether all the guesses are justified or not, many people believe the Central Intelligence Agency to be America's worldwide terrorist arm. As an ally, Greece is essential to NATO because the Eastern Mediterranean Basin is vital for the defence of the West. A Greek move into the communist camp would be a hard blow to American strategy. And the West already faces a serious potential threat when the 82-year-old Tito will no longer rule Yugoslavia.

There are five ethnic groups in Yugoslavia, and they have always lived in tension, if not outright hostility. The deepest rift is between the Serbs and the Croats—two very different races historically, culturally and by religion. Over the past 50 years, they have found a few occasions to massacre each other. The fear is that, in the event of Tito's demise, the Russians will exploit the delicate situation to regain influence over Yugoslavia—which would give them a powerful status in the Adriatic, and create an intolerable state of affairs for the West.

This is one of the complications arising from recognition of nationalism as the only factor in the maintenance of monolithic political states. Yugoslavia was created in 1918, out of a myth of apparent common language and nationality,

66

while ignoring other vital interests, because national self-determination was then thought to be as holy as the Ten Commandments. But the idyll of the multi-national or bi-national state lost ground. Czechoslovakia—the most liberal of the new states—was unable to build a multi-national state based on true equality even though it had strong minorities; it could be a model democracy, but had to give preference to the Czechs, thereby alienating the Slovaks and earning the hostility of the Sudeten Germans. Henlein, the Nazi leader of the Sudeten minority, declared in 1938: "We want to go home, to the Reich." What was the meaning of "home"? The Sudeten Germans had never been citizens of the German Reich since it was founded in 1871.

BUBER ON BI-NATIONALISM

Cyprus was part of the Ottoman Empire until 1878, when Turkey ceded the island to Great Britain. But the Greek population, the majority on the island, demanded "Enosis"—union with Greece—even though the bi-national settlement held the seeds of prosperity for the entire population of the island. And this obstinate demand resulted in tragedy for all.

Among the Jews of mandatory Palestine, there was a faction that, in the light of geographic and demographic realities, argued in favor of a bi-national state, based on cooperation between the ethnic groups for the benefit of the country as a whole. One of the faction's most energetic supporters was Martin Buber. In "Dividing Line",* an interesting booklet published recently, A.F. Simon records a conversation with Buber—the year he died—on the bi-national problem, among other things.

Simon doubted the endurance of the bi-nationalism principle, after the experiences of places where it had failed in the 40 years since Buber and his colleagues had prescribed it for Palestine. The geo-political situation and other concepts had changed (apparently a hint at the exaggerated view of self-determination). Simon went on to mention the examples of Canada, Ireland and Cyprus—but there are other places like Belgium, Czechoslovakia and South Africa—where there were prior conditions for successful bi-nationalism, but they gave way to hostile rift and zealous nationalism. The fact that, in most cases, tragedy afflicted all parties, did not influence stubborn opinions. And, after three wars, the circumstances of Palestine were more difficult.

Buber replied: "For me, bi-nationalism is only a stage of a more comprehensive objective: a Jewish-Arab federation in the region, or a part of it. We may now have to start with a pact based on a relative separation between the national areas of residence." He seems to have been referring to separate states.

The answer didn't satisfy Simon. After all, Buber always "supported the myth of a nation's link with its land, and what is the place of the link under these conditions?

From direct examination, Simon concludes that Buber "left too many questions for which he had no satisfactory answers. And it was these that are likely to put an end to our complacency, and reawaken our conscience from its tendency to slumber."

The same thought applies to other nations—like Cyprus—which, because of sterile hate and jealousy, cannot solve their problems.

[From New Outlook, October 1974]

LESSONS FROM CYPRUS

(By Meir Pa'il)

Dr. Meir Pa'il is former Commander-in-Chief of the Central Officers' School in the Israel Defense Forces. Recently he left the IDF, with the rank of Colonel, to become a Member of the Knesset (Moked List). Last month he was awarded the Itzhak Sadeh Prize for Literature on Military Problems.

A confrontation between two nationalist movements cannot be resolved by clinging to chauvinist ideals, nor by submitting to U.S. arbitration, nor yet by establishing territorial facts. As the Cyprus affair indicates, the best solution to such a conflict is territorial compromise.

----

*"Dividing Line". Nationalism, Zionism and the Jewish-Arab dispute in the philosophy of Martin Buber—by Auiva Ernst Simon. Published by the Arab Studies Center. Givat Haviva. 60 pages. Cit. pp. 47-48, 39.

The violence and drama that recently gripped Cyprus deserve a thorough study, though the affair is not over yet, and it is likely that further unexpected developments will occur on the island and round the Aegean Sea.

So far, there are four lessons to be learned from the Cyprus affair:

A. The recent events, which were largely influenced by the long-standing national friction between the Greeks and Turks on the island and in the periphery of the Aegean Sea, seem to be leading to the partition of Cyprus into a Turkish sector in the north and a Greek sector in the south. Cyprus may remain an independent state—but this time it will be an independent federative state, composed of two separate autonomous national republics, each with considerable political powers. Perhaps the island will actually be divided between Turkey and Greece, or else developments might lead to the establishment of two entirely independent states in Cyprus (though this seems less likely at the moment).

At all events, the idea of "Greater Cyprus" has failed totally: there will be no independent "Greater Cyprus" and certainly no "Greater Cyprus" annexed to Greece. This proves once more, and bitterly, the validity of the notion that the best solution to a prolonged confrontation between two zealous nationalist movements is territorial compromise.

B. Fate seemed to mock the Greek leaders of the Greek-Cypriot National Guard, who staged a coup d'etat in order to remove President Makarios and replace him with a Greek nationalist regime to turn Cyprus into an independent Greek State or annex it to Greece under the slogan of "Enosis".

Blinded by their nationalist ideal and their profound faith in its importance, they did not see the obvious: that Turkey, near-by and relatively strong, could not accept Cyprus being turned into a Greek State.

Thus they themselves, the Greek nationalists, supported by the Colonels' regime in Greece, caused the Turkish invasion of Cyprus. This, in turn, brought about the partition of Cyprus and the shattering of the Greek nationalist ideal of "Enosis"; it also caused the defeat of the Greek National Guard officers in Cyprus as well as the collapse of the Colonels' regime in Greece, which reached the verge of an open and disastrous war with Turkey.

C. Does the Turks' behavior in Cyprus prove that, in the final analysis, the use of force and the establishment of territorial facts are the decisive factors?

There is no doubt that Turkey's decision and ability to use troops in Cyprus helped to advance her interests on the island and strengthen the political status of the Cypriot-Turkish minority.

For all that, we should bear in mind Turkey's relative restraint in the use of force in Cyprus. After all, from the military point of view, the Turkish troops (land, sea and air) could gain control over all of Cyprus. And surely there are Turkish nationalist zealots who advocate taking control of the whole island, as in the 16th century Turkish conquest of Cyprus.

To be sure, Turkey's restraint is not due to pure humanitarian considerations, but rather to the limitations imposed by the super-powers that support Turkey's present actions in Cyprus: the U.S. was interested in Makarios' removal and ready to risk Turkish involvement in Cyprus so long as Greece was not pushed out of NATO and out of the system of alliances with the U.S. The USSR, which suffered politically and strategically from Makarios' ouster, is prepared to come to terms with the Turkish invasion of Cyprus, hoping to disrupt and split NATO. This situation created a favorable international background for Turkey to establish territorial facts, so long as Turkey has the wisdom to limit her aspirations from the start, without illusions of a "Greater Turkish Cyprus".

Clearly, the establishment of territorial facts is restricted by the dictates of the international balance of power in the region. This, too, is a lesson worth remembering.

D. All the evidence suggests that the Greek National Guard officers' coup in Cyprus was supported by Nixon's administration, in order to get rid of President Makarios who had recently strengthened his political ties with the USSR to develop a neutral Cypriot policy—a "Third-World" type of foreign policy.

Indeed, all the signs indicate that the U.S. Government suspected that Makarios' removal by the Greek officers would lead to a Turkish invasion, that it would bring about partition of the island and a political solution out of line with the expectations of the nationalistic Greek officers in Cyprus and Greece.

But it seems that the Turkish invasion of Cyprus, and the danger of a wider war between Turkey and Greece in the Thrace region, led to upheavals in the Greek government beyond the expectations of the American policy-makers.

The fall of the Greek junta was not in the interest of the U.S.; the junta was toppled by strong pressures of elements in the Greek army who wished to avoid a full-scale war with Turkey. The U.S. backed, perhaps even suggested, the res-rotation of Karamanlis to the Greek Premiership as an alternative to the junta, hoping to retain Greece within NATO and the American sphere of influence.

But the relative success of the Turks in Cyprus and the rage in Greece caused and still cause deep political shocks: the return of political exiles (Mikis Theodorakis), the release of political prisoners, and the public return of Andreas Papandreou to Greece and perhaps even to power. These events may prompt Greece to sail beyond the exclusive spheres of influence of NATO and the U.S., in the manner of De Gaulle's France.

Of course, such a development is not inevitable. But it is possible, which proves that human history is hard to plan or predict, even for the leaders of the Great Powers.

[From the Washington Star-News, Dec. 17, 1974]

CYPRIOT IMPASSE

On the surface, the prospects for a negotiated settlement on Cyprus declined in the first few days after the return of Archbishop Makarios. This was because the president of the shattered island republic, was anything but conciliatory in his initial crowd-pleasing appearances before his Greek Cypriot supporters.

He seemed to rule out the kind of agreement that might be acceptable to Turkey and the Turkish Cypriots when he rejected "any solution involving transfer of populations and amounting to partition of Cyprus." His only conciliatory gestures were toward Greek Cypriot opponents—presumably those who backed the July coup against him, which led to the Turkish invasion and the present Greek Cypriot plight. For good measure, Makarios snubbed Glafkos Clerides, the former acting president who has played an outstanding role in negotiating communal issues with the Turks.

Makarios perhaps was carried away by the emotion of his return to Nicosia, or was using rhetorical overkill to solidify support among Greek Cypriots. H now says Clerides will be given written instructions for conducting further negotiations with the Turks. The archbishop turned down a request by Vice President Denktash, leader of the Turkish Cypriot community, for face-to-face talks, on grounds of Makarios's legal status as president of the whole island. That is just as well, since Clerides with a sufficient mandate can be expected to function as a more realistic negotiator. Makarous apparently must provide such a mandate under terms of a secret agreement reached in Athens among Greek and Greek Cypriot leaders.

The post-invasion facts on Cyprus, with the Turkish army in control of 40 percent of the island, put the Turks in a seemingly insuperable bargaining position. Turkey and the Turkish Cypriot minority want a federated Cyprus divided geographically into autonomous zones. The separation of the warring communities and much movement of population already have taken place and are unlikely to be reversed except for territorial adjustments. The alternative to a negotiated federation of autonomous cantons would appear to be a continuance of the present de facto partition. Ultimately, a settlement on Cyprus must be sanctioned by Ankara, currently without a government, and Athens, where parliamentary government has just been restored.

Makarios can keep stirring up his adherents for a return to the Greek-dominated Cyprus that evolved from the 1959 constitution, but that is a dream. The sooner he settles for realistic negotiations and political conciliation the better it will be for uprooted Cypriots of both ethnic communities, as well as for their sponsors in Greece and Turkey.